African External Finance in the 1990s

edited by
Ishrat Husain
John Underwood

The World Bank
Washington, D.C.

Manufactured in the United States of America
First printing October 1991

Library of Congress Cataloging-in-Publication Data

African external finance in the 1990s / edited by Ishrat Husain, John Underwood.
p. cm. -- (A World Bank symposium)
Includes bibliographical references.
ISBN 0-8213-1926-4
1. Debts, External--Africa, Sub-Saharan. 2. Debts, External--Africa. 3. Investments, Foreign--Africa, Sub-Saharan. 4. Investments, Foreign--Africa. 5. Export credit--Africa, Sub-Saharan. 6. Loans, Foreign--Africa. I. Husain, Ishrat, 1941- . II. Underwood, John M., 1944- . III. Series.
HJ8826, A364 1991
336.3'435'096--dc20 91-30428
CIP

Foreword

Most African governments and donors now broadly agree that achieving sustained economic growth depends not only on continuing economic and financial policy reforms but also on a wide array of other action needed to deal with long-term development problems. The World Bank, in partnership with other donors, is supporting initiatives by African countries to deal with these long-term issues—to build the capacity of African institutions, to strengthen human resource development, to improve governance, and to stop environmental degradation.

These initiatives will require time to take shape and bear fruit. In the meantime, the international community will need to provide substantial external resources to support adjustment and growth in *Sub-Saharan Africa*. The availability of external financing assumes critical importance in the light of tightened budgetary constraints in many donor countries, almost complete withdrawal of commercial bank lending to developing countries, severe competition for foreign direct investment, dwindling flows of export credits, and stagnant concessional resources at the disposal of multilateral institutions.

To help shed some light on these issues, the World Bank initiated a research project, building on the framework of its Long-Term Study *(Sub-Saharan Africa: from Crisis to Sustainable Growth)*. This research project sought to assess the likely availability of external financial resources needed to achieve significant perspective economic growth in Sub-Saharan Africa. This volume summarizes the findings of that project. It also provides an empirical basis for the long-term financial planning that successful reform and development require.

Given the need to provide substantial aid and debt relief to Sub-Saharan Africa, donors and creditors are justifiably concerned with ensuring that their aid is used effectively to support reforms and viable and efficient investments. From its perspective, the World Bank is concerned with ensuring that limited aid resources are allocated where and when they are most needed to support reform and growth.

To this end, the World Bank has since 1987 chaired a partnership of donors and creditors that seeks attempts to coordinate and channel assistance to Sub-Saharan Africa. Within this framework—the Special Program of Assistance, or SPA—donors and creditors meet twice yearly to review the performance of low-income heavily indebted African countries and to monitor the financing requirements, including debt rescheduling and write-offs, of countries where reform programs are strong enough to merit SPA support. Through the SPA, donors and creditors allocate additional adjustment support where it is needed, report on collective efforts to improve aid quality, and discuss development issues linked to adjustment. This partnership has become of the most effective examples of aid coordination. The successful completion of its first three-year phase led to agreement on the second phase for 1991-93.

The experience of the SPA shows that external resources can be mobilized if African countries intensify and strengthen their economic policy reform and adjustment efforts. Progress in this regard is encouraging, with some thirty Sub-Saharan countries now engaged in the adjustment process. Trade, investment policies, and regulatory frameworks will be streamlined, and private saving and investment will be encouraged through financial liberalization. Public investment programs will complement private sector initiative and concentrate on infrastructure deficiencies and human resource development.

For this strategy to succeed, African countries need to adopt and maintain strong domestic policy measures that should reduce their on dependence on external aid by the end of this decade. But in the immediate future, their resource needs will continue to grow, and ways must be found to mobilize these resources, including measures to reduce Africa's debt burden.

It should be understood that stronger adjustment efforts, including increased saving, by African countries will not be sufficient to ensure continued growth and development. The studies in this volume show that, despite improvements in investment efficiency, domestic savings, and export volume, the financial requirements of adjusting countries in Sub-

Saharan Africa cannot be fully met without new money and further debt relief.

Recognizing the magnitude of the task ahead, the Global Coalition for Africa—a new international mechanism to help build consensus on African issues—has taken up aid flows to Sub-Saharan Africa as a major issue and, furthermore, has adopted the estimates presented in this volume as a starting point. Thus, the output of this research project has already provided valuable, practical guidance to policy-makers. I hope that the publication of the results in this volume will expand their usefulness to others, both in African and in donor countries.

Edward V. K. Jaycox
Vice President, Africa Region
The World Bank

Acknowledgments

The editors gratefully acknowledge the contributions of several people to the production of this symposium volume. David Stewart was instrumental in organizing the symposium, with help from Clifford Papik. Bruce Ross-Larson led the editing team, with Vince McCullough and Meta de Coquereaumont. Stephanie White organized the production team and provided editing support. Rose Vo and Michael Betteridge did the word processing. Thanks are also due to Edward V. K. Jaycox and Stanley Fischer, who encouraged us to undertake this project, and the members of the World Bank's Research Committee for agreeing to provide financial support.

Contents

Contributors

Joseph Abbey
Ambassador of Ghana to the United States of America

Paul Acquah
African Department, International Monetary Fund

Robert Ayres
External Affairs Department, World Bank

Richard Brun
Cofinancing and Financial Advisory Services, World Bank

Richard Carey
Organisation for Economic Cooperation and Development

Kevin Chang
Professor, New York University

Stijn Claessens
International Economics Department, World Bank

Lawrence Cockcroft
Overseas Development Institute

Jorge Culagovski
Africa Technical Department, World Bank

Robert Cumby
Professor, New York University

Asli Demirguc-Kunt
International Economics Department, World Bank

Stephen Denning
Southern Africa Department, World Bank

Refik Erzan
International Economics Department, World Bank

Victor Gabor
Asia Country Department III, World Bank

Maria Cristina Germany
Africa Technical Department, World Bank

Sudarshan Gooptu
Cofinancing Financial Advisory Services, World Bank

Joshua Greene
Research Department, International Monetary Fund

Charles Humphreys
Africa Technical Department, World Bank

Ishrat Husain
Chief Economist for Africa, World Bank

Ronald Johannes
International Economics Department, World Bank

G.G. Johnson
Exchange and Trade Relations Department, International Monetary Fund

Ellen Johnson-Sirleaf
Equator Bank, Washington, D.C.

Yvonne Jones
Cofinancing and Financial Advisory Services, World Bank

Anthony Killick
Overseas Development Institute

Kathryn Larrecq
Resource Mobilization Department, World Bank

Samuel Malaba
Reserve Bank of Zimbabwe

Francis Nyirjesy
Equator Bank, Washington D.C.

Mufutau Lyiola Raheem
Professor, University of Ibadan, Nigeria

Roger Riddell
Overseas Development Institute

Emanuel Tumusiime-Muteble
Ministry of Planning and Economic Development, Uganda

John Underwood
International Economics Department, World Bank

Marcel Yondo
Former Finance Minister, Cameroon

Introduction

John Underwood
Ishrat Husain

External financing for Sub-Saharan Africa is a vexing problem with no easy solutions. The region's macroeconomic policies, domestic savings, and efficiency of resource use—all generally poor—impinge heavily on the size, growth, and timing of external finance. The papers in this symposium volume assume that structural adjustment efforts in most African countries will be intensified and strengthened. Macroeconomic imbalances and microeconomic distortions will be minimized if not eliminated. Trade, investment policies, and regulatory framework will be streamlined. Private savings and investment will be encouraged through financial liberalization. Public investment programs will complement private sector initiative and concentrate on infrastructural deficiencies and human resource development. Since the Bank's report, *Sub-Saharan Africa, From Crisis to Sustainable Growth* (World Bank 1989a), tackles these issues well, we only restate the essential ingredients of a strategy for resuming growth.

The international economic environment is clearly important for Sub-Saharan Africa. It drives the prices of African exports, the demand for those exports, and the effective interest rate countries pay. Today, the international environment is beset with more than the usual uncertainties. First, the growth of the industrial countries in the 1990s—and the corresponding growth of markets for African exports and of available financing—will depend on key policy decisions of industrial country governments. It is not obvious how long the slowdown in industrial countries will last and what policy responses will be forthcoming. Nor is it obvious what effects the emergence of regional trading blocks in Asia, Europe, and North America will have on nontraditional exports from Africa. Second, and related to the previous point, is the evolution of interest rates and exchange rates among major world currencies. The increase in nondollar interest rates and the depreciation of the U.S. dollar, if allowed to continue unabated, would create significant pressures on the external payments position of many African countries. Corrective measures by the major players, the largest industrial countries, can help mitigate the adverse effects. Third, the prices of non-oil primary commodities are projected to decline in the 1990s, causing a stagnation or fall in export earnings, depending upon the gains from volume growth. There probably will not be a strong reversal in trends, at least in the first half of the 1990s, so any expectations about a favorable international economic environment would be misplaced. African policymakers should proceed with this base scenario in mind. Fourth, the short-term dislocation caused by the Middle East crisis has affected most oil-importing countries in Africa, and the speed and ease of recovery from this external shock will also be a factor.

The natural and human resource endowments and initial conditions of African countries must be taken into account in considering external finance requirements. With a few exceptions, countries in Sub-Saharan Africa fall into the low-income category. Despite this, there are wide divergences in initial conditions and in endowments. At one extreme are the poor Sahelian countries, where the rigors of natural adversity and a harsh physical environment limit the options in development strategies. At the other extreme are countries such as Botswana and Mauritius, where good economic policies and management have already made a difference. In between are other countries—Nigeria, Cameroon, Kenya, Zimbabwe, and Cote d'Ivoire—where the potential for expanding on human and physical endowments is promising.

Significantly, success in using external resources has an impact on their supply. Official aid will continue to be the major component of external resource flows to most countries in the region. Questions about the effectiveness of aid have concerned the international development community. The climate for official development assistance (ODA) in donor countries, already chilled by internal budgetary pressures, can improve substantially if resources are used well and if aid is coordinated well. This theme has been repeated since the early 1950s, but today the perceived lack of coordination remains a powerful deterrent to mobilizing ODA. In recent years, some progress has been made—both at the country and the regional level—in improving the effectiveness and coordination of aid. Experience with the Special Program of Assistance for Sub-Saharan Africa (SPA) and with country consultative groups and roundtables has been rewarding. But much still needs to be done. Several of the papers here provide useful insights about aid coordination and suggest practical means to achieve better results.

The record

Sub-Saharan Africa's economic disaster has been well documented. As the paper by Culagovski and colleagues shows, per capita real gross domestic product (GDP) declined by almost 20 percent in the region between 1974 and 1984. That is the greatest sustained development failure of the century, and it has not yet been conclusively reversed. Since 1984, economic growth has picked up—but it lagged behind population growth until 1989.

Growth has varied widely from country to country. Average GDP growth from 1961 to 1987 was 8.3 percent a year in Botswana but a negative 2.2 percent a year in Uganda. The region's poor growth was not a statistical anomaly caused by reversals in one or two countries. Between 1968 and 1988, only 10 of 40 Sub-Saharan African countries reached an average growth rate of more than 5 percent a year. In half those 40 countries, economic growth fell short of population growth. Since 1980 only nine countries have managed to achieve real per capita income growth.

Domestic investment and savings

Domestic investment and savings followed the same downward pattern with one important exception. In 1974-80 gross domestic investment relative to output rose in all major groups of Sub-Saharan African countries. Excluding Nigeria (at the peak of its oil boom), gross national savings as a share of output dropped in the same period. The difference was made up by use of a larger volume of external resources. And the end result, too often, was a debt crisis. Returns on investments were too low to meet the debt service on borrowed resources.

Some of the factors contributing to low efficiency of investment are highlighted by Culagovski and colleagues: price distortions, poor public sector management, and inadequate institutional and human capital development. In addition, they note, investment data may have been inflated by the inclusion of recurrent public expenditures financed by foreign project aid; borrowed resources financed consumption.

Since 1980, investment and savings have both declined as a share of output in Sub-Saharan Africa. Between 1981 and 1988, investment averaged about 17 percent of GNP and gross national savings about 8 percent of GNP. At the same time, the gap between investment and savings widened. This difference—the region's use of external resources,—averaged less than 4 percent of GNP in 1967-73; it reached almost 9 percent of GNP in 1988. Sub-Saharan Africa's net use of external resources has thus increased, but the resources have come to support a lower level of investment.

Patterns of external resource flows

External finance has grown dramatically as a share of GDP and gross domestic investment in Sub-Saharan Africa (table 1.1). In 1970 external financing was about one-fifth of gross domestic investment, and in 1988 one-half. The rise in external financing relative to GDP has been even more dramatic. At 8 percent of GDP in 1988, net external resource flows about equalled the region's gross national savings.

During the last three decades, the four major types of African external finance have been (1) concessional official development assistance (ODA), (2) nonconcessional bilateral official and officially guaranteed finance, predominantly from or guaranteed by export credit agencies, (3) nonconcessional multilateral development bank lending, and (4) commercial bank lending without an external guarantee (representing true commercial bank exposure to African country risk). Foreign direct investment (FDI) was not a major source of external financing for the region between 1970 and 1990 (see Cockroft and Riddell). External equity investment in Sub-Saharan Africa has been negligible; most of the countries have very limited equity markets. Official external financing has generally predominated, but the pattern has varied across time and recipient countries. The sparse data for the 1960s indicate that external financing of relatively small current account deficits, 2 to 4 percent of GDP, was largely official, roughly half of which was concessional.

Table 1.1: ***Net Resource Flows to Sub-Saharan Africa*** **as a Share of GDP and Gross Domestic Investment** (percentages)

	1970		*1975*		*1980*		*1985*		*1988*	
	Share of		*Share of*		*Share of*		*Share of*		*Share of*	
Flow type	*GDP*	*GDI*	*GDP*	*GDI*	*GDP*	*GDI*	*GDP*	*GDI*	*GDP*	*GDI*
ODA [a]	1.7	11.5	2.5	11.9	2.5	12.8	3.8	31.4	6.8	42.7
Other Official Finance	0.2	1.4	0.6	2.9	0.6	2.9	0.2	1.8	0.3	2.0
Private	1.2	8.2	1.2	5.6	2.0	10.3	-0.2	-1.7	0.7	4.6
Total	**3.2**	**21.1**	**5.1**	**24.4**	**5.6**	**28.3**	**3.7**	**30.3**	**8.0**	**50.6**

Note: OECD Data. Excludes technical cooperation grants.

Source: IBRD and OECD.

During the 1970s nonconcessional official and officially guaranteed lending played a large role (figure 1.1). A few countries gained access to commercial bank credit, usually during or following commodity booms. Two countries, Nigeria and Cote d'Ivoire, received 60 percent of all syndicated credits from commercial banks to the Sub-Sahara. These nonconcessional official and, to a lesser extent, private resources fed the 1974-1980 investment boom.

After 1970 ODA remained roughly constant at around 2 to 4 percent of GNP until the late 1980s. By then, other forms of financing had collapsed, and ODA jumped to 7 percent of GDP (excluding technical cooperation grants). Bilateral ODA also became more concessional. It moved from half grants and half loans in the early 1970s to more than 80 percent grants in the late 1980s.

Burden of external debt

With its surge of borrowing and subsequent reschedulings, Sub-Saharan Africa became the worlds's most indebted region in relative terms. As Husain and Underwood show, its $160 billion of debt, while far less than the $430 billion debt of Latin America, is a larger burden. Sub-Saharan Africa's GNP is less than a sixth of that in Latin America. Scheduled debt service for the region was more than 50 percent of exports in 1989, as high as the ratio for Latin America. Actual debt service payments relative to exports were smaller in Africa (24 percent) than in Latin America (27 percent). These lower cash debt service payments are a measure of the smaller and weaker economies in Sub-Saharan Africa.

Over the last decade, 30 of the Sub-Sahara's 44 countries have run into debt servicing difficulties, as evidenced by arrears and reschedulings. The causes were poor policies, inefficient use of borrowed resources, as well as some external shocks. The most important shocks were the unexpectedly low real prices for primary commodity exports (Krumm 1986). The inability of African countries to maintain

Figure 1.1 ***Net Resource Flows to Sub-Saharan Africa***

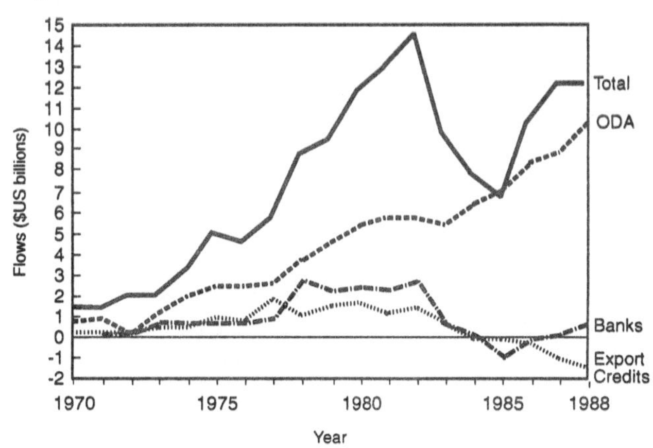

export market shares exacerbated the negative effect of the price declines. The rise in real interest rates in the 1980s, roughly 4 percentage points above average rates in the 1970s, had less of an impact. Excluding Nigeria, only a quarter of the region's debt was at floating rates in 1980, compared with 80 percent in Latin America. Sub-Saharan Africa's debt is dominated by official creditors (more than four-fifths in most countries, compared with about a third in Latin America), and official-source debt in the 1970s was mainly fixed-rate.

Twenty-seven Sub-Saharan countries are severely indebted, and 24 of them are low-income countries. Perhaps the best illustration of debt-servicing difficulties is the discrepancy between actual and scheduled debt service. Over the last five years, debt service paid has averaged about 40 percent of the debt service due. The difference was rescheduled or accumulated as arrears, often regularized through subsequent reschedulings. Past reschedulings resulted in the capitalization, at market rates, of large amounts of nonconcessional official bilateral debt. Today, an estimated 35 percent of such debt of low-income African countries consists of capitalized interest. Even the most generous cash-flow relief through rescheduling may not resolve debt difficulties. The best way to solve a debt problem is to grow out of it. But a large public debt can deter private investment and act as a disincentive to policy adjustment. Without investment and adjustment, the path to restored growth may be rocky.

The strategy for resumption of growth

Should we expect Sub-Saharan Africa's economic results to be different in the 1990s from those of the 1980s? Africa's physical infrastructure is in a state of decay. Roads, railroads, government buildings, school facilities, and power and communications systems are dilapidated. Educational achievement levels and the quality of schools have deteriorated in many countries. Population trends are alarming; if current rates of increase continue the region's population will double every 20 years, worsening pressure on infrastructure and the environment.

In spite of these difficult initial conditions, there are reasons for optimism about the Sub-Sahara's future. Most African governments have recognized the urgency and importance of major economic reforms. As Culagovski and colleagues note, 28 Sub-Saharan countries had economic adjustment programs agreed with the World Bank and 27 with the IMF at the end of 1989. Carey writes that donor agencies in developed countries are serious about increasing the return on ODA contributions. Together, governments and donor agencies can forge a viable strategy for restoring growth.

The major elements of a new growth strategy were outlined in the World Bank study, *Sub-Saharan Africa: From Crisis to Sustainable Growth*. The report set as a target a steady increase in real GDP growth rates to a sustainable 5 percent a year by 2000. Beyond continuing economic adjustment for growth, it identified four major components of a strategy for the 1990s: (1) building the capacity of African institutions, (2) developing human resources, (3) improving economic governance, and (4) halting environmental degradation. The report details the types of policy changes required of African governments and external donors if the new strategy is to succeed. (Culagovski and colleagues present a framework for projecting the implied external financing requirements implicit in achieving the study's targets).

External setting

The external setting, based on projections made before the Middle East crisis, is assumed to be relatively favorable. OECD country growth rates are assumed to average almost 3 percent a year through 2000. Real interest rates are projected to average about 3.5 percent, compared with almost 5.5 percent in the 1980s. The terms of trade of oil importing countries are projected to decline by 0.6 percent a year. Real oil prices are projected to rise by about 3 percent a year from their level immediately before the Middle East Crisis. Culagovski and colleagues note that each dollar increase in the oil price raises the external financing requirements of oil-importing countries by $240 million annually, after taking into account the demand-dampening effects of higher prices. The financing requirements of the five oil exporters reduced, but not enough to offset the increased financing needs in other Sub-Saharan African countries.

Policy stance

While Culagovski and colleagues do not explicitly include policy variables in their model, they set key parameters that implicitly assume that Sub-Saharan governments adopt and maintain strong policy measures. Real exchange rates are assumed to depreciate by 2-3 percent a year. Investment levels are projected to rise to 20 percent of GDP by 1995 and 25 percent by 2000. The efficiency of investment is to increase dramatically (one dollar of investment is projected to produce 21 cents a year of additional output in 2000, up from 15 cents in 1985-88). The income elasticity of imports is assumed to be one. Export volume growth, negative over the last decade, is to be about 5 percent a year. Gross domestic savings rise from their current 11 percent of GDP to 20 percent in 2000 (averaging roughly 16 percent over the decade).

Policy actions that would be necessary to improve the efficiency of investment include: foreign trade liberalization, with reductions in quantitative restrictions and domestic price controls, to shift capital to more productive uses; the reduction or elimination of directed credit; and improvements in the composition of public expenditures, especially public investment. Such investment should complement, not substitute for, private investment. Policies that would help to raise investment include reducing public sector deficits to free up resources for private investment and lowering overvalued exchange rates to encourage investment in traded goods production. Policies that would contribute to higher savings rates include financial liberalization and restrictive credit policies to combat inflation.

Some observers have questioned whether, despite good policies, the growth rates of exports, domestic savings rates and the incremental capital-output ratios underlying these projections would be difficult to achieve at the aggregate level or in individual countries. Others have raised concerns about the political feasibility of these objectives. Much will depend on the credibility of the governments undertaking economic reforms and their success in striking a social consensus in implementing the reforms. It is unrealistic to expect that the pattern of economic performance in all the countries would be smooth, linear or unidirectional. Some countries would show some progress and then relapse into inaction. Others would move forward but erratically. Outside and policy factors would impinge on the final outcome in ways that cannot be clearly predicted. But it is certain that countries with a record of aborted reforms and unsuccessful remedies would have a harder task in achieving the growth rates of key parameters implied in these projections.

Financing needs

Culagovski and colleagues project that achieving the 5 percent target growth rate for Sub-Saharan Africa by 2000 would require \$28 billion to \$30 billion annually in gross external financing (in 1988 dollars). Gross financing is defined as the amount needed to meet the net import bill and debt service payments coming due. As a share of GDP, these gross foreign financing requirements fall from 18 percent of GDP at the beginning of the decade to 13 percent at the end.

IDA-only countries require roughly three-quarters of the total. Most of their gap represents the difference between imports and exports. In contrast, the gross financing needs of the middle-income African countries are driven by debt-servicing requirements. These countries are projected to run trade surpluses.

There are two key questions about these projections of external financial requirements in the 1990s. The first is whether the supply of available foreign financing can match the demand. The second is what amounts and forms of foreign financing would leave Sub-Saharan Africa with a level of external liabilities that could be serviced on a sustainable basis.

The potential supply of external finance

Bilateral concessional assistance

Carey describes the significance of bilateral ODA in Sub-Saharan Africa. As the most important source of external finance, bilateral assistance to Sub-Saharan Africa from countries in the Development Assistance Committee (DAC) reached more than \$10 billion in 1989. One-quarter of the total came in the form of technical cooperation grants that are often not recorded in recipients' balance of payments statistics. Even without these grants, DAC bilateral assistance now makes up more than half the net external resource flows to the Sub-Sahara. Roughly 80 percent of DAC assistance is now in grant form, up from 50 percent in the early 1970s.

Carey points out a common misconception about ODA in the 1980s, while the real growth rate of ODA over the decade was minimal, the cause was a sharp decline in ODA from high-income oil exporting countries, commensurate with the drop in their petroleum earnings. ODA flows from DAC countries continued to increase at about 3 percent a year in real terms. Sub-Saharan Africa benefited not only from the growth in ODA from DAC countries but also from a shift of ODA funds in favor of the region. Sub-Saharan Africa now receives more than 30 percent of total ODA, up from less than 10 percent at the beginning of the 1960s.

The Bank's study of Sub-Saharan Africa concentrated on the ODA resources needed to support growth. It suggested that ODA must increase 4 percent per year in real terms if Africa is to meet its growth objectives. Carey tested the feasibility of this goal, as applied to bilateral ODA. He assumes a reasonable value for the key parameter, the share of ODA to GNP in donor countries (0.35 percent), and sets OECD GNP growth at 3 percent a year in real terms. He found that achievement of the goal would require a relatively modest increase in Sub-Saharan Africa's share in bilateral ODA, from roughly 31 percent currently to 34.5 percent by the end of the decade, so the goal is feasible. But he points out that this achievement would be far from automatic. It would require significant efforts--on the part of aid recipients to use concessional funds more effectively, and on the part of donors to mobilize resources and to provide assistance in forms that allow for efficient use.

Multilateral assistance

The outlook is less favorable for expanded multilateral development bank assistance. Despite a highly constrained financing environment in the 1980s, the principal sources of multilateral assistance—IDA, the EEC, and the African Development Fund (ADF)—substantially increased their transfer of resources to the region, as Larreq demonstrates. The substantial increases, especially over the last three years of the decade, cannot be sustained. The underlying funding of the institutions will continue to grow only modestly. Multilateral disbursements are likely to slow significantly in the second half of the 1990s, unless future replenishments of IDA and ADF take place at relatively higher levels in real terms. The effectiveness of the International Development Association (IDA) in assisting the low-income countries—both in growth and poverty allevation—is by now well established. While bilateral ODA disbursements could reasonably meet the Bank study's target, overall ODA net disbursements are likely to fall short of that goal in absence of a compensatory offset in concessionary multilateral funds.

The International Monetary Fund (IMF) is the major international financial institution that is not a development bank. At the end of 1989, IMF claims on Sub-Saharan Africa stood at $6.4 billion, about 2.5 percent of the region's total external liabilities. As Acquah and Edo point out, the IMF has been flexible in adapting instruments and policies to changes in the international environment. Specifically, the Structural Adjustment Facility and the Enhanced Structural Adjustment Facility have allowed the IMF to provide concessional resources to low-income countries with prolonged balance of payments difficulties. About SDR 2.3 billion of such funds had been committed to Sub-Saharan African countries as of July 1990, with SDR 1.7 billion disbursed.

In the 1990s Acquah and Edo see the IMF's main role as a catalyst for external funding from other sources. IMF policy advice and assistance in the formulation and implementation of adjustment programs will help countries attract funds from donors and creditors. The IMF will continue to provide funding to countries that request its support and have strong adjustment programs; this will take place through its SAF, ESAF, and other facilities. But the revolving nature of its resources means that, over the decade, the IMF itself is not likely to be a major supplier of net external financing for Sub-Saharan Africa.

Commercial bank lending

Commercial bank lending has never been a major source of external financing for most Sub-Saharan African countries. Long-term commercial bank debt makes up only $22 billion, or 16 percent, of the region's total debt. Nyirjesy and Johnson Sirleaf write that of the 44 countries, 15 account for 97 percent of commercial bank borrowing. Nigeria and Cote D'Ivoire together account for 60 percent.

Commercial bank long-term lending to Sub-Saharan Africa dropped sharply during the 1980s. Nyirjesy and Johnson Sirleaf note that commercial bank disbursements fell from $4 billion in 1980 to less than $2 billion in 1988. Net of principal repayments, disbursements fell from almost $3 billion in 1980 to less than $500 million in 1988. Excluding an estimated $475 million in net lending to the private sector in Cote d'Ivoire (which may have been guaranteed externally and do not appear in creditor data), net flows from commercial banks to Sub-Saharan countries were negative in 1988.

In discussions with international bankers, Nyirjesy and Johnson Sirleaf found virtually no commercial bank interest in new sovereign lending to African countries. New, tighter mandatory provisioning and capital adequacy rules reduce the return on loans to African countries, while the perceived risk has grown. A few bankers saw opportunities in lending to the mining sector or to other strong export sectors, but the volume of lending is expected to be miniscule. For the most part, bankers will try to collect as much as possible on outstanding claims that remain at risk.

Short-term trade finance

Brun and Gooptu review the experience of Sub-Saharan Africa with short-term trade finance. (Credits are defined as short-term if their original maturity is less than one year.) Most of this trade finance takes the form of short-term credits from commercial banks in OECD countries to commercial entities in African countries. Total short-term debt (excluding interest arrears on long-term debt) fell from $12.5 billion in 1984 to $9 billion in 1989. Part of the decline resulted from a reclassification of liabilities. Short-term credits in arrears were rescheduled into long-term claims in Nigeria. Debt swaps reduced trade credit arrears in Zambia. Other countries were unable to renew revolving credit lines.

As Brun and Gooptu write, African countries use short-term trade finance for two main purposes. One is to import commodities (especially oil) and consumer goods (capital goods imports are usually financed with longer term credits). The other is pre-export finance. Since most of these countries are primary goods exporters, their access to short-term trade lines is crucial.

Brun and Gooptu highlight how the African countries have coped with the squeeze on short-term credit. Some simply pay more. Some African countries have been paying effective rates of London Interbank Offered Rate (LIBOR) plus 6 percentage points or more on trade credits secured by cash deposits in creditor banks. Other countries resort to barter trade, countertrade, or pre-export finance schemes. All of these more exotic forms of trade finance have turned out to be extremely expensive. Fees of 20 percent of the value of the goods are common. As a result of their experiences with such alternatives, many Sub-Saharan countries are now trying to regain access to more traditional forms of trade finance.

Trade finance can make an important marginal contribution to Sub-Saharan Africa in the 1990s. If it grows in proportion to projected external trade, it will provide an annual average of $1 billion in net external inflows. More important, access to appropriate forms of trade finance can raise the region's efficiency in participating in the international economy.

Export credits

Demirguc-Kunt and Erzan show that more than 20 percent of all external resource flows to Sub-Saharan Africa between 1973 and 1980 were officially supported export credits. These export credits were more important for low-income countries than for middle-income ones, which financed a large share of capital goods imports with sovereign loans from commercial banks. Most low-income countries were able to tap the commercial bank market only with a third-party guarantee.

As Demirguc-Kunt and Erzan explain officially supported export credits have posed a moral hazard. Since guarantees were equally priced across broad categories of borrowing countries, exporters could select the riskiest projects in the riskiest countries. The borrowers paid the risk premium in higher import prices. Export credit agencies, often under pressure to support domestic manufacturers, ignored these problems and suffered the financial losses.

New export credits, which disappeared almost completely in the 1980s, now show some signs of life. They could emerge as a useful and important form of financing provided the problems that have plagued their activities can be overcome. More flexible pricing mechanisms, cooperation with multilateral development banks, and developing country reforms will help. Even so, the net annual flows to Sub-Saharan Africa from such credits are unlikely to exceed $1 billion a year over the next decade.

Foreign direct investment

Foreign direct investment (FDI) has declined as a source of external resource flows. In the latter half of the 1980s FDI accounted for just 2.3 percent of flows to the region. This is in sharp contrast to other regions, where recovering FDI now makes up a substantial portion of net inflows.

In their review of prospects for FDI in Sub-Saharan Africa, Cockroft and Riddell cite opportunities in the energy and mineral sectors. Other potential flows may go to the tourism industry and to manufacturing projects with privileged access to external markets.

Cockroft and Riddell conclude that there is no realistic prospect for a large increase in FDI flows. Indeed, African countries must work hard to maintain current levels of FDI flows (about $1 billion annually). The authors cite both external and internal factors for this pessimstic conclusion. The external: the poor outlook for prices of African commodity exports and the increased competition from other regions. The internal: uncertainty surrounding commitment to adjustment programs, high levels of external debt, and other factors that limit short-term growth prospects. The successful implementation and liberalization of domestic and foreign trade regimes in coun tries such as Nigeria, Zimbabwe, Kenya, Cote d'Ivoire, and Cameroon offer the best hopes for attracting FDI flows to Africa.

Return of flight capital

Chang and Cumby estimate that Sub-Saharan private residents hold about $40 billion in assets in industrial countries. While these estimates are based on data with big shortcomings, they tend to confirm the hypothesis that African residents are a potentially important source of external finance in the 1990s. But the same factors that lead to a pessimistic conclusion about FDI apply to private capital reflows. There is no evidence of reflows in response to the adjustment efforts of African governments in recent years. A sustained history of good economic policies and sound economic management will be important to both FDI and private capital. Countries that persist with adjustment programs may find themselves on a virtuous circle, attracting FDI and capital reflows—like Mexico.

Cash-Flow Benefits of Debt Relief

Sub-Saharan African countries will derive large cash-flow savings as a result of debt relief arrangements in the 1990s. Applying programs and procedures currently in place to roll over principal payments and capitalize interest payments will reduce external financing needs by about $4 billion a year in 1991-95. Culagovski and colleagues derive this estimate on the assumption that concessional debt relief programs will be extended to a wider set of countries. Specifically, they assume that Nigeria will reschedule its debts to bilateral official creditors at the Toronto terms. They also assume that virtually all bilateral ODA debt is forgiven and that debt service arising from Toronto term reschedulings are not subsequently rescheduled. As a result, the cumulative impact of debt reschedulings turns slightly negative in the late 1990s, as payments due under the old Toronto-term reschedulings are larger than amounts consolidated in new reschedulings.

Overall assessment of external finance

Culagovski and others estimate that projected financing sources will fall short of estimated needs by about $3.5 billion over the next decade. They project that more than half of the gap will occur in low-income IDA-only countries. The gap occurs largely because of the limited outlook for expansion of multilateral concessional assistance. As Larreq demonstrates, multilateral funds programmed for the 1990s were essentially brought forward and used in the 1980s. The consistently optimistic assumptions underlying the estimates by Culagovski and colleagues mean that their estimate of the potential external resource shortfall in Sub-Saharan Africa in the 1990s may be at the low end. Higher oil prices, lower commodity prices, or a slippage in industrial support for ODA would add to the gap. The likely range of external resource flows to Sub-Saharan Africa in 1995, from analysis in the papers in this volume, appears in table 1.2. Under all likely circumstances, official source grants and concessional loans will make up the bulk of net resource flows. Official flows are doubly important because their availability, along with appropriate policy measures by the recipient countries, will influence private sources, especially short-term and foreign direct investment inflows.

External Viability

If Sub-Saharan African countries are to gain external viability over the next decade, debt service must be brought in line with available external resources. External viability means that debtor countries can, with sustainable growth at or close to potential, meet their external resource needs (including debt service payments) without reschedulings or accumulations of arrears. External viability does not imply necessarily that a country has unrestricted access to all forms of external finance. Countries with poor short-term growth prospects may need to meet debt-service payments from net export earnings (likely to be negative) and capital inflows at appropriately concessional terms.

If external viability is not forthcoming, the optimistic assumptions concerning adjustment and investment are called into question. While annual reschedulings may ease the cash-flow constraint, uncertainty about a country's ability to meet future debt service payments discourages adjustment and deters private investment, particularly that in tradable goods production.

As Husain and Underwood show, external viability for Sub-Saharan Africa would require additional measures equivalent to an annual reduction in scheduled debt service of about $6 billion, or 35 percent of scheduled debt service. This is mainly for the most severely indebted low-income African countries. These measures can take the form of further reductions in debt or debt-service payments or further increases in highly concessional ODA. Burden-sharing among creditors is likely to be simplified if the assistance comes as concessional debt relief tailored to the circumstances of individual debtor countries. Further debt relief tailored in this manner could increase external resources for Sub-Saharan Africa in the 199Os. But the terms of that relief are important, because further cash-flow relief could fill financing needs but be detrimental to growth.

Relaxing the External Finance Constraint

Given that external resources available in the 1990s are very likely to fall short of the "minimum" proposed in the Bank's study of Sub-Saharan Africa, how can policymakers relax this external constraint? The answers fall into three basic categories: actions to (1) increase domestic savings, (2) increase the external resources, and (3) increase the efficiency of resource use. Most policy measures that positively affect one of these goals will also have a positive impact on the others. Culagovski and colleagues have already assumed a substantial increase in domestic savings rates and in the efficiency of investment. The suggestions below go beyond the improvements projected there or take account of the risk that their optimistic assumptions on concessional resource inflows may not materialize.

More efficient financial intermediation including liberalization of financial sectors and reduction in public sector deficits can help raise savings rates and

Table 1.2 ***Likely range of net flows of external resources to Sub-Saharan Africa in 1995 by type (billions US$)***

Type of flow	Annual Average Actual 1989	Projected 1995 Low	Projected 1995 High	change (%) 1989-95 Low	change (%) 1989-95 High
Official-source	11.1	12.7	15.3	2.3	5.5
Concessional loans	3.7	4.2	4.8	2.1	4.4
Multilateral	2.2	2.5	2.8	2.2	4.1
Bilateral	1.5	1.7	2.0	2.1	4.9
Nonconcessional Loans	0.8	0.5	1.0	-7.5	3.8
Multilateral	0.6	0.5	0.8	-2.9	4.9
Bilateral	0.2	0.0	0.2	n.a.	0.0
Grants	6.6	8.0	9.5	3.3	6.3
Private-source	1.8	-0.7	2.7	n.a.	7.0
Long-Term loans	1.1	-1.2	0.3	n.a.	19.5
Commercial banks	0.3	-0.5	0.0	n.a.	n.a.
Guaranteed export credits	0.9	-0.3	0.5	n.a.	-9.3
Other	-0.1	-0.4	-0.2	n.a.	n.a.
Short-Term	-0.2	0.0	0.9	n.a.	n.a.
Foreign direct investment	0.9	0.5	1.5	-9.3	8.9
Total	12.9	12.0	18.0	1.2	5.7
Projected Gap:		7.0	1.0		
(Mean)		(4.0)			

Note: Net disbursements on a cash basis, after rescheduling.

Table 1.3: *Potential Access to External Flows by Type in 2000*

	PRIVATE				OFFICIAL			
Types of Country Groups	FDI	Commercial banks	Suppliers/ buyers credits	s/Official export credits	Multilateral non-con-cessional	Bilateral concessional	Multilateral concessional	Official grants
Oil producers[a]	Yes	Yes	Yes	Yes	Yes	No	No	No
Mineral exporters[b]	Yes	Yes	Yes	Yes	No	No	No	No
Diversified Economies[c]	Yes	Yes	Yes	Yes	No	No	No	No
Agricultural Exporters[d]	No	No	No	Yes	Yes	Yes	Yes	No
Other developing countries[e]	No	No	No	No	No	No	Yes	Yes
Sahelian countries[f]	No	No	No	No	No	No	Yes	Yes
Small economies[g]	No	No	No	No	No	No	Yes	Yes

a. Nigeria, Gabon, Angola, Congo, Cameroon.
b. Botswana, Zaire, Zambia, Liberia, Sierra Leone, Guinea.
c. Zimbabwe, Mauritius, Kenya, Swaziland.
d. Uganda, Sudan, Tanzania, Cote d'Ivoire.
e. Benin, Burundi, CAR, Chad, Ethiopia, Mozambique, Rwanda, Somalia, Togo.
f. Senegal, The Gambia, Mali, Chad, Mauritania, Burkina, Niger.
g. Comoros, Cape Verde, Djibouti, Guinea Bissau, Sao Tome, Equatorial Guinea, Seychelles.

the efficiency of investment. Nyirjesy and Johnson Sirleaf suggest ways in which African countries could take advantage of the presence of foreign banks with domestic operations to increase the efficiency of domestic resource mobilization.

Since ODA resources will make up the bulk of external resource flows to the Sub-Sahara in the 1990s, more efficient use of these concessional inflows is a key factor in achieving sustainable growth. Killick finds that much of the ODA received by the region has been ineffective in developmental terms. He cites recipient and donor country policies as the key. Among his recommendations for more effective future use of ODA are improvements in aid coordination, less use of aid for political or commercial ends, and more official funding of nongovernmental organizations (NGOs) where they are more efficient in delivering aid.

Feinberg and Killick discuss the concepts of political conditionality, Feinberg in regard to the IMF and IBRD, and Killick in regard to bilateral development assistance. Both see pitfalls in attempts to implement lending or aid programs with this requirement. Feinberg, however, notes that the charter of the European Bank for Reconstruction and Development explicitly calls for political conditionality. Other multilateral and bilateral institutions may be under pressure to follow suit. Killick and Feinberg see "good governance" as important in improving the efficiency of resource use in Africa.

Policies that relax the constraints on FDI can provide many benefits to the Sub-Sahara. While the volume of net new external resources resulting from changed policies may be small, FDI can bring needed managerial skills and new technology with gains far greater than measured by the foreign exchange inflow. External support is available to countries interested in increasing FDI inflows. The Multilateral Investment Guarantee Agency provides guarantees for qualifying FDI inflows and promotes FDI by matching interested investors with potential projects. The Foreign Investment Advisory Service, a joint venture of MIGA and the International Finance Corporation (IFC), reviews FDI regulations in developing countries and provides country-specific advice on policy and regulatory reform designed to attract FDI inflows. The IFC often cofinances projects with foreign investor involvement.

Equity investment, without the management component implicit in FDI, is another channel through which Sub-Saharan African countries can, at the margin, increase foreign resource inflows. The lack of well-developed, functioning equity markets in Sub-Saharan Africa will limit the scope of foreign equity investment to minimal amounts in the 1990s. With the help of the IFC, many African countries are in the process of improving accounting rules, clarifying business codes, and undertaking other reforms necessary for efficient equity markets.

By 2000 oil exporters should have access to a variety of forms of private and official nonconcessional funding (table 1.3). At the other extreme, the access of Sahelian countries to external funding will probably be limited to highly concessional official sources. Countries in the middle, like agricultural exporters, should have access to a mix of official concessional and nonconcessional funds.

Managing external risk

As Claessens and Qian show, Sub-Saharan African countries are exposed to three major types of external risk: (1) currency risk (from movements in the cross rates for major currencies), (2) interest rate risk, and (3) commodity price risk. The region is particularly vulnerable to commodity price fluctuations because of the large share of commodities in total exports. It is less vulnerable to interest rate fluctuations than are other developing regions because a large share of its external liabilities consist of concessional, fixed-rate debt. The region may be less vulnerable to currency risk because the currency composition of its debt is minimizing portfolio of net external liabilities for Sub-Saharan Africa would contain a large component of commodity-price-linked liabilities. Hedging against commodity price risks could not only reduce the region's vulnerability to external shocks. It could also result in a larger inflow of external resources if creditors recognized that African countries' ability to service external liabilities was better matched with its debt service obligations.

Conclusions

Sub-Saharan Africa's demand for external capital will heavily depend on its ability to export, and world commodity markets will be the most important factor determining export earnings. On the basis of a set of relatively optimistic assumptions concerning external conditions, one of the papers in this volume puts Sub-Saharan Africa's gross external financing needs at $30 billion annually in the 1990s, almost 15 percent of GNP. Where will these resources come from? ODA will grow. But this growth will be more modest than in the second half of the 1980s. Despite competing claims, including those of Eastern Europe, the volume of ODA for Sub-Saharan Africa is likely to depend on events in the recipient countries.

Debt relief will be part of the answer. Cash-flow relief, which has been and will be substantial, may meet financing targets--but more concessional relief may be required to reduce the negative incentive effects of the existing debt in many countries. Commercial bank lending, foreign direct investment, and the return of flight capital probably will not be part of the answer.

The analysis leads to two essential points.

(1) Sub-Saharan Africa must help itself by raising its domestic savings rate. Foreign resources need to become less of a substitute for, and more of a complement to, domestic savings.

(2) Sub-Saharan Africa, with the help of donors, must use its external resource receipts more wisely. The quality and efficiency of domestic investment need to improve.

External finance will be in short supply and cannot be squandered as it often was in the past. Efficient external resource use will be a major determinant of Africa's economic success in the 1990s.

Note

1. The authors are the Lead Economist and Division Chief respectively, Debt and International Finance Division, the World Bank. The views expressed in this chapter are those of the authors and should not be attributed to the World Bank, its Board of Directors, its management or any of its member countries.

References

World Bank 1989a. *Sub-Saharan Africa: From Crisis to Sustainable Growth*. Washington, D.C.

—. 1989b. *World Debt Tables* 1989, Appendix III.

Part I

Africa's Financing Needs

African Financing Needs in the 1990s

Jorge Culagovski
Victor Gabor
Maria Cristina Germany
Charles P. Humphreys

To achieve GDP growth of 5 percent a year by 2000 (proposed in *Sub-Saharan Africa: From Crisis to Sustainable Growth)*, Africa could require average gross external capital of $28-29 billion a year in 1991-2000—both as inflows of new financing and reductions in debt-service obligations. About half would finance net imports of goods and services (other than interest) needed for current production and investment for future growth, the other half debt-service payments on past borrowing.

These needs can be met with no nominal increase in gross external resources, roughly $28 billion in 1988. But the composition of these resources will change drastically. By 2000 formal debt relief will be negligible as most debt will be ineligible for further rescheduling under current debt-relief options. New financing would make up nearly all the resources (compared with about 83 percent in 1988-89). If aid flows double over the decade, they would cover two-thirds of the resource transfers. Nonconcessional borrowing at recent levels and a doubling of net foreign direct investment would still leave a financing gap averaging $3-4 billion a year.

Even this level of external capital will not achieve the growth target without changes in domestic policies. In particular, reforms are needed to raise domestic investment to an equivalent of 25 percent of GDP—and to achieve a dramatic improvement in the efficiency of capital.

To estimate external resource requirements a two-gap model is used, in which the gap between domestic savings and gross investment, plus obligations to repay past loans, must equal the difference between imports and exports of goods and services (including interest obligations). This gap is financed by gross external capital or foreign savings—including debt relief to reduce debt service obligations.

Economic change and evolution

About 30 years ago colonialism was ending in Africa, and public resources were channeled mainly into industrialization. Agriculture, a way to provide raw materials and tax revenues, took second place, and many governments spent heavily on social sectors and infrastructure. The development strategy, supported by donors, included a dominant role for the government.

At first, this strategy seemed to pay off. Strong export demand and high investment—financed from export earnings, commercial borrowing, and aid—boosted GDP growth. But the strategy began to show its failures as countries stumbled after the first oil shock in 1973-74. (See Annex table 1). In the 1970s most African countries expanded public consumption and investment. Instead of raising savings, they financed much of this with foreign funds, taking advantage of heavier borrowing based on high export prices and negative real interest rates in international markets.

However, the increase in investment did not translate into higher output growth later, as might have been expected. By the mid-1970s Africa's performance was lagging behind that of other developing countries. By the 1980s output began to decline.

The drop in output was caused partly by the low efficiency of investment. High population growth, oil price and rising international interest rates (there was another in 1979-80) shocks, war and drought contributed to the crisis in Africa, but weak economic management was also to blame. Questionable domestic policies and lack of policy implementing capacity hindered improved economic performance.

As the crisis deepened, many African countries

Table 2.1 ***Evolution of key economic indicators for Sub-Saharan Africa, 1967-88 (average annual percentage change, unless otherwise indicated)***

	1967-73	*1974-80*	*1981-84*	*1985-87*	*1988*
GDP	7.0	2.7	-1.1	2.6	2.5
Export volume	17.1	0.2	-7.5	2.1	1.2
Import volume	4.3	7.6	-6.8	-0.7	-2.8
GDI (percent of GNP)[a]	16.7	22.3	16.7	15.0	16.6
GNS (percent of GNP)[a]	13.0	17.2	9.0	8.8	8.0
Private consumption	4.1	1.8	1.1	1.3	2.2
Gross ODA (percent of GNP)	3.2	3.6	4.2	6.6	8.9
Terms of trade index (1980=100)	83.9	84.4	101.3	83.0	74.2
GNY					
Total	3.9	4.5	-1.1	0.7	2.4
Per capita	1.2	1.7	-4.1	-2.4	-0.9

a. Refers to 1966-73

b. Refers to 1970-73

Source: World Bank data files.

began reform programs, which resulted in some improvements in the real exchange rate, real interestrates, fiscal balances, trade liberalization, pricing and public management, and other policies, and helped raise efficiency of investment. Aggregate GDP growth in the region began to recover in the second half of the 1980s, reaching 3.6 percent in 1989, compared with -1.1 percent in 1981-84, despite low investment rates.

Export performance is improving, but import volumes are still declining, albeit at a slower pace. Gross domestic investment and national savings, which reached a low in 1983-85, are no longer falling as a percentage of GNP (although the gap between the two is about the same as in the early 1980s). Private consumption began to recover in 1985-87 and improved in 1988, as stronger output growth was channeled more into consumption than savings.

The response to reforms is more evident when reforming countries are examined separately. For countries eligible for the Special Program of Assistance (SPA), which began in late 1987 and covers most reforming countries,data through 1990 show that output grew at an average 4 percent a year in the 20 core SPA countries in 1988-90 (23 countries have received assistance from the SPA, but Somalia and Zaire are now inactive, and Zambia became eligible only in 1990). Exports and gross domestic investment of the 20 expanded even faster; gross domestic savings continued to grow as a share of GDP; and the decline of real per capita consumption was almost arrested.

Countries outside SPA either deteriorated or stagnated (table 2.2). In 1988-90 output growth continued to slow and averaged 2.2 percent a year. Exports expanded slightly faster than GDP; investment increased moderately; gross domestic savings fell as a share of GDP; and real per capital consumption continued to decline.

To compensate for low national savings, and help underwrite increased imports, donors have stepped up ODA contributions, which reached about 14 percent of the SPA countries' GNP in 1985-88, or almost three times that of 1970-73. This increasing recourse to outside resources for growth and development reflects the difficulties for African economies to achieve sustainable growth.

Distorted policies that discouraged and limit the scope for domestic savings, plus high interest on

Table 2.2 ***Selected performance indicators, Sub-Saharan Africa, 1980-90. (annual average percentage change, unless otherwise specified)***

	1980-84	*1985-87*	*1988-90*
GDP			
SPA core countries	1.0	3.2	4.0
Other countries a,b/	3.3	3.2	2.2
Export volume			
SPA core countries	-0.6	3.0	3.7
Other countries	1.3	2.0	2.4
GDI/GDP ratio (percent)			
SPA core countries	18.4	16.7	19.3
Other countries	23.9	21.2	19.6
GDS/GDP ratio (percent)			
SPA core countries	2.9	4.0	4.9
Other countries	8.9	9.3	8.8
Terms of trade index (1987=1)			
SPA core countries	1.055	1.064	0.939
Other countries	1.208	1.058	1.024

Note: Other countries include Somalia, Zaire, and Zambia and exclude Angola, Comoros, Djibouti, Equatorial Guinea, and Swaziland because of incomplete data.

Source: World Bank data files.

foreign debt, have substantially reduced Africa's capacity to finance investment. The decline in national savings has been caused by growing negative savings of the public sector and a small decline in private savings, while net factor payments abroad have been increasing. The public sector deficits have resulted mainly from weak revenue performance and the high share of government consumption in GDP.

Public consumption and investment have continued, despite dwindling national savings, as external resources have been used to finance growing fiscal deficits on current and capital budgets (table 2.3). As a result, the investment-savings gap has increased from 3.7 percent of GNP in 1966-73 to 7.4 percent in 1985-88. In 1966 almost 90 percent of investment was financed by Sub-Saharan Africa's savings, in 1988 only 50 percent. The persistent widening of this gap has been mainly in IDA-only countries (countries eligible to borrow IDA credits but not IBRD loans).

The decline in African savings can be explained by: 1) falling income, which leaves fewer resources for public and private consumption and savings, 2) the government's negative savings resulting from growing recurrent budget deficits, and 3) some misclassification of foreign inflows, making domestic savings look lower than they are.

Although the inadequacy of funds for investment in Africa is understood, inadequate demand for investment is just as important in explaining low levels of investment. This is because of low and uncertain returns on private domestic assets (caused by distorted economic and financial policies and political animosity) and the lack of public investment projects attractive to international or bilateral lenders and donors. The weak demand for domestic investment is evident in large capital flight from Africa, which may have amounted to US$40 billion in 1976-87—equivalent to about half the total official development assistance received during the same period. Had this capital been invested in the region, it could have raised the investment rate by an average 2 percent of GDP during the period. If investment and output follow a linear function, this capital flight would have caused an output loss of about 30 percent of GDP by 1987. This suggests that stagnant investment and output resulted from poor demand for investment—as well as inadequate national savings and external financing.

In fact, net external flows to Africa almost doubled as a percentage of GNP in the past two decades. Net loan disbursements plus grants and net foreign investment rose from 6 percent of Sub-Saharan Africa's GNP in 1970 to 10.9 percent in 1988 and have become more concessional, up from less than half in 1970 to five-sixths in 1988.

Estimated financing requirements

The Banks' study, Sub-Saharan Africa: From Crisis to Sustainable Growth, assumed real GDP growth during the 1990s of 4-5 percent a year, annual export volume growth of over 5 percent, an import elasticity falling to about 1.1 by 2000, investment rising to 25 percent of GDP, and an incremental capital-output ratio declining from about 7:1 in 1990 to 5:1 by 2000. These targets for the whole of Africa, more optimistic than historical trends, are consistent with the experience of successful countries in (and out) of Africa and with recent improvements in reforming countries. The key assumption—a dramatic improvement in savings performance to around 20 percent of GDP by 2000—would reduce the dependence on net external financing from 10 percent of GDP to 5 percent by the end of the decade.

The requirements are based on "the most likely" outcome in *World Development Report 1990*, which assumes that industrial countries will grow at 3 percent a year in the 1990s. The projections use an import elasticity of one, and reserves are targeted to rise to three months of imports by 2000. Compared with 1988-90, the terms of trade index for the region (excluding Nigeria) is projected to increase slightly (substantially for Nigeria). For IDA-only countries, the index would remain below 1988-90, declining slightly over the decade. Bilateral ODA flows are assumed to grow in line with nominal GNP in the OECD countries. Multilateral ODA flows in the early 1990s stem from present arrangements, and after 1993 are assumed to grow at the same rate as bilateral aid, except for the IMF. Private transfers are assumed to decline to zero by 2000.

The gross foreign financing requirements for Africa, before debt relief or the accumulation of new arrears, are projected to average about $28 billion a year (in nominal prices) in 1991-2000, or about $50 per capita annually (figure 2.1). This compares with estimated gross financing of $27-28 billion in 1988 and $24-25 billion in 1982, implying that the financing needs can be met with no nominal increase in gross external capital, so foreign financing would be equivalent to only about 12-14 percent of all capital flows to the developing world in 1988.

In real terms (deflated by projected import prices), the gross external financing requirements would average about one-fourth less than nominal requirements. As African economies continue to grow, gross external financing requirements would also decline as a share of GDP—from about 18 percent in the early 1990s to around 13 percent by 2000 (figure 2.2), after which gross external financing requirements could continue to rise in nominal terms while declining as a share of GDP.

Table 2.3 ***Investment and savings, Sub-Saharan Africa,*** **1966-88 (average annual percentage of GNP)**

	1966-73	*1974-80*	*1981-84*	*1985-87*	*1988*
Gross domestic investment	6.7	22.3	16.7	15.0	16.6
Gross national savings	13.0	17.2	9.0	8.8	8.0
Gap (investment minus savings)	3.7	5.1	7.7	6.2	8.6

Source: World Bank data files.

Figure 2.1 ***Gross Financing Requirements of Sub-Saharan Africa, 1989-2000***

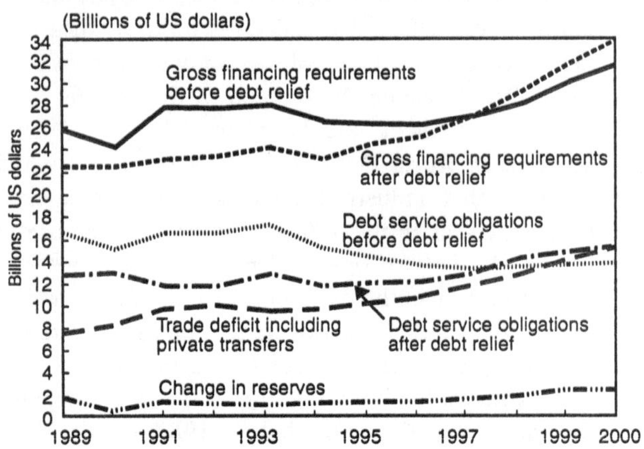

Figure 2.2 ***Gross Financing Requirements of Sub-Saharan Africa, 1989-2000***

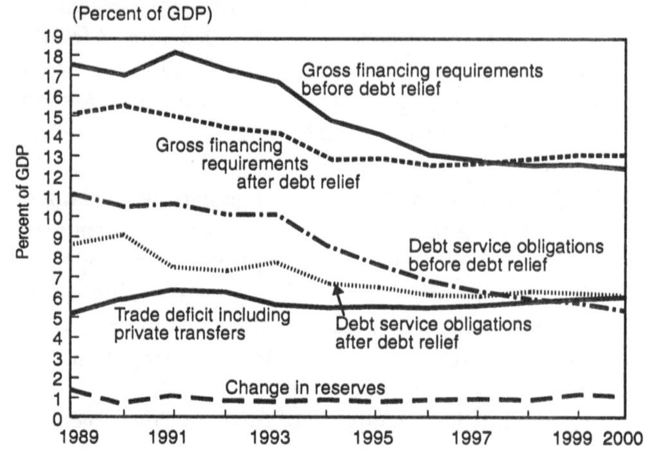

This financing comprises what is needed for improved growth and future development (the trade gap of goods and nonfactor services) and requirements to deal with past borrowing (debt-service obligations). The 1990-97 requirement tracks the debt-service obligations: high in the early years, declining in the middle years, and stabilizing after 1997. In the last part of the decade it rises as the trade deficit widens because export growth lags behind imports (owing mainly to the low growth for Nigerian oil exports), the terms of trade decline for oil-importing countries, and the base for projecting import values is about a third larger than export values.

Debt service obligations—before rescheduling and additional arrears—account for more than half the gross external financing requirements in the first half of the 1990s, falling to about 40 percent by 2000. In 1982 they were roughly a third and in 1988 about 75 percent. These figures show that the external financing problem in Africa is more than a structural imbalance of imports and exports—and that debt relief is important as a source of financing.

Changes in underlying assumptions and targets will affect the projections, mostly because of their impact on the trade balance. For instance, if the GDP growth target were one percentage point higher in each year (implying that the target proposed in Sub-Saharan Africa: From Crisis to Sustainable Growth would be achieved by 1995)—and there were no improvement in import efficiency—gross financing requirements would rise by 20-25 percent, or by an average of $6-7 billion a year. If the assumed export growth were one percentage point higher each year (bringing it closer to that of other developing countries)—and there were no offsetting increases in imports—those requirements would fall by about 15 percent, or some $4 billion a year on average. If the terms of trade index were one percentage point below the base case in each year (but still resulting in a slight improvement over the period), gross financing requirements would rise by about 15 percent, or an average of $4-5 billion a year. And if policy reforms improved efficiency enough to lower import elasticity by 10 percent, gross financing requirements would fall by over 5 percent, or almost $2 billion a year. (Each dollar increase in oil prices could raise financing requirements by $250 million a year, but this would be more than offset by an increase in export revenues of $750 million at current export levels).

Table 2.4 ***Past and projected key economic indicators, Sub-Saharan Africa,*** **1985-88, 1995, 2000 (average annual percentage change unless indicated otherwise)**

	1985-88	*1995*	*2000*
Domestic indicators			
Real gross domestic product (GDP)	2.6	4.0	5.0
Real gross domestic investment (GDI)	-6.9	8.7	7.7
GDI (percent of GDP)	14.0	20.7	25.0
Gross domestic savings (percent of GDP)	11.4	16.6	20.0
Real consumption per capital	-0.7	0.1	1.3
Real gross national income (GNY)	-1.8	4.2	5.4
Real GNY per capita (1988 US$)	314.0	304.0	334.0
Real effective exchange rate	-4.0[a]	-3.3	-3.4
ICOR (1988, 1994, and 1999 prices)	6.8	4.9	4.8
Trade indicators and official development assistance			
Import elasticity	-1.6	1.0	1.0
Import volume	-4.0	4.1	5.0
Imports (percentage of GDP)	22.9	33.1	39.3
Export volume	1.9	3.6	4.3
Exports (percentage of GDP)	20.3	29.0	34.3
Import prices	6.3	4.6	5.4
Export prices	-4.6	4.8	5.9
Terms of trade index (1988=100)	111.5	103.5	107.5
Real gross ODA	13.9	3.3	1.1
Gross ODA (percentage of GDP)	5.9	8.6	9.0
Debt service indicators before debt relief			
Debt service ratio (percentage of exports)		-26.5	15.7
Debt service (percentage of GDP)		-7.8	5.4

Note: a. Median for about three-fourths of the Sub-Saharan countries, 1986-88.
Source: World Bank data files and projections.

Projections by groups of countries

Some countries—especially the poorest—have more severe financing needs than others, like oil exporters. Moreover, aggregate estimates may underestimate regional needs because they assume that surpluses in some countries can be used to offset deficits in others, which is unlikely. In lieu of estimates for each country, countries can be grouped by their prospects and needs.

More than 75 percent of the region's gross financing needs are accounted for by IDA-only countries and are driven not by debt service but by a widening trade deficit, which more than doubles in current terms in the 1990s. So, narrowing the requirements cannot be achieved by short-term measures. Because exports cover less than $3 of every $4 of imports, export growth will have to be a third higher than import growth rate—or 8-10 percent a year—for a sustained period to lower the nominal trade gap, and exports would have to grow faster if terms of trade decline. If policy reforms are effective (and if the trade environment in the industrial countries is favorable), the trade gap may begin to narrow after the end of the decade if export growth continues to accelerate. Optimistic? Yes, but successful developing countries have achieved those rates.

Prospects for the middle-income countries and Nigeria in the 1990s contrast sharply with low-income countries; middle-income countries (based on data for Cameroon, Congo, Côte d'Ivoire and Zimbabwe) account for 20 percent of total requirements and decline in the 1990s in real terms and as a percentage of GDP. Their requirements are not driven by trade but by debt service, which rises during the decade as payments for nonconcessional obligations contracted in the second half of the 1980s become due. Debt relief could fill much of the financing gap. If creditors grant more generous debt relief than the Toronto terms of the Paris Club assumed in the model, the need for new financing would be much less.

Nigeria needs an average annual gross financing (before debt relief) of $2.4 billion only in 1991-95. Starting in 1996 Nigeria would generate an inceasing surplus, which with declining debt-service obligations would mean a fall in its requirements. After debt relief (including reductions of commercial bank debt) Nigeria would need an annual average of only $1.1

Table 2.5 ***Past and projected financing and debt relief, Sub-Saharan Africa*** **1985-88, 1995, and 2000 (average annual percentage of GDP unless indicated otherwise)**

	1985-88	*1995*	*2000*
Total foreign financing required			
Billions of U.S. dollars	14.8	26.5	32.0
Percentage of GDP	10.2	14.2	12.7
Gross foreign inflows projected, of which:	10.1	11.9	11.9
Loan disbursements	6.5	6.2	5.8
Official transfers	3.1	5.0	5.3
Direct foreign investment	0.4	0.7	0.8
Net debt relief [a]		1.2	-0.7
Residual financing gap	0.1	1.1	1.5
Memo items:			
Debt service indicators *after* debt relief			
Debt service ratio (percentage of exports)	31.2	22.5	17.7
Debt service	6.5	6.6	6.1

Notes: a. Net of moratorium obligations on consolidated amounts.
b. Debt relief and accumulation of arrears have already been taken into account in calculating financing requirements because historical debt service is shown as payments, not obligations.
Source: World Bank data file and projections.

billion in 1991-92.

Projected financing sources

The major possible financing sources include gross loan disbursements from all lenders, official transfers, debt relief net of additional moratorium debt service, and direct foreign investment (table 2.6 and figure 2.3). Private transfers are treated as resources, included in the current account balance

Total gross loan disbursements, net official transfers, and direct foreign investment are assumed to grow at annual average nominal rates of 3-4 percent, 7 percent and 10 percent, respectively. Gross disbursements of nonconcessional loans are assumed to remain constant, in nominal prices, at the 1988 level. As a result, the share of gross loan disbursements and official transfers in total financing (including debt service reduction) would rise from 65 percent to 87 percent by the end of the decade. The share of direct foreign investment would double in the 1990s, but because the base is small, its contribution to total requirements remains low (6 percent in 2000). Relief of official debt is assumed, for all countries, at the most favorable terms allowed under the Toronto Terms of the Paris Club. Moreover, reduction of commercial debt is assumed through London Club rescheduling and a combination of buybacks at deep discounts, swaps, and other arrangements. Total debt relief would nevertheless dwindle gradually and become negative by 1998, as repayment of previous debt consolidations fall due.

Table 2.6 ***Possible sources of financing, Sub-Saharan Africa, 1991-2000*** **(annual averages in billions of dollars)**

	1991-95	*1996-2000*	*1991-2000*
Gross loan disbursements	10.8	13.3	2.1
of which concessional	6.1	8.3	7.2
Official transfers	8.4	11.6	10.0
Direct foreign investment	1.1	1.9	1.5
Debt relief [a]	3.9	-0.4	1.7
Residual gap	3.3	2.5	2.9
Total financing	27.5	28.9	28.2

Note: a. Net of moratorium debt service on rescheduled debt.
Source: World Bank projections.

There are two other reasons for the small contribution of debt relief to total financing resources: about a fourth of Africa's debt is multilateral and not eligible for debt relief, and all new borrowing is assumed to be ineligible for rescheduling.

Based on these assumptions, only about 90 percent of the requirements would be met—implying a residual gap of an average $3-4 billion a year. This suggests the need for stronger reforms, export promotion, more efficient use of imports, and additional resources—that is, more favorable debt relief and larger capital inflows, especially from the private sector.

Figure 2.3 ***Financing by Source in Sub-Saharan Africa, 1989-2000***

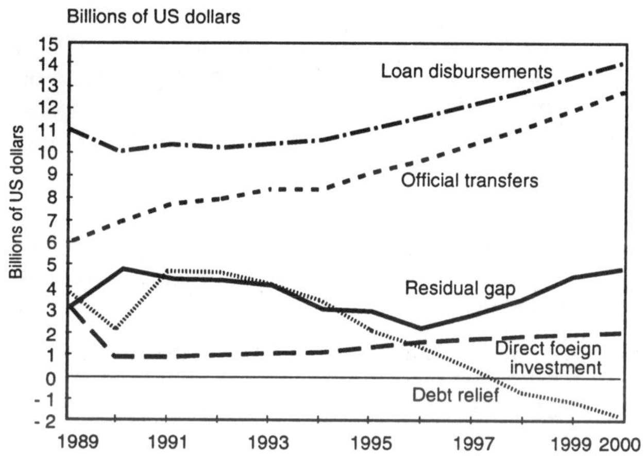

Note

This paper is based on Jorge Culajovski; Victor Gabor; Maria Cristina Germany; and Charles Humphreys, *African Financing Needs in the 1990s* PRE working paper number 764, forthcoming 1991. This paper explains in more detail the issues related to savings, investment, and efficiency of capital. It also describes, in the annex, the general assumptions used in the projections and the sensitivity results to changes in major assumptions.

References

Chang, Kevin P.H., and Robert E. Cumby. 1990. "Capital Flight in Sub-Saharan African Countries." World Bank, Washington, D.C.

Corden, Max W. 1990. "Macroeconomic Policy and Growth. Some Lessons of Experience." *Annual Conference on Development Economics.* Washington, D.C.: World Bank.

Deaton, Agnus. 1989. "Savings in Developing Countries." *Annual Conference on Development Economics.* Washington, D.C.: World Bank.

Dornbusch, Rudiger. 1990. "From Stabilization to Growth." *Annual Conference on Development Economics.* Washington, D.C.: World Bank.

Fischer, Stanley, and Vinod Thomas. 1990. "Policies for Economic Development." World Bank Working Paper 459. Washington, D.C.

Khan, Mohsin S. 1987. "Macroeconomic Adjustment in Developing Countries. A Policy Perspective." *Research Observer.* No. 1.

Organization for Economic Cooperation and Development (OECD). 1989. *Development Co-operation in the 1990's.* Paris.

Pfeffermann, Guy P., and Andrea Madarassy.1989. "Trends in Private Investment in Thirty Developing Countries". IFC Discussion Paper No.6. Washington, D.C.

United Nations Development Programme (UNDP) and World Bank. 1989. *African Economic and Financial Data.* Washington, D.C.

——. 1989. *Africa's Adjustment and Growth in the 1980s.* Washington, D.C.

World Bank. 1989. Sub-Saharan Africa: From Crisis to Sustainable Growth. Washington, D.C.

——. 1989. *World Debt tables, 1989-90.* Vols. 1 and 2 and underlying data files. Washington, D.C.

——. 1989. *World Development Report 1989.* Washington, D.C.

——. 1989. *World tables,* 1988-89 edition and underlying data files. Washington D.C.

——. 1990. *World Development Report 1990.* Washington, D.C.

——. 1990. *Special Program of Assistance: Proposal for the Second Phase.* Washington, D.C.

——. 1990. *Adjustment Lending Policies for the Recovery of Growth.* Policy and Research Series No.14. Washington, D.C.

——. 1990. *World tables.* 1989-90 edition. Wash ington, D.C.

Yeats, Alexander J. 1989. "Do African Countries Pay more for Imports? Yes." World Bank Working Paper 265. Washington, D.C.

Comment

S.M.T. Malaba

To achieve the 5 percent G.D.P. growth target by the year 2000 proposed in Sub-Saharan Africa: From Crisis to Sustainable Growth the quantitative scenario in the paper shows that Sub-Saharan Africa could require a gross external capital inflow, before debt relief of US$28-29 billion a year on average, for 1991-2000 (or US$21 billion a year in 1990 dollars). This compares with an estimated gross external capital inflow of about US$27 billion in 1988, before debt relief on new arrears.

The paper looks very closely at the reform programs and policies that must be undertaken by the developing counbtries for the adjustment process to succeed. The structural adjustment programs in the subregion will depend crucially on the growth of exports. An analysis of these exports shows that the markets are in the developed countries and so for any export growth in Sub-Saharan Africa, there is need for the developed countries to reform their trade and protectionist policies to allow for increased entry of exports into their markets.

The model in this paper depends critically on an annual growth rate of over 50 percent a year, and hence the state of the global economic environment is a very important variable. This is of great importance when one takes into account the fact that there has been a continued decline in the prices of primary commodities leading to a deterioration in the terms of trade. Furthermore, the developed economies have been pursuing a monetary policy stance that has encouraged high interest rates in order to fight inflation. This of course has further worsened the heavy debt burden of the developing countries. It is therefore necessary for the paper to emphasize more the need for an improved global economic environment and the key role that the policies of the industrial countries have in achieving this healthy environment.

Africa's financing needs during the 1990s cannot be looked at in isolation from the various regional economic integrations taking place in Europe and the Americas. The impact of such economic integrations on the growth potential of Sub-Saharan Africa should be seriously looked into. There is hence a need for countries in the subregion to design their structural adjustment programs in a manner that will promote and increase regional and bilateral trading arrangements. This will encourage more open trading policies, which will foster the structural adjustment process in the subregion.

It is generally acknowledged that reform and financing go hand in hand. Failure to link the key parameters to the policy reform means that the paper does not adequately address how much reform is required and the implications of the reform measures.

There is no dispute about the need for reform. The question is about the speed and quantum of such reform. It is also important not to over generalize on the structural adjustment programs for the Sub-Saharan Region as the design of the reform measures need to be more specific.

The paper very correctly notes that the financing problems in Africa are more than a structural imbalance of exports and imports. It therefore indicates the importance of debt relief measures as a source of financing. Failure to take cognizance of this point would mean that the financial requirements of the subregion would have been estimated.

The paper needs to address much more critically the ability of the subregion to realistically mobilize US$28-29 billion a year in the face of declining resources of finance from official sources, direct foreign investment, commercial banks and the likes.

It also needs to examine the emergence of Central and Eastern Europe as a major competitor for external financial resources. As Eastern Europe embarks on economic and political reform, its needs for financial and technical assistance will also increase. Any increased assistance to Eastern Europe is likely to result in less assistance to other developing countries, despite statements to the contrary by the developed countries.

Africa's financing needs in the 1990s cannot be looked at without an analysis of the implications of the Gulf crisis, which resulted in very high oil prices and recession among the industrialized countries. The high oil prices will have a devastating impact on the economic performance of the low- and middle-income oil importing countries. The Gulf crisis implies additional financial resources over and above the estimated US$28 billion per annum. It is highly unlikely that oil prices will drop to below US$20 per barrel after the crisis, so the impact of the current

Gulf crisis will be felt both in the short and medium term. There will therefore be need for concessional assistance to countries in the subregion. Unless the structural adjustment program being undertaken are funded adequately, they cannot be effective or sustainable. Inadequate funding will make it difficult for African countries to stick to the adjustment programs. On the other hand, a prolonged spiralling of oil prices will result in a world recession which will affect the demand of exports from the subregion at a time when the countries are embarking on structural adjustment programs. It is therefore important that the paper incorporates two scenarios to take account of the potential impact of the Gulf crisis. One scenario would assume the Gulf crisis to be short in term, and the other assumes longer in term.

The Problem of Sub-Saharan Africa's Debt—and the Solutions

Ishrat Husain
John Underwood

Countries in Sub-Saharan Africa are among the most indebted of developing nations. Many are severely indebted to official bilateral creditors. Others, like Nigeria, are indebted to commercial banks. And some, including Botswana and Swaziland, have no debt problems. Who are Sub-Saharan Africa's external creditors? How big is the debt? Is there a debt overhang? How big is the region's need for debt relief in the context of external financing needs? What is the impact of the official response to the debt crisis on the external financial situation of African countries? And what measures could strengthen the debt strategy?

The size of the debt

At the end of 1990 Sub-Saharan Africa's debt was about $161 billion or 12 percent of the debt of all developing countries (table 3.1). Compared with Latin America's debt of $428 billion, this appears small. Yet, standard debt indicators show that Sub-Saharan Africa is as seriously indebted as Latin America. In 1988 debt was 112 percent of Sub-Saharan Africa's GNP, and 48 percent of Latin America's. In the same year, Sub-Saharan Africa made debt service payments equal to 24 percent of exports, Latin America 27 percent. This second statistic does not mean a lighter debt burden in Africa. Scheduled debt service payments were about 50 percent of export earnings in both regions. The lower debt service payments in Africa reflect weaker and poorer economies.

Debt-servicing difficulties are pervasive across the continent. Thirty of the 44 countries in the region have resorted to rescheduling, mainly official bilateral debt reschedulings at the Paris Club. Twenty-four Sub-Saharan African countries are classified, on the basis of objective indicators of debt burden, as severely indebted (World Bank 1989). Only three (Burundi, Ghana, and Kenya) among those severely indebted have not rescheduled or run up arrears in the past eight years.

Poverty and related structural weaknesses

What makes Sub-Saharan Africa's debt a bigger burden than that of other highly indebted regions? Greater poverty and the more serious structural weaknesses of African economies are the main causes. Only 11 are classified as middle-income (with per capita incomes of more than $480 annually), most in the lower range. The other 33 countries are in the low-income category. Only five (Cameroon, Côte d'Ivoire, Gabon, and Zimbabwe) are borrowers from the IBRD on market terms. The rest borrow from IDA, the concessional window of the World Bank Group.

Differences between low-income African countries and severely indebted middle-income countries are considerable (table 3.2). Only three Sub-Saharan African countries are severely indebted middle-income countries: Congo, Côte d'Ivoire, and Senegal. Low-income African countries are smaller than the middle income countries. Without a diversified export base, it is difficult for them to adjust to changing world economic conditions. With higher population growth, per capita income growth is more difficult, and education and health demands are greater. Infant mortality is twice that of middle income severely indebted countries, and only two-thirds or so of the school-age population attend primary school. Investment is low and less productive.

Origins of the debt problem

One reason for the region's debt difficulties is falling export prices. Many countries, including oil producers like Nigeria, borrowed on the assumption that high prices for their major commodities would persist or that price declines would be temporary (Krumm 1986). In fact, excluding Nigeria, Sub-Saharan Africa's terms of trade declined by 25 percent in 1980-88, and low-income Africa's export volume is now lower than in 1970 (Greene 1989). Primary commodity production problems added to debt problems in countries such as the Congo and Zambia.

Poor policies in many African countries have magnified these difficulties. Unable to diversify exports in the short run, they are ill equipped to cope with external shocks. These problems and the unmanageability of debt are reflected in aggregate economic data. Nominal GDP per capita declined from $612 to $485 in the 1980s, and the nominal value of exports declined over the same period. Debt troubles, a drag on government adjustment efforts and on recovery in private investment, are now more than a symptom of growth problems in Sub-Saharan Africa. Empirical evidence shows that a debt overhang (where reduction in the face value of debt would likely increase the expected value of future debt service payments) is more probable in Africa than in any other region (Claessens 1988 and Cohen 1989). The solution is not simple: it must take into account the wide range in the sources and terms of African debt.

The diverse nature of African debt

Twenty-four of the 26 severely indebted low-income countries are found in Sub-Saharan Africa. So, too, are three severely indebted middle income countries. Only nine African countries are neither seriously nor moderately indebted: Botswana, Burkina Faso, Djibouti, Lesotho, Mauritius, Rwanda, Seychelles, Swaziland and Chad (although a unique set of internal circumstances has led to debt difficulties in Chad, despite favorable debt indicators).

All but six countries are classified as official-source borrowers, of which three are mainly indebted to multilateral creditors (table 3.3). None is severely indebted. Another 21 are mainly (and most severely) indebted to bilateral creditors. Another 14, classified as mixed official borrowers, are less severely indebted and tend to hold heavily concessional debt unlike official-source borrowers, which tend to have debt at harder terms.

Nigeria owes almost half its debt service to private creditors, while six countries (Congo, Côte d'Ivoire, Niger, Sudan, Seychelles, and Zimbabwe) are mixed private/official borrowers. All but Sudan are middle-income countries and all six have heavily nonconcessional debt. For most other countries, scheduled debt service is owed to bilateral official creditors.

The debt of African countries is shown by type of economy (or major export) in tables 3.4 to 3.10. Five oil-exporting countries have mainly bilateral nonconcessional and private-source debt and face debt servicing difficulties despite their oil resources. Mineral exporters, such as Zaire and Zambia, have mainly nonconcessional bilateral official debt, reflecting limited creditworthiness in their heavy borrowing period, and except for Botswana, all face immense debt servicing difficulties. Agricultural exporters are less homogeneous. Sudan and Côte d'Ivoire once had access to much bilateral nonconcessional and commercial bank credit. The remainder (Ghana, Malawi, and Uganda) borrowed chiefly from official sources and at softer terms, with Malawi and Uganda having repeated reschedulings and arrears problems. Four countries classified as diversified economies (Kenya, Mauritius, Swaziland, and Zimbabwe) also borrowed from diversified sources and have avoided the serious debt servicing difficulties common to African countries with concentrated sources of export earnings. Countries of the Sahel have fragile economies dependent on capricious weather and most have debts mainly to official creditors, with a heavily concessional component. Debt of small African economies, which have little or no access to private markets, is mainly official—and half have highly concessional debt. Of the least developed economies, all except Rwanda have had servicing difficulties on debt that is highly official and concessional. In all groupings there is a movement from private toward official debt. Excluding arrears, private debt (mainly to commercial banks) dropped from 40 percent of total Sub-Saharan African debt in 1980 to 25 percent in 1989.

With few exceptions, African multilateral debts were fully serviced in 1989 (table 3.11). Private creditors were paid more than half the amount due, while bilateral official creditors were last in line, receiving about a quarter. Since then, Nigeria has limited payments on its private debt, while most other

African countries have virtually suspended payments to private creditors. However, most countries try to fully service valuable active short-term trade credits, even when they are accumulating arrears on long-term debt owed to the same creditors.

The share of variable interest rate denominated debt is gradually declining. The average cost of new funds has almost halved, and the proportion of concessional debt has increased significantly. On the other hand, the risk has become more concentrated among official creditors, and the debt structure has become less flexible as preferred creditors have a rising share in net flows to the countries in this region.

The need for debt relief

Debt relief for adjustment

Is there an economic rationale for concessional debt relief for Sub-Saharan Africa? The most persuasive pro arguments (Claessens and Diwan 1989) are centered around debt overhang and liquidity constraints—that is, around the perverse incentive effect of a large debt outstanding on the willingness of the country to adjust and invest and on the willingness of the creditors to provide new financing. Without an injection of liquidity, additional investment is costly to the debtor as current consumption must be reduced—unattractive after austerity has lowered per capita consumption and income over the past decade. Moreover, the more indebted a country is, the larger the share of future benefits of austerity and investment will be to creditors. So, as the share of output a debtor has to transfer overseas increases, further austerity for the sake of future growth becomes less attractive. What is the best outcome for creditors? It is an adequate amount of debt relief on the assurance that the benefits will be invested in additional capacity to service debt in future years.

Progress has been considerable in many African countries in the past few years to improve the structure of incentives, efficiency, and competitiveness. They have made major efforts to maintain realistic exchange rates, pay remunerative prices to agriculture producers, dismantle state ownership of enterprises, and promote the private sector.

Serious adjustment efforts of 23 low-income African countries have been recognized by donors and creditors; they are eligible for external support under the World Bank-sponsored Special Program of Assistance (SPA). Nigeria, although a low-income country, is not currently eligible under the SPA because it is an IBRD borrower, but its adjustment efforts have been recognized by the international community. In the SPA countries, inflation has been contained while fiscal deficits have been curtailed. The pace of progress has not been rapid enough, however, to avert a decline in per capita incomes. And without adequate external support at appropriate terms, adjustment in highly indebted countries is likely to fail.

Financing requirements for growth

To achieve a 4 percent annual growth rate of GDP (5 percent by the end of the 1990s), total investment in Africa will have to average 21 percent of GDP during the period (see chapter 2). Domestic savings are projected to average 16 percent of GDP, compared with 11 percent now. Foreign savings required to support the investment rate would average 6 percent of GDP, a high rate because of the poor prospects for world prices of most primary commodities exported by Africa and the need to restore a minimum level of imported raw materials and capital goods for investment. Even so, per capita income is projected to grow by less than one percent annually and per capita consumption will stagnate. All this assumes successful and sustained adjustment programs and an average annual level of foreign savings to finance Sub-Saharan Africa's recovery over the next decade of around $11 billion.

Gross foreign financing available to Sub-Saharan Africa is projected to be about $22 billion—50 percent loans, 40 percent grants, and 10 percent foreign direct investment with a large share of the loans coming from official sources. Because of budget constraints in donor countries, an increase in official concessional assistance relative to donor GNP seems unlikely. Few African countries are likely to be able to borrow from market sources during the decade, and anyway such debt is inappropriate for most low-income African countries, given their short-term growth prospects. Such external financing would leave $11 billion available for debt service, which could average $16-$18 billion during the decade, taking into account debt relief measures to date.

The goal of African adjustment programs is for growth with external viability. This viability implies that debtor countries can meet import bills, scheduled pdebt service, and other external resource needs from export earnings and financial inflows, without recourse to rescheduling or external payments arrears. If Africa is to achieve external viability over the next decade, additional measures will be required equivalent to an annual reduction in debt service of about $6 billion, or an average 35 percent of scheduled debt service—the difference between scheduled debt service of about $17 billion and the $11 billion available for debt service. For the most severely indebted of the low-income African countries, additional measures averaging roughly 70 percent of currently scheduled debt service would be required.

In the next five years, about 25 percent of exports is the maximum amount of debt service that can be expected, which suggests debt service payments averaging about $11 billion over the decade. This 25 percent debt service ratio should not be seen as a target, since some countries might understate exports or discourage export expansion, believing that higher exports attained will mean higher debt servicing payments. Moreover, country circumstances differ greatly. Kenya and Burundi, for example, are severely indebted and have high debt servicing ratios but have chosen to fully service their debt and attract new flows. All this helps to identify in quantitative terms the magnitude of debt relief required by Africa in the context of successful adjustment programs, to relate this to debt relief to date, and to estimate additional requirements for external viability.

These estimates need to be qualified further. The weight of Nigeria, Côte d'Ivoire, and Zaire, accounting for roughly half of the total scheduled debt service payments, is significant. Some countries that do not have credible adjustment programs will not be eligible for debt relief. Others may not need additional relief beyond that already available. The capacity to service debt depends on the volume of real net capital inflows including external assistance. If non-debt creating flows, including official grants and the repatriation of flight capital, exceed the amounts assumed for these flows in our projections, then the requirements for debt relief will be reduced. Moreover, if oil prices were to increase, a few African countries would require less external assistance, but most of the severely indebted low-income countries will face serious financing constraints. Most important, if marginal domestic saving rates are higher in the future, the need for external resources can be reduced or growth rates accelerated. Given the decline in per capita incomes in the 1980s, the case for faster growth through higher investment and higher domestic savings is more persuasive.

What should be the qualifications for debt relief? The starting point should be a low per capita income—say, the IDA eligibility level of $480. There should also be an economic adjustment program approved by the IMF and the World Bank—and on track. Also taken into account should be the severity of debt burden. All these criteria are in line with the Special Program of Assistance (SPA) for Africa.

The policy response

How can this relief be structured? Who provides it and in what proportions?

Multilateral creditors

In 1989 multilateral institutions (excluding the IMF) were owed $31 billion by Sub-Saharan Africa (30 percent of the total) and accounted for $2.6 billion of the region's scheduled debt service (15 percent of the total). Of this, two-thirds was principal repayment, one-third interest. This compares with a multilateral debt burden in 1980 of $8 billion and $1 billion of debt service.

Debt service cannot be divorced from the availability of new loans and ODA grants, an important consideration for multilateral institutions. These institutions increased loan disbursements to Sub-Saharan Africa from $1.7 billion in 1980 to $3.8 billion in 1989, of which a growing proportion is concessional (about two-thirds today). As a result, multilateral net lending flows (disbursements less repayments) increased from $1.5 billion to $2.8 billion, and net transfers have also remained positive at $1.8 billion. More than $2 billion is provided as ODA grants by multilateral institutions. IMF net purchases have turned negative, reflecting repurchases resulting from large IMF programs in the early 1980s.

The IBRD has stopped nonconcessional loans to most African countries, while increasing concessional funds. New IBRD loans to Sub-Saharan Africa (excluding Nigeria) have virtually dried up in the past three years. The IBRD's negative flows are more than offset by $1.3 billion in net new flows from IDA, which should increase to over $1.6 billion a year in fiscal years 1991 to 1993. Not only are aggregate flows positive, but in each country with an adjustment program, IDA lending is larger than IBRD repayments.

Is it appropriate for IDA-only countries to service nonconcessional multilateral debt? In September 1988 the Governors of the World Bank earmarked 10 percent of IDA reflows and investment income to eligible countries in proportion to their IBRD interest payments. Extra IDA adjustment credits of about $100 million have been provided to 10 Sub-Saharan African countries. Funds provided under IDA's interest financing facility are equivalent to about 60 percent of their annual IBRD interest obligations. Norway and Sweden also made grants for IBRD debt service in four African countries. Funds available will allow IDA to provide new credits up to 100 percent of scheduled IBRD interest payments and as IBRD debt is paid, the percentage of interest covered under this program should rise. In the long term this program is self-limiting because most IBRD debt to IDA-only countries should be repaid by the end of the 1990s.

The IMF has also increased its soft loan capabilities—the Structural Adjustment Facility (SAF) and the Enhanced Structural Adjustment Facility (ESAF)—to offset reduced nonconcessional lending. By April 1990 the first had committed $638 million (and disbursed $493 million) to 20 countries. By the same date, the second had approved eight arrangements for severely indebted low-income countries, committing $1.6 billion, of which $875 million had been disbursed. As funds by the two facilities are disbursed over the next few years, the IMF's negative flows would also be reduced. These concessional disbursements will have the effect of replacing outstanding purchases at market-related terms with debt at concessional terms and result in a lower debt and debt servicing burden for African countries in the future.

A few IDA-only countries, with poor economic performance and policies, have accumulated large arrears to multilateral institutions, and, at most, only limited IDA lending is maintained. Until these countries make credible economic reforms, additional funds are unlikely to be well spent to reduce debt burdens. Countries taking difficult measures to reform their economies, such as Zambia and Sierra Leone, have received sympathetic support from creditors. The two available mechanisms, the collaborative support group and the IMF "rights approach" (see chapter 6), could be used in both cases.

For multilateral creditors, the preferred strategy remains the provision of new money at concessional terms to countries making serious adjustment, leveraging this new money with cofinancing and coordinated financing with other creditors, allocating funds for buyback of commercial debt, and in effect subsidizing the interest payments falling due on previously contracted nonconcessional debt. The gradual replacement of IDA for IBRD lending and of SAF/ESAF for conventional IMF credit in the debt stock of recipient countries over the next few years will alter the composition of debt and debt service in favor of more concessional multilateral debt and easy terms of servicing.

Bilateral creditors

Africa's main creditors are official bilateral lenders. These creditors are owed $73 billion, including claims they have guaranteed on which the scheduled debt service payments are about $10 billion annually, or over 50 percent of the total. The largest single group of creditors is the Paris Club, whose members are owed $51 billion or almost 40 percent of the region's outstanding debt. Much progress has been made in reducing the official bilateral debt burden of African countries. It can be divided into three main initiatives.

Increased flow of concessional aid

Sub-Saharan Africa is now the major aid-receiving region. From less than 10 percent of total ODA in 1960, it accounted for more than 30 percent by the late 1980s (World Bank 1989). In the 1980s bilateral aid to the region grew 4.3 percent per year, compared with growth in total DAC ODA of 2.9 percent a year. The volume of net ODA flows to Sub-Saharan Africa in constant prices and exchange rates rose from $8.9 billion in 1978 to $14.7 billion in 1988. The first phase of the SPA provided an additional flow of quick-disbursing concessional funds to 23 countries of $6 billion in 1987-90. With the second phase now formulated (for 1991-93), the target of almost $8 billion over the three year cycle appears probable.

Debt forgiveness by official bilateral creditors. Thirteen OECD countries have announced or implemented plans to cancel or convert bilateral loans owed by various low-income African countries into grants (table 3.12). Debt forgiven or converted for African countries since 1987 is roughly $7 billion, virtually all of which was concessional, arising from earlier ODA activities. Scheduled debt service payments in 1990 were lower by roughly $400 million as a result of ODA debt forgiveness, but the impact on overall debt service has been small because of the highly concessional nature of these loans. Moreover, most beneficiary countries would have rescheduled these payments anyway. Typically, concessional debt service is rescheduled on concessional terms, thereby increasing the grant element and reducing the burden. Countries that do not reschedule their debt have benefitted more substantially from ODA loan forgiveness. Debt forgiveness also represents an emerging consensus among the official bilateral community not just to reschedule but to reduce the stock of debt.

Still unresolved is the source of funding for debt cancellations or conversions. It is not much good if donors rely on recycling earlier aid to fund new programs or use budgetary aid allocations for this purpose and in turn reduce new aid allocations by a comparable amount of forgiveness. But if the level of new grants and concessional loans remains the same (adjusted for projected growth), debt forgiveness has positive effects in terms of net flows available to the beneficiary country, without reducing aid flows to other countries.

Paris Club reschedulings

The Paris Club has eased the terms on rescheduled official bilateral debt for severely indebted low-income countries. The most recent reschedulings for 17 low-income African countries included the cancellation of one-third of the amount consolidated, very long maturities (25 years), and a reduction in interest rates. More than $5 billion have been consolidated under these Toronto terms since October 1988 (table 3.13), resulting in a cash flow savings of about $100 million annually. There are three main reasons for the limited amount of these cash flow savings:

(1) The concessions apply only to debt maturing in a given period—an average of 16 months.

(2) The standard reschedulings granted to low-income African countries by the Paris Club already provide 100 percent rescheduling of principal and interest.

(3) Not all potentially eligible debt has been included under the arrangements: some is debt service on loans past the cutoff dates, and some previously rescheduled debt has not been rescheduled.

The cash flow relief in relation to the original contractual terms of agreements is nevertheless significant. For these 17 African countries the cash flow savings were almost $5 billion. While reschedulings are necessary for cash flow relief, they add to the buildup of debt. About 40 percent of the long-term nonconcessional debt of rescheduling countries in low-income Africa owed to the Paris Club at the end of 1988 represented capitalized interest. With repeated Toronto-term reschedulings, debt service payments due to Paris Club creditors would be about 20 percent lower, compared with repeated standard reschedulings. Some creditor countries reschedule nonconcessional debt by extending maturities and charging moratorium interest at market rates. If they either canceled one-third of the consolidated amount or reduced the interest rate by 3.5 percentage points, the reduction in the present value of scheduled debt service would increase to 30-33 percent.

In the past, Paris Club creditors have dealt with Sub-Saharan Africa's debt problems on a flow basis. Because reschedulings cover only the debt service coming due over the consolidation period (16 months for Toronto reschedulings), only about an eighth of the eligible debt has been touched. An alternative would be to reschedule the entire stock of debt under agreements containing recapture clauses, tied to favorable exogenous events, to avoid a debt reduction that is, ex post, excessive. (The recent proposal by the UK's then Chancellor of the Exchequer, John Major, discussed below, would incorporate debt stock restructuring into Paris Club reschedulings for low-income countries.)

Eleven African countries owed more than 25 percent of total 1989 debt service to bilateral creditors outside the Paris-Club—OPEC countries, the CMEA, and a host of others (table 3.3). Some borrowers are accumulating arrears that add to the debt stock and debt service obligations. More needs to be done through rescheduling, cancellations, or reductions in principal and interest (perhaps through new concessional lending).

Private creditors

Except in Nigeria, private creditors have played a small part in the external financing of Africa. The long-term debt owed to them by all Africa was $34 billion in 1989 ($22 billion excluding Nigeria) or less than 15 percent of the total excluding interest arrears. Scheduled debt service payments on long-term bank debt were $8.2 billion ($4.3 billion excluding Nigeria) or one-third of the total due, but the actual payments were only $4.2 billion ($2.2 billion excluding Nigeria). In 1980 the private creditors' share of total debt service (excluding Nigeria) was 43 percent.

Apart from Nigeria, others (including Benin, Mozambique, and Niger) have excessive commercial debt. The IDA debt-reduction facility, set up in 1989, will provide grants up to $10 million each to countries with adjustment programs to buy back or exchange commercial bank debt at a discount, and 14 African countries with commercial bank debt of $1.6 billion have requested grants. Only one, of $10 million, has been approved for Niger, with other countries providing supporting grants. Much of the delay in approvals is due to reluctance of banks to participate, partly to avoid setting precedents for other countries where their exposure is larger.

Nigeria's debt to private creditors (excluding loans guaranteed by official creditor agencies) was $12 billion at the end of 1989. Debt-servicing payments (after rescheduling of promissory notes and agreements with commercial banks and the Paris Club) will account for roughly 40 percent of exports of goods and services in 1992—clearly untenable.

The debt burden of a few countries is divided among bilateral, multilateral, and private creditors.

For them, equal burden-sharing in debt relief or new flows would be preferable, rather than action by any single group of creditors.

Direct foreign investment and capital flight

In addition to increased aid flows and reduced debt service payments, there are other options for meeting external financing needs in the 1990s, including increased foreign direct investment (FDI) and reflows of flight capital (mainly for Nigeria).

FDI flows to Africa, estimated at less than $500 million annually during the past three years, account for about 5 percent of net flows. FDI investment has not been sought aggressively by African countries as a source of financing, technology transfer, managerial skills, or market penetration. The inflows, modest compared with other developing regions, have been concentrated in a few key sectors, such as oil and mining, and in a few countries, mainly Nigeria, Gabon, and Kenya. The potential for attracting larger flows is great but unexploited because of political instability, poor economic policies, poor governance, and inadequate human resources and physical infrastructure. Competition for FDI, particularly from East European countries, is fierce. And some Sub-Saharan African countries—such as Nigeria, Côte d'Ivoire, Cameroon, Kenya, and Zimbabwe—will have to change their policies to attract foreign investors. Others, especially the Sahelian countries, will continue to rely on official grants and concessional flows and should not count on large FDI inflows.

The same is true of flight capital reflows. Cumby and Chang suggest that $20-$30 billion is held in African residents' deposits abroad, but mostly by Nigerians. If Nigeria can attract some of these deposits back, the pressure on ODA flows will be eased, but the prospects in the short run do not appear promising unless economic stability and investor confidence are restored.

Assessment of the policy response

Of the $6 billion shortfall in the ability of Sub-Saharan African countries to service debt and scheduled debt service payments, low-income countries (excluding Nigeria) account for about $5 billion (table 3.14). Promised ODA debt cancellation will reduce the difference by $400 million. Toronto-term reschedulings could reduce scheduled debt service by another $2.3 billion. That still leaves $2 billion. Officially supported debt and debt service reduction operations could reduce the $1 billion debt service due to commercial banks on long-term loans to severely indebted low-income African countries. All of this means that policy responses, even if fully implemented, are not adequate to restore external viability to many low-income African countries. The problem will be worse in the second half of the 1990s. The concessional options of Toronto-term reschedulings have relatively short grace periods. The principal payments due under these reschedulings add to scheduled debt service payments after 1995. This bulge in debt service affects current assessments of external viability when it is recognized as too large to be met from available external resources.

At the September 1990 meeting of the Commonwealth Secretariat in Trinidad, Britain's then Chancellor of the Exchequer, John Major, proposed a more concessional approach to Paris Club reschedulings of the bilateral official debt of low-income countries. He proposed that Paris Club creditors cancel two thirds of the stock of eligible debt and reschedule the rest over 25 years with five years of grace. Interest due during the first five years would be automatically capitalized, providing further cash-flow relief; later payments would be graduated and related to the debtor country's ability to pay.

If these Trinidad terms were adopted, the scheduled debt service of low-income African countries would fall by $4 billion and come close to restoring external viability to low-income Africa. But, a few countries do not have adjustment programs and would not benefit from debt reduction; others have debt servicing difficulties greater than the average for low-income Africa. If two-thirds debt reduction had been applied in past reschedulings (with no change in grace periods), eight low-income African countries would have faced debt service ratios above 50 percent in 1989 (Equatorial Guinea, Guinea-Bissau, Liberia,

Mozambique, Sao Tome and Principe, Somalia, Sudan and Zaire). Moreover, if donors allocated funds from aid budgets for concessional reschedulings and reduced new allocations for other purposes, the impact of debt relief on external viability would be neutralized.

Nigeria and two of the severely indebted middle-income countries in Africa (Congo and Côte d'Ivoire) account for much of the remaining $1 billion difference between scheduled debt service and likely ability to service debt. All are oil exporters, and their need for debt relief will depend on oil prices. All three could benefit from officially supported commercial bank debt and debt service reductions. Currently, these countries are not eligible for concessional relief on their bilateral official debt, mainly hard-term export credits. Unless oil prices rise significantly, some concessional relief on their official bilateral debt (assuming strong adjustment programs) may be necessary to restore external viability.

Conclusion

Debt difficulties in Africa are a symptom of deeper structural problems and poor economic policies. Countries undertaking structural adjustment and bringing about a turnaround in economic policies deserve conditional assistance, and growth in levels of real aid flows needs to be maintained in the 1990s. Even allowing for exceptional efforts to raise domestic savings, adequate funding for the adjustment programs of low-income African countries would require continuing expansion in the real value of ODA flows during the 1990s, partly by expanding the SPA for low-income debt distressed countries in Africa. The SPA should also be reinforced by extending coverage to lower middle-income countries that adopt adjustment programs.

There is also a need for more concessional debt relief for low-income countries. External viability could be achieved by most countries if scheduled debt service payments were no greater than actual payments in recent years (25-30 percent of exports). Achieving this goal in the most severely indebted low-income African countries will require more comprehensive and more concessional reschedulings by their main creditors—official bilateral agencies. Ideally, the reduction in the present value of nonconcessional bilateral loans through reschedulings should equal the grant element in new loans and grants extended to these debtors by the same creditor governments. There are two arguments in favor of concessional debt relief. First, it fits better with equitable burden-sharing among creditors and donors. Second, the future availability of extra concessional assistance flows for debt service would always be in doubt.

Multilateral creditors should continue to increase net flows on concessional terms to support adjustment and development efforts, leverage other types of assistance, provide funds for buying back commercial debt, and refinance interest payments on their nonconcessional loans on easy terms. Private creditors are most exposed in Nigeria, where a combination of a Brady-type deal, debt-equity swaps, and other reschedulings would ease the debt servicing problem. In other countries, the IDA debt reduction facility, along with other donors, could finance the buyback of commercial bank debt at deep discounts and so reach a comprehensive settlement.

Foreign direct investment flows and the repatriation of flight capital have been neglected in Africa so far, but they potentially have a useful role to play in Nigeria and a few other countries. Many poorer and less diversified economies will continue to rely on official development assistance for the major share of their external financing needs. This differentiated approach to capital flows—matching the appropriate type of financing with the right subgroup of countries—is the key to the efficient allocation of limited external resources available for Africa and for their effective use.

References

Claessens, Stijn. 1988. The Debt Laffer Curve: Some Estimates, World Bank, International Economics Department.

Claessens, Stijn, and Ishac Diwan. 1989. "Conditionality and Debt Relief." World Bank PRE Working Paper No. 213, 1989.

Cohen, Daniel. 1989. "Is the Discount on the Secondary Market a Case for LDC Debt Relief?" World Bank Working Paper No. 132. Washington, D.C.

Greene, Joshua. 1989. "External Debt Problem of Sub-Saharan Africa." *IMF Staff Papers* 36 (December): 836-74.

Krumm, Kathie. 1986. "The External Debt of Sub-Saharan Africa: Origins, Magnitude, and Implications for Action." World Bank Working Paper No. 741. Washington, D.C.

World Bank. 1989. *World Debt Tables, 1989-90 Edition*. Washington, D.C.

Table 3.1 ***Sub-Saharan Africa's external debt, end-1989***
(US$ billions)

Total external debt	161
Total debt service [a]	11
Debt/GNP (percent)	112
Debt/exports (percent)	352
Debt service/exports (percent)	24
Memo items:	
Latin American debt/GNP (percent)	48
Latin American debt/exports (percent)	261
Latin American Debt service/exports (percent)	27

[a]. Debt service on a cash, rather than scheduled, basis.
Source: World Bank, *World Debt Tables*, 1990-91 edition.

Table 3.2 ***Structural differences between severely indebted low-income countries and severely indebted middle-income countries***

	Severely indebted countries	
Indicator	*Low-income*	*Middle-Income*
Annual population growth (percent)	3.2	2.0
GNP per capita (1988 US dollars)	288	1,632
Gross domestic investment/GDP (percentage on current prices, 1987-88)	14	22
Exports as a share of GDP (percent 1987-88)	18	16
Share of manufacturing in exports (percent 1987-88)	8	43
Infant mortality (deaths per 1000 live births, 1987)	110	55
Primary school enrollment (percentage of age group 1986)	67	103
Official development assistance (share of GDP, 1987)	8.2	0.6
Long-term official debt (as percntage of debt, 1989)	67	35

Source: World Bank data files.

Table 3.3 ***Structure of scheduled debt service on Sub-Saharan Africa's long-term debt in 1989*** [a]
(percentage share unless otherwise noted)

Country	Official									Private L		
	Multilateral			Bilateral [b]								
	IBRD/IDA	Other	Total multilateral	Paris Club	OPEC [c]	CMEA	Other	Total Bilateral	Total official	Commercial Bank [d]	Other	[illegible] s)
Total Sub-Saharan Africa	9.2	5.7	14.8	41	3.2	6.4	1.7	52.5	67.3	29.5	3.2	[illegible]
less Nigeria	10	8.4	18.4	40.7	4.9	6.3	2.6	54.5	72.9	26.6	.5	[illegible]
Mainly official debt	10.	10.3	20.5	44.6	5.5	8.9	3.5	62.4	82.9	17	0	[illegible]
Large multilateral debt	1.3	31.3	62.6	29.2	3.4	1	0	33.4	96	4	0	[illegible]
Botswana	36.9	29.8	66.7	27.4	14.5	0	0	31.9	98.6	1.4	0	[illegible]
Cape Verde	.9	54.0	55.1	25.2	6.5	11.2	0	42.1	97.2	2.8	0	[illegible]
Swaziland	28.5	27.6	56.1	34.1	0	0	0	34.1	90.1	9.9	0	[illegible]
Large bilateral debt	7.2	8.7	15.9	47.6	5.8	11.1	3.7	68.2	84.1	15.8	0.1	[illegible]
Cameroon	15.3	8.3	23.5	46.1	1.7	0	3.2	51.1	74.7	25.3	0	[illegible]
Central African Republic	4.5	22.9	27.1	37.4	4.5	1.4	17.9	61.2	88.3	11.7	0	[illegible]
Equatorial Guinea	1.4	14	15.4	48.3	0	4.9	28.7	81.8	97.2	2.8	0	[illegible]
Ethiopia	6.6	3	9.6	34.2	1	29	6.4	70.7	80.3	18.8	.9	[illegible]
Gabon	.7	4.7	5.4	64.7	.9	0	.1	65.7	71.1	28.9	0	[illegible]
Guinea	7.6	6.6	14.1	30.7	5.2	31.9	10.6	78.4	92.5	7.5	0	[illegible]
Guinea-Bissau	2.8	21.5	24.3	34.5	8.3	.9	10.8	54.5	78.8	21.2	0	[illegible]
Lesotho	5	38.2	43.3	50.4	3.4	0	.8	54.6	97.5	2.1	0	[illegible]
Madagascar	3	5.4	8.4	46.5	10.5	21.3	.2	78.5	86.9	13.1	0	[illegible]
Mauritania	8	24.6	32.6	28.3	29.1	0	.1	57.5	90.1	9.9	0	[illegible]
Mozambique	.2	3	3.2	32	3.6	50.7	1.3	87.6	90.8	9.2	0	[illegible]
Niger	3.1	14.4	17.4	42	5.4	0	4	51.4	68.8	31.1	0	[illegible]
Sao Tome and Principe	.7	20.9	21.6	44	0	9.7	12.7	66.4	88.1	11.9	0	[illegible]
Senegal	4.9	17.2	22.1	44.3	14.2	.1	1	59.6	81.8	18.3	0	[illegible]
Sierra Leone	6.9	10.7	17.5	61.4	0	0	11.1	72.3	89.8	10.2	0	[illegible]

Table 3.3 ***Structure of scheduled debt service on Sub-Saharan Africa's long-term debt in 1989 (continued)***

(percentage share unless otherwise noted)

	Official									Private			TOTAL		
	Multilateral				Bilateral [b]										
Country	IBRD/IDA	Other	Total multi-lateral	Paris Club	OPEC [c]	CMEA	Other	Total Bilat-eral	Official	Commercial Bank [d]	Other	Priv.	All types of creditors (US$, mil.)	Concessional	Non-con-cessional
Somalia	3.8	17.1	20.9	46.1	22.58	5.4	4.5	78.4	99.3	.7	0	.7	114	50.4	49.6
Tanzania	24.3	6.7	31	27.2	12.9	14.7	6.4	61.2	92.2	7.8	0	7.8	327	44.3	55.7
Togo	5.2	21.7	26.9	48.1	3.8	0	0	52	78.8	21.2	0	21.2	76	30.8	69.2
Uganda	8.3	18.1	26.4	14.7	2.4	8.3	33.5	59	85.3	14.5	.2	14.7	172	31.8	98.2
Zaire	3.1	4.1	7.2	71.3	1.3	0	1.7	74.4	81.6	18.3	0	18.4	1,164	11.6	88.4
Zambia	17.6	11.1	28.7	48.2	3.4	14.4	2.7	68.6	97.3	2.7	0	2 .7	522	16.9	83.1
Mixed official borrowers	20.5	14.7	35.2	34.2	4.3	.9	2.7	42	77.2	22.8	0	22.8	1,520	27.5	72.5
Benin	4.6	18	20.9	39.7	1.6	2.9	2	46.3	67.2	32.8	0	32.8	89	25.5	74.5
Burkina Faso	6.4	37	41.6	31.3	4.7	0	6.2	42.1	83.7	16.2	0	16.2	68	46.4	53.5
Burundi	20.8	32.2	38.8	22.3	10.1	2.8	6	41.2	80	20	0	20	47	56.9	43.1
Chad	2.4	21.6	42.4	29.6	4	0	0	33.6	76	24	0	24	13	53.6	46.4
Comoros	.9	28.8	32.3	8.5	19.5	0	4.9	32.3	64.6	35.4	0	35.4	16	54.9	45.1
Djibouti	4.3	24.9	25.8	12.2	27.2	0	0	39.4	65.3	34.7	0	34.7	21	63.4	37.1
Gambia, The	12.1	34.9	39.2	23.4	14.4	0	0	37.8	77	23	0	23	21	50.2	49.3
Ghana	28.3	14.2	26.3	37.4	2.4	3.4	3.1	46.3	72.6	27.5	0	27.5	241	27.2	72.7
Kenya	25.4	6.9	35.2	35.8	2.5	0	2.5	10.9	76	24	0	24	616	15.7	84.3
Liberia	28.3	17.5	42.9	39.6	2	0	1	42.7	85.6	14.4	0	14.4	124	27.6	72.7
Malawi	25.4	17.8	46.1	36	0	0	1.2	37.2	83.1	14.7	0	14.7	78	26.1	73.7
Mali	28.3	32.1	42.7	8.8	29	2	2	41.9	84.7	15.3	0	15.3	49	70.8	29.4
Mauritius	10.8	11.9	43.9	35.4	2.3	0	5.1	42.8	86.7	13.3	0	13.3	102	24.9	75.1
Rwanda	31.9	19.6	31	20.4	1.9	0	2.6	40.9	71.9	28.1	0	28.1	34	57.6	42.4

Table 3.3 ***Structure of scheduled debt service on Sub-Saharan Africa's long-term debt in 1989 (continued)***

(percentage share unless otherwise noted)

Country	IBRD/IDA	Other	Total multilateral	Paris Club	OPEC [c]	CMEA	Other	Total Bilateral	Official	Commercial Bank [d]	Other	Priv.	All types of creditors (US$, mil.)	Concessional	Non-concessional
	Official									Private			TOTAL		
	Multilateral				Bilateral [b]										
Mixed private/official borrowers	8.3	2.2	10.5	38.2	1.5	4.4	.9	44.9	55.4	38.9	5.6	44.6	10,020	5.3	94.7
Congo	2.1	4.9	7.1	35.8	1	.35	2.7	43.1	50.2	49.8	0	49.8	979	7.9	92.1
Cote D'Ivoire	16.8	3.9	20.7	33.7	0	0	.1	33.8	54.5	45.4	.1	45.5	1,629	5.4	94.6
Nigeria	7.6	.4	8	41.5	0	6.5	.6	48.6	56.6	35	8.4	43.4	6,027	1.5	98.5
Seychelles	3.3	13.2	16.6	16.6	7	0	1.7	25.5	42.1	58.3	0	58.3	30	17.5	28.5
Sudan	2.4	6	8.4	28.3	15.2	1.6	1.1	46.3	54.6	45.4	0	45.4	908	25.7	74.6
Zimbabwe	14	4.5	18.5	38	.9	0	.1	39	57.5	30.1	12.4	42.5	447	6.9	93.2

Note: (I) More than 60 percent of scheduled debt service owed to official creditors: "country with mainly official debt, " and within that category, (Ia) more than 50 percent of scheduled debt service owed to multilateral creditors: "country with large multilateral debt," (Ib) more than 50 percent of scheduled debt service owed to bilateral official creditors: "country with large bilateral debt," (Ic) the remaining countries with mainly official debt: "mixed official borrowers;" (2) more than 40 percent of scheduled debt service owed to private creditors: "mixed private/offical borrowers." No sub-Saharan African countries were classified as (3) "countries with mainly private debt" because none owed 60 percent or more or scheduled debt service to private creditors.

[a] Shares are based on a total excluding the IMF.

[b] Includes estimates of guaranteed obligations.

[c] OPEC includes: Algeria, Ecuador, Gabon, Indonesia, Iran, Iraq, Kuwait, Libya, Nigeria, Qatar, Saudi Arabia, United Arab Emirates, and Venezuela.

[d] Bank data include commercial bank loans to private nonguaranteed borrowers.

Table 3.4 ***African oil exporters*** [a]

(US$ millions)	Debt Stock and Debt Service [b]					Percent shares				
	Debt Stock			1989 Debt Service		Debt Stock			1989 Debt Service	
Type of Creditor	1970	1980	1989	Scheduled	Cash	1970	1980	1989	Scheduled	Cash
TOTAL	916	14,355	43,926	8,081	2,684	100	100	100	100	100
Official	756	4,827	29,450	4,954	1,158	82.5	33.6	67	61.3	43.1
Multilateral	263	1,150	5,035	716	628	28.7	8	11.5	8.9	23.4
IBRD/IDA	253	932	4,033	571	518	27.6	6.5	9.2	7.1	19.3
Other	10	218	1,002	145	110	1.1	1.5	2.3	1.8	4.1
Bilateral	493	3,677	24,415	4,238	530	53.8	25.6	55.6	25.4	19.7
Paris Club	454	2,880	21,769	3,438	434	49.6	20.1	49.6	42.5	16.2
Oil Exporters	0	155	190	24	4	0	101	.4	.3	.1
CMEA	4	173	1,665	428	11	.4	102	3.8	5.3	.4
Other	35	469	791	348	81	3.8	3.3	1.8	4.3	3
Private	160	9,528	14,476	3,127	1,526	17.5	66.4	33	38.7	56.9
Commercial Banks [c]	142	9,526	9,923	2,887	1,292	15.5	66.4	22.6	35.7	48.1
Other	18	2	4,553	240	234	2	0	10.4	3	8.7
Memo Item: IMF	0	96	260		18					

Note: Small differences between scheduled and cash debt service payments are the result of interest and exchange rate movements and scheduled adjustments. Large differences imply arrears and reschedulings.

[a] Oil exporters include Cameroon, Congo, Gabon, and Nigeria. Data for Angola are not available.

[b] Excludes interest arrears on long-term debt; debt service on long-term debt only.

[c] Includes short-term and non-guaranteed long-term debt.

Table 3.5 ***African Mineral Exporters*** [a]

	Debt Stock and Debt Service [b]					Percent shares				
(US$ millions)										
	Debt Stock			1989 Debt Service		Debt Stock			1989 Debt Service	
Type of Creditor	1970	1980	1989	Scheduled	Cash	1970	1980	1989	Scheduled	Cash
TOTAL	1,510	9,414	17,778	2,153	451	100	100	100	100	100
Official	1,127	6,804	14,812	1,885	412	74.6	72.3	83.3	87.6	91.4
Multilateral	106	1,136	4,232	378	165	7	12.1	23.8	17.6	36.6
IBRD/IDA	106	882	2,588	208	74	7	9.4	14.6	9.7	16.4
Other	0	254	1,644	170	91	0	2.7	9.2	7.9	20.2
Bilateral	1,021	5,668	10,580	1,507	247	67.6	60.2	59.5	70	54.8
Paris Club	741	4,129	7,964	1,247	154	49.1	43.9	44.8	57.9	34.1
Oil Exporters	6	266	421	51	26	.4	2.8	2.4	2.4	5.8
CMEA	170	499	885	146	40	11.3	5.3	5	6.8	8.9
Other	104	774	1,310	63	27	6.9	8.2	7.4	2.9	6
Private	383	2,610	2,966	298	39	25.4	27.7	17.7	12.4	8.6
Commercial Banks [c]	34	2,598	2,962	268	38	2.3	27.6	16.7	12.4	8.4
Other	349	12	4	0	1	23.1	.1	0	0	.2
Memo Item: IMF	0	1,004	1,993		425					

Note: Small differences between scheduled and cash debt service payments are normally the result of interest and exchange rate movements and schedule adjustments. Large differences imply arrears or reschedulings.

[a] Mineral exporters include Botswana, Guinea, Liberia, Sierra Leone, Zaire, and Zambia.

[b] Excludes interest arrears on long-term debt; debt service on long-term debt only.

[c] Includes short-term and non-guaranteed long-term debt.

Table 3.6 ***African agricultural exporters*** [a]

	Debt Stock and Debt Service [b]					Percent shares				
(US$ millions)										
		Debt Stock		1989 Debt Service		Debt Stock			1989 Debt Service	
Type of Creditor	1970	1980	1989	Scheduled	Cash	1970	1980	1989	Scheduled	Cash
TOTAL	1,586	15,427	33,196	3,354	1,705	100	100	100	100	100
Official	1,379	10,602	22,285	2,072	756	86.9	68.7	67.1	61.8	44.3
Multilateral	245	2,271	8,562	660	505	15.4	14.7	25.8	19.7	29.6
IBRD/IDA	235	1,406	6,388	440	384	14.8	9.1	19.2	13.1	22.5
Other	10	865	2,174	220	121	.6	5.6	6.5	6.6	7.1
Bilateral	1,134	8,331	13,723	1,412	251	71.5	54	41.3	42.1	14.7
Paris Club	896	4,527	8,663	1,038	122	56.5	29.3	26.1	30.9	7.2
Oil Exporters	66	1,711	2,867	190	9	4.2	11.1	8.6	5.7	.5
CMEA	94	612	742	85	15	5.9	4	2.2	2.5	.9
Other	78	1,481	1,451	99	105	4.9	9.6	4.4	3	6.2
Private	207	4,825	10,911	1,282	949	13.1	31.3	32.9	38.2	55.6
Commercial Banks [c]	105	4,795	10,890	1,281	948	6.6	31.1	32.8	38.2	55.6
Other	102	30	21	1	1	6.4	.2	.1	0	.1
Memo Item: IMF	0	941	2,445		578					

Note: Small differences between scheduled and cash debt service payments are normally the result of interest and exchange rate movements and schedule adjustments. Large differences imply arrears or reschedulings.

[a] Agricultural exporters include Cote d'Ivoire, Ghana, Malawi, Sudan, Tanzania, Uganda.

[b] Excludes interest arrears on long-term debt; debt service on long-term debt only.

[c] Includes short-term and non-guaranteed long-term debt.

Table 3.7 ***African diversified exporters*** [a]

	Debt Stock and Debt Service [b]					Percent shares				
(US$ millions)										
	Debt Stock			1989 Debt Service		Debt Stock			1989 Debt Service	
Type of Creditor	1970	1980	1989	Scheduled	Cash	1970	1980	1989	Scheduled	Cash
TOTAL	704	4,624	9,326	1,201	1,044	100	100	100	100	100
Official	374	2,291	6,658	846	692	53.1	49.5	71.4	70.4	66.3
Multilateral	93	793	3,156	364	319	13.2	17.1	33.8	30.3	30.6
IBRD/IDA	92	612	2,452	279	259	13.1	13.2	26.3	23.2	24.8
Other	1	181	704	85	60	.4	3.9	7.5	7.1	5.7
Bilateral	281	1,498	3,502	482	373	39.9	32.4	37.6	40.1	35.7
Paris Club	281	1,464	3,219	439	344	39.9	31.7	34.5	36.6	33
Oil Exporters	0	0	113	22	10	0	0	1.2	1.8	1
CMEA	0	0	0	0	0	0	0	0	0	0
Other	0	34	170	21	19	0	.7	1.8	1.7	1.8
Private	330	233	2,668	355	352	46.9	50.5	28.6	29.6	33.7
Commercial Banks [c]	105	1,731	2,347	299	269	14.9	37.4	25.2	24.9	25.8
Other	225	602	321	56	83	32	13	3.4	4.7	8
Memo Item: IMF	0	361	508		252					

Note: Small differences between scheduled and cash debt service payments are normally the result of interest and exchange rate movements and schedule adjustments. Large differences imply arrears or reschedulings.

[a] Diversified economies include Kenya, Mauritius, Swaziland, and Zimbabwe.

[b] Excludes interest arrears on long-term debt; debt service on long-term debt only.

[c] Includes short-term and non-guaranteed long-term debt.

Table 3.8 ***African Sahel countries*** [a]

(US$ millions)	Debt Stock and Debt Service [b]					Percent shares				
	Debt Stock			1989 Debt Service		Debt Stock			1989 Debt Service	
Type of Creditor	1970	1980	1989	Scheduled	Cash	1970	1980	1989	Scheduled	Cash
TOTAL	487	4,278	10,635	1,002	583	100	100	100	100	100
Official	455	3,199	9,565	819	418	93.4	74.8	89.9	81.7	71.7
Multilateral	30	960	4,036	266	197	6.2	22.4	38	26.5	33.8
IBRD/IDA	26	510	2,194	58	55	5.3	11.9	20.6	5.8	9.4
Other	4	450	1,842	208	142	.8	10.5	17.3	20.8	24.4
Bilateral	425	2,239	5,529	553	221	87.3	52.3	52	55.2	37.9
Paris Club	235	1,295	3,138	374	147	48.3	30.3	29.5	37.3	25.2
Oil Exporters	17	469	1,570	160	69	3.5	11	14.8	16	11.8
CMEA	80	193	379	2	1	16.4	4.5	3.6	.2	.2
Other	93	282	442	17	4	19.1	6.6	4.2	1.7	.7
Private	32	1,079	1,070	183	165	6.6	25.2	10.1	18.3	28.3
Comm. Banks [c]	32	1,065	1,070	183	165	6.6	24.9	10.1	18.3	28.3
Other	0	14	0	0	0	0	.3	0	0	0
Memo Item: IMF	0	301	586		155					

Note: Small differences between scheduled and cash debt service payments are normally the result of interest and exchange rate movements and schedule adjustments. Large differences imply arrears or reschedulings.

[a] Sahelian countries include Burkina, Chad, The Gambia, Mali, Mauritania, Niger, and Senegal.

[b] Excludes interest arrears on long-term debt; debt service on long-term debt only.

[c] Includes short-term and non-guaranteed long-term debt.

Table 3.9 ***Small African Economies*** [a]

	Debt Stock and Debt Service [b]					Percent shares				
(US$ millions)										
	Debt Stock			1989 Debt Service		Debt Stock			1989 Debt Service	
Type of Creditor	1970	1980	1989	Scheduled	Cash	1970	1980	1989	Scheduled	Cash
TOTAL	17	458	1725	163	85	100	100	100	100	100
Official	17	364	1577	122	60	100	79.5	91.4	74.8	10.6
Multilateral	4	126	875	45	31	23.5	27.5	50.7	27.6	36.5
IBRD/IDA	4	33	345	4	4	23.5	7.2	20	2.5	4.7
Other	0	93	530	41	27	0	20.3	30.7	25.2	31.8
Bilateral	13	238	702	77	29	76.5	52	40.7	47.2	34.1
Paris Club	13	120	384	48	20	76.5	26.2	22.3	29.4	23.5
Oil Exporters	0	31	144	15	8	0	6.8	8.3	9.2	9.4
CMEA	0	31	73	3	0	0	6.8	4.2	1.8	0
Other	0	56	101	11	1	0	12.2	5.9	6.7	1.2
Private	0	94	148	41	25	0	20.5	8.6	25.2	29.4
Comm. Banks [c]	0	94	148	41	25	0	20.5	8.6	25.2	29.4
Other	0	0	0	0	0	0	0	0	0	0
Memo Item: IMF	0	24	25		7					

Note: Small differences between scheduled and cash debt service payments are normally the result of interest and exchange rate movements and schedule adjustments. Large differences imply arrears or reschedulings.

[a] Small economies include Cape Verde, Comoros, Djibouti, Equatorial Guinea, Guinea-Bissau, Lesotho, and Sao Tome and Principe

[b] Excludes interest arrears on long-term debt; debt service on long-term debt only.

[c] Includes short-term and non-guaranteed long-term debt.

Table 3.10 ***Other Least Developed African Countries*** [a]

	Debt Stock and Debt Service [b]					Percent shares				
(US$ millions)										
	Debt Stock			1989 Debt Service		Debt Stock			1989 Debt Service	
Type of Creditor	1970	1980	1989	Scheduled	Cash	1970	1980	1989	Scheduled	Cash
TOTAL	448	4389	16791	1661	671	100	100	100	100	100
Official	442	3580	15286	1424	522	98.7	81.6	91	85.7	77.8
Multilateral	96	1112	5416	185	165	21.4	25.3	32.3	11.1	24.6
IBRD/IDA	95	751	3404	55	59	21.2	17.1	20.3	3.3	8.8
Other	1	361	2012	130	106	.2	8.2	12	7.8	15.8
Bilateral	346	2468	9870	1239	357	77.2	56.2	58.8	74.6	53.2
Paris Club	277	1606	5623	633	263	61.8	36.6	33.5	38.1	39.2
Oil Exporters	5	303	1271	106	20	1.1	639	7.6	6.4	3
CMEA	53	249	2469	455	62	11.8	5.7	14.7	27.4	9.2
Other	11	310	507	45	12	2.5	7.1	3	2.7	1.8
Private	6	809	1505	237	149	1.3	18.4	9	14.3	22.2
Comm. Banks [c]	6	809	1501	234	146	1.3	18.4	8.9	14.1	21.8
Other	0	0	4	3	3	0	0	0	.2	.4
Memo Item: IMF	0	306	563		158					

Note: Small differences between scheduled and cash debt service payments are normally the result of interest and exchange rate movements and schedule adjustments. Large differences imply arrears or reschedulings.

[a] Other least developed economies include Benin, Burundi, CAR, Ethiopia, Madagascar, Mozambique, Rwanda, Somalia, and Togo

[b] Excludes interest arrears on long-term debt; debt service on long-term debt only.

[c] Includes short-term and non-guaranteed long-term debt.

Table 3.11 ***Debt Service on Long-Term Debt, Sub-Saharan Africa, 1989***

	Scheduled debt service (US$ billion)	Share (percent)	Debt service paid (US$ billion)	Share (percent)	Paid/ scheduled (percent)
Total	17.6	100.0	7.2	100.0	41.0
Official	11.9	67.3	4.0	55.2	33.7
Multilateral	2.6	14.8	2.0	27.8	77.0
Bilateral	9.2	52.5	2.0	27.4	21.4
Paris Club	7.2	41.0	1.5	20.5	20.6
OPEC	0.6	3.2	0.1	2.0	25.7
CMEA	1.1	6.4	0.1	1.8	11.5
Other	0.3	1.9	0.2	3.0	65.8
Private	5.8	32.7	3.2	44.8	56.1
Commercial Banks	5.2	29.5	2.9	39.9	55.6
Other	0.6	3.2	0.4	4.8	61.4

Source: World Bank, Debtor Reporting System.

Table 3.12 ***Cancellation of ODA Debt of Sub-Saharan Africa, 1978-89 (Millions of dollars)***

Donor Country	1978-86	1987-89	1990	Total
Belgium	0	184	0	184
Canada	176	53	730	959
Denmark	194	136	15	345
Finland	49	0	0	49
France	100	0	3,300	3,400
Germany	1,284	1,315	587	3,186
Italy	79	0	0	79
Japan	20	18	0	38
The Netherlands	144	58	0	202
Norway	4	7	0	11
Sweden	189	3	13	205
United Kingdom	175	68	0	243
United States	0	0	282	282
All Donors	2,414	1,842	4,927	9,183

Note: Data for some donor countries may contain non-ODA debt cancellation. For Japan, amounts represents grants provided to fund debt service payments. Not all of the announced cancellations have gained final approval from donor governments. Some donor governments provided mainly grants and had little or no ODA claims to cancel.

Table 3.13 ***Toronto-Term Reschedulings Benefiting African Countries***

	Date of reschedule	Amount consolidated (US$ million)	Length of consolidation period [a] (months)	Net cashflow savings[b] (US$ million)	Decrease in present value of scheduled debt service [c] (US$ million)
Mali	Oct.'88	63	16	*	4
Madagascar	Oct.'88	197	21	2	25
Tanzania	Dec.'88	481	6	6	96
Central African Republic	Dec.'88	26	18	1	4
Niger	Dec.'88	44	12	1	11
Senegal	Jan.'89	142	14	3	28
Uganda	Jan.'89	42	18	2	8
Guinea	Apr.'89	116	12	*	5
Mauritania	Jun.'89	110	12	2	15
Togo	Jun.'89	76	14.5	1	15
Benin	Jun.'89	157	13	*	12
Zaire	Jun.'89	1,530	13	26	197
Chad [c]	Oct.'89	40	15	*	4
Guinea-Bissau	Oct.'89	26	15	*	4
Mali	Nov.'89	16	26	*	1
Senegal	Feb.'90	107	12	1	23
Equitorial Guinea [c]	Mar.'90	6	0	*	1
Tanzania	Mar.'90	200	12	3	42
Mozambique	Jun.'90	707	30	30	155
Central African Republic	Jun.'90	4	12	*	1
Togo	Jul.'90	84	12	3	16
Madagascar	Jul.'90	139	12	2	20
Zambia	Jul.'90	965	18	14	136
Niger	Sep.'90	116	28	4	30
Total or average:		5,394	15.8 [d]	101	853

[a] The period over which debt service payments coming due are consolidated and subject to rescheduling. Payments falling due after the consolidation period are not rescheduled. The consolidation period normally starts at or slightly before the date of the rescheduling, often coinciding with a Fund program.
[b] Relative to the previous standard rescheduling for low-income countries, a 20-year maturity with 10 years of grace. A discount rate of 9 percent was used to calculate present values.
[c] Bilateral arrangements outside the Paris Club.
[d] Excluding the bilateral arrangements outside the Paris Club.
* Means less than 1 million.

Table 3.14 ***Low-Income African Countries Effect of Debt Relief on Scheduled Debt Service (billions of US dollars)***

Average scheduled debt service, 1991-95	8.2
Estimated debt service capacity	3.5
Difference	4.7
Effect of ODA debt cancellation	0.4
Remaining difference	4.3
Toronto-term rescheduling	2.3
Remaining difference	2.0
Trinidad-term rescheduling	4.0
Remaining difference	0.3

Comment

Mufutau Iyiola Raheem

The paper raises several interesting and relevant issues and again brings to the fore the severity of the debt problem, its implications for the African economies, and what needs to be done in order to contain the problem. In the immediate past, the debt of the low-income African nations was not generally considered a major issue warranting urgent and far-reaching international attention—for many reasons.

First a large proportion of the debt of these countries is owed to official creditors (governments and multilateral lending institutions, such as the Bank and the Fund). Second, the region's total debt is relatively small when compared with that of other regions in Latin America and Asia (less than 12 percent of the total). But the ratio of Africa's outstanding debt to exports of goods and services was about 331 percent in 1988, compared with about 148 percent in 1980. The rate of increase in the debt burden in Sub-Saharan Africa is greater than that of other developing countries. Many countries in the region have a stock of debt whose value is equivalent to their GDP, while some like Somalia and Zaire carry a debt level of between 125 and 165 percent of their GDP, few countries (e.g. Zambia) are burdened with debt more than 2.5 times the GDP. It is on record that about 25 countries rescheduled their debt 105 times between 1980 and 1988. It seems that despite their already worsened situation, African debtor countries have been refraining from invoking total repudiation of their debt service obligation.

The debt problem is not new in Africa but the present situation is more severe.

Husain and Underwood rightly indicate the heterogeneous nature of the external debt problem in the region and divide the region into country groups on the basis of several analytical characteristics—such as the severity of the debt burden, the predominant creditor source, rescheduling and nonrescheduling countries, as well as per capita income. This approach complements the classification adopted by the IMF, which categorizes the region into three groups: the market borrowers; the official borrowers; and the diversified borrowers. Thus, as a result of this heterogeneity, the international community of donors and creditors is not following a generalized across-the-board approach but intervenes selectively. Opinion in some circles is that this approach may not be doing much to solve the region's debt problem. A more comprehensive approach is believed to be more relevant to Africa.

A growing number of countries in the region (about 30) has instituted far-reaching economic reforms because of severe economic imbalances. Accessing the existing debt relief facilities is conditional upon implementing strong adjustment measures.

Two observations can be made at this point. These are the underfunding of adjustment efforts and fatigue with the adjustment. Given the experience of the African adjusting countries, the adjustment programs are grossly underfunded. Most of the promised new money in the adjustment package has often not come in. External capital inflow to the region has been negligible. It would seem that international capital is refraining from coming to Africa. This shortfall in capital flows has severely reduced the probability of success of the adjustment programs in restoring growth. I support the suggestion of the authors that it is essential that the resolve and willingness of the African countries to pursue serious economic reforms and restore growth should be complemented by an adequate inflow of external resources on terms and conditions that are commensurate with the current economic standing of these countries. This support is based on the fact that political willingness and commitment to carry out reforms depend on the availability of sufficient external resources to minimize the short-term transitional cost of adjustment.

A new but dangerous development in some African countries is adjustment fatigue. This fatigue is setting in as more and more African countries reach the point where further austerity in the absence of meaningful economic growth has become politically and economically untenable.

The paper raises the issue of capital flight, no longer restricted to Latin America. As inefficient macroeconomic policy is common in Africa, the emergence of capital flight in the region is not surprising. It has been analyzed somewhere that capital flight can contribute to the accumulation of external debt. An indication is given in the paper that the region's requirements for debt relief will be reduced if the non-debt creating flows, including official grants and repatriation of flight capital, exceed the amount assumed for these flows in the projections made. The possibility of this happening is remote because the unstable macroeconomic environment, the political instability, and other factors will continue to deter capital inflows, including direct foreign investment.

The paper also highlights lucidly the problem of debt overhang and import strangulation in the region. As of 1987, real imports were only two-thirds their 1980 level in Sub-Saharan Africa, reflecting the impact of higher debt service obligations. On the other hand, export earnings are only marginally above their 1977 levels. The effect of this is to delay or prolong the adjustment required for growth resumption.

A quick review and assessment of the existing international facilities aimed at reducing the intensity of the debt crisis is in order. This effort is considered necessary since Husain and Underwood's paper does not critically assess the relevance and adequacy of most of these facilities to the needs of the debt-distressed African countries. From the time of its inception in 1986, the Structural Adjustment Facility (SAF) appeared inadequate (SDR2.7 billion) relative to the financial needs of the countries that qualified for assistance under the facility. Hence the establishment of Enhanced Structural Adjustment Facility (ESAF) in 1987 with about SDR 6 billion. Of the 62 countries to use the resources, 34 are from Sub-Saharan Africa. The number of countries that have so far benefited from this arrangement has not been encouraging.

According to this paper, only 20 Sub-Saharan countries had made use of the SAF while about 8 countries had benefited from the ESAF as at end April 1990. While the loan agreements under ESAF have lagged considerably, many African countries have criticized the tough conditionality attached to ESAF resources. The point that is not always considered by the international creditor bodies is that many of the affected countries lack administrative capabilities to implement adjustment programs.

Another related facility from the Fund's stable is the Contingency and Compensatory Financing Facility (CCFF). This facility is specifically created to give ready assistance to countries experiencing adverse external shocks. The importance of this facility comes to the fore when it is noted that emergence of external shocks can compound the debt crisis of the affected countries. The combined access under the CCFF amounts to 105 percent of quota. As of April 1989, none of the countries in Sub-Saharan Africa had made use of the facility.

The SPA program of the World Bank was established in 1987. Its focus is low-income debt distressed countries in Sub-Saharan Africa. At the outset, the program involved 15 countries and has now been extended to cover 21 countries. The achievement so far regarding the use of the facility has been very negligible at best. A casual observer would have the impression that the program is moving slowly. To get the program well rooted, there is an urgent need to speed up specific commitments on the part of the donor countries and bodies. As more and more countries become eligible to drawn on SPA resources, the need for a rapid augmentation of its resource base becomes more urgent.

The principle of official debt forgiveness has already been conceded for the low-income countries. The Toronto menu of options expressly covers this. The first few countries that benefited from the Toronto rescheduling terms include Central African Republic, Madagascar, Mali, Niger, and Tanzania. But the practical impact of these measures has been limited. Even though about 14 Sub-Saharan countries have been granted rescheduling on Toronto terms, the resultant cash relief amounts to only an estimated US$400 million a year.

The key and novel feature of the Brady Plan is the recognition of the need for official backing of schemes that are designed to achieve voluntary, market-based debt (or debt-service) reduction. At the same time, the new strategy preserves important elements of the (previous) Baker plan approach such as the clauses that negotiations are to proceed on a case-by-case basis and that participation is made conditional on the pursuit of an IMF-approved economic adjustment program. However, the Brady initiative is of only limited relevance to Sub-Saharan Africa. On a broader scale, the size of the transactions is small and limited to only a few countries. Given the structure of the African debt problem, measures to exchange old debt for new securities as a way of assisting debtor-countries to come to terms with a more sustainable debt-service profile may be less realistic. It is becoming increasingly realized that a reduction in bank debt may, on its own, be grossly insufficient to provide the scale of financial relief required by the affected countries.

It is surprising that the paper does not specifically cover the activities of the African Development Bank (ADB)) vis-a-vis the debt problems of Sub-Saharan countries. Concessional lending from ADB has come from African Development Bank Fund. Under the 5th. Replenishment of the Fund in November 1987, its financial resources were doubled to about US$2.7 billion over the five years ending 1992. Even though its resource base is meager when compared with the needs of its member countries, it continues to increase its concessional lending over the years. How the ADB can be assisted in terms of enhancing its financial resources should be an urgent issue to be considered by African member countries as well as participating foreign countries and institutions.

There are two other issues which one expects a background paper on African debt crisis to raise if only tangentially. These are negative net financial flows from the Fund to Africa as well as the arrears problems. Some African countries borrowed extensively from the Fund in the late 1970s and early 1980s as a way of coping with the balance of payments crisis. Since then, many SSA countries have become prolonged users of IMF resources. The Fund currently has programs with about 29 African countries. The net financial flows from the Fund have been declining of late, as repayments became due on the past borrowing. There was a net resource flow to the Fund to the tune of US$426 million in 1985, $895 million in 1986, and about $364.5 million in 1988. Due to the inability of many Sub-Saharan countries to service their debt as due, massive arrears were accumulated. The mounting arrears has been blocking the affected countries from having access to new credit lines. For instance, of total arrears to the Fund of some US$4 billion, about $2.7 billion are owed by Sierra Leone, Somalia, Zambia, the Sudan, and Liberia. Consequently, most of the countries have been declared ineligible to use Fund resources.

Furthermore, the paper does not discuss in detail the trend of debt accumulation in the region as well as the composition and structure of its external debt and how the structure has been changing over the years. The adequacy as well as the coverage of the debt data used in the paper needs to be re-examined. Most of the information is from the World Debt Tables published by the World Bank. The limitations of this information base are well known. There may be a need to supplement the existing data with those from the Bank for International Settlement and the Organization for Economic Cooperation and Development to have a more clearer and comprehensive picture of the problem.

Last, the importance of having sound debt management capability on the part of the borrowing countries in Africa was not emphasized in the paper.

Part II

Official External Finance

Prospects for Bilateral Concessional Assistance

Richard Carey

Bilateral aid from the Development Assistance Committee (DAC)[1] is the most important source of external finance for Sub-Saharan Africa. In 1989 it reached $10.4 billion (in current prices), of which around a quarter was technical cooperation. Multilateral aid was roughly $5 billion. DAC bilateral aid is a complex river system, with 18 sources spreading across the African political and economic landscape. That some part of the flow never reaches its destination, or with great effect, is hardly surprising.

One implication of the macroeconomic and financial projections in the World Bank's (1989) study, *Sub-Saharan Africa: From Crisis to Sustainable Growth*, is a radical increase in the productivity of investment in Africa. The study calls for a revolution in Sub-Saharan Africa, focusing on the "governance system," domestic resource mobilization, and private sector development and confronting the huge problems of poverty, environment, population, education, and primary health care. This is an ambitious but essential agenda. Given the reliance on aid in the region, it implies a radical improvement in the orientation and productivity of aid.

The quality of aid has long been a preoccupation of the DAC, and in the 1980s bilateral donors experienced a "prise de conscience" on the need for aid coordination to support adjustment and policy reform, especially in Africa. Even so, without a cultural revolution among aid donors, pouring more aid into the system will create more swamp rather than irrigate a widening and deepening process of social and economic transformation.

The record

Over the past 20 years Sub-Saharan Africa has been the major aid-receiving region. From less than 10 percent of total ODA in 1960, it accounted for more than 30 percent by the early 1980s—largely at the expense of North Africa and India, which suggests that the aid community believes that its greatest mission and challenge lies in Africa (table 4.1). Despite the static volume of total world ODA—stemming from the dramatic rise of OPEC ODA in the 1970s and then a fall in the 1980s—ODA to Sub-Saharan Africa rose in real terms by over 3 percent a year between 1980-81 and 1988-89 (figure 4.1).

After 1983 there was a strong donor response to the "crises" in many countries, later to be defined and targeted through the Special Program for Africa (figure 4.2). The response was most dramatic from the multilateral institutions, with IDA being the

Figure 4.1 ***ODA to Sub-Saharan Africa***

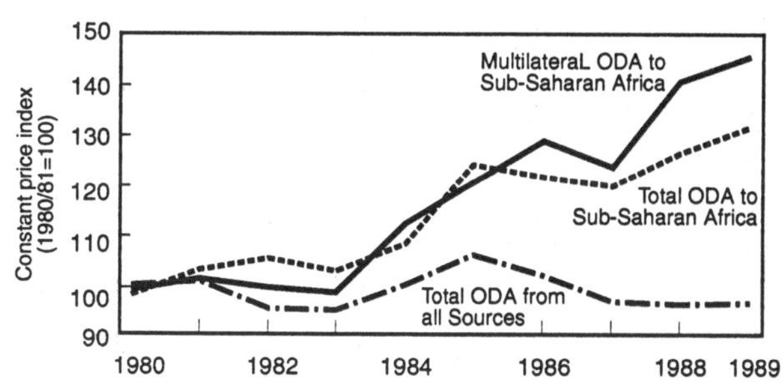

1. The index of ODA is based on net disbursements at 1988 prices and exchange rates.

2. Real annual growth rates 1980/81-88/89:

Total ODA to SSA:3.2 percent
Mult. ODA to SSA:4.4 percent
Total ODA :0.5 percent

Table 4.1 ***Average annual net disbursements of ODA to Sub-Saharan African countries from all sources by region and income group***

	Percentage of total ODA			*Percentage of GNP*		
	1960-61	*1970-71*	*1984*	*1960-61*	*1970-71*	*1984*
Asia	44.8	47.1	28.2	1.6	1.3	0.8
Sub-Saharan Africa	9.0	18.7	30.8	1.9	2.9	5.4
Low-income countries	7.8	13.0	25.6	2.5	3.6	10.5
Somalia	0.6	0.4	1.4	12.0	9.0	27.1
Sahel group[a]	0.2	2.7	5.4	0.4	7.4	21.4
Lesotho	0.1	0.2	0.4	7.3	12.6	17.5
Tanzania	0.6	0.9	2.2	4.1	4.3	14.3
Sudan	0.5	0.1	2.4	1.8	0.4	7.5
Rwanda	0.2	0.4	0.6	6.1	10.5	10.5
Kenya	1.1	1.0	1.7	5.5	3.8	7.7
Zaire	2.2	1.5	1.2	7.3	5.3	10.1
Ethiopia	0.5	0.7	1.4	1.9	2.4	7.7
Ghana	0.1	0.9	0.8	0.3	2.9	5.1
Lower middle-income countries	1.0	3.7	3.4	0.6	1.4	1.1
Congo	--	0.3	0.4	0.1	5.8	5.3
Cameroon	0.1	0.8	0.7	0.7	4.8	2.7
Côte d'Ivoire	--	0.8	0.5	0.3	3.6	1.9
Nigeria	0.8	1.7	0.1	1.0	1.0	0.1
Upper middle-income countries	0.3	2.1	1.8	3.7	15.5	9.2
Reunion	--	1.6	1.3	--	25.8	20.1
Latin America	9.9	16.0	12.7	0.5	0.6	0.5
Europe	9.3	2.8	1.5	1.4	0.4	0.3
Oceania	--	4.2	3.7	--	16.2	13.7
Total	100.0	100.0	100.0	1.7	1.2	1.1

-- Zero or negligible.
Note: Net ODA from bilateral DAC and OPEC sources; net concessional resources from multilateral programs (excluding multilateral development bank nonconcessional lending).
a. Comprises Burkina Faso, Cape Verde Islands, Chad, Gambia, Mali, Mauritania, Niger, and Senegal.
Source: OECD (1989a).

Figure 4.2 ***ODA to SPA Countries***

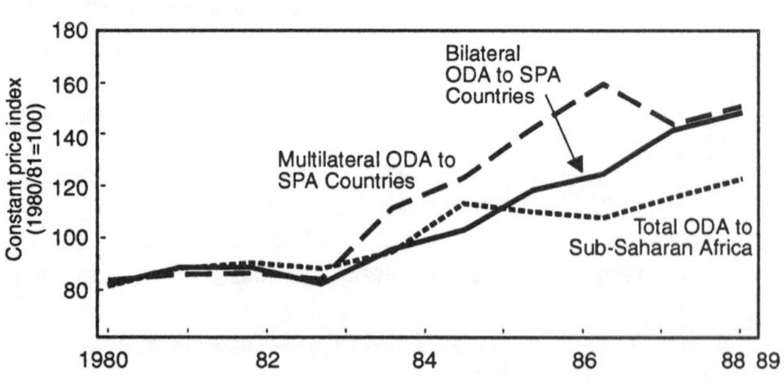

1. The index of ODA data is based on net disbursements at 1988 prices and exchange rates.

2. Real annual growth rates 1980/81-88/89:
Bilat. ODA to SPA: 5.2% 1980-83 bilat. ODA: 0.2% mult. ODA: 0.1% 1983-86 bilat. ODA: 6.2% mult. ODA: 1.2%
Mult. ODA to SPA: 5.4% 1983-86 bilat. ODA: 9.5% mult. ODA: 10.7%

leading force. But bilateral donors' efforts have been sustained, and with the fall-off in multilateral disbursements in 1988-89, the bilateral and multilateral efforts have been almost equal over the period. This attention-shift in 1983 chanced the geographical distribution of DAC ODA, and there was a further shift toward SPA countries after 1986 (figure 4.3).

Around 40 percent of the total flow was to the more populous countries, including some with big problems in the 1980s (Sudan, Mozambique and Ethiopia) and some that have not begun to implement effective adjustment programs. Not included in this group is Nigeria, despite its huge population. Without Nigeria's rising oil revenues, the donor community would face a major challenge in Nigeria, which has recently become IDA-eligible.

The remainder of the recipient order seems reasonably predictable on the basis of population size and income levels. A major exception is Reunion (which the DAC classifies in the *Sub-Saharan African*

Figure 4.3 ***DAC ODA to Sub-Saharan Africa***

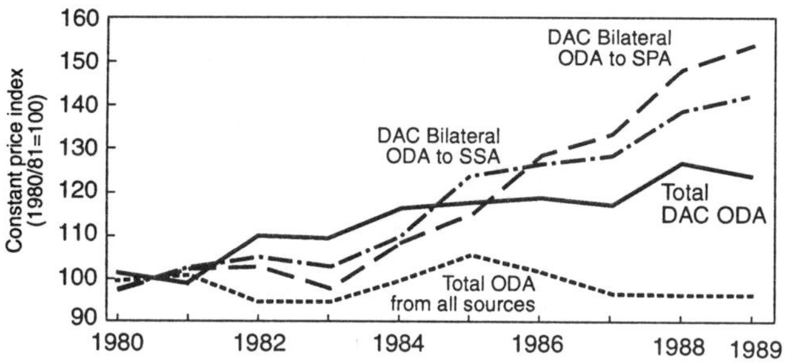

1. The index of ODA data is based on net disbursements at 1988 prices and exchange rates.

2. Real growth rate of DAC Bilateral ODA to SSA: 1980/81-88/89: 4.3 percent 1980-83: 1.9 percent 1983-86: 7.0 percent 1986-89:4.1 percent

region). Botsuana is also a well aided country given its population size and income level. To a lesser degree this is also the case with Angola. The overall geographical distribution of aid is surprising when set against individual donor programs. Here historical associations and particular interests or affinities emerge. Also, there is little country concentration. Many recipients get small amounts from individual donors, which despite the predominance of the region has implications for policy attention that recipient programs might get from donor agencies. Individual donor concentration shows the importance placed on Sub-Saharan Africa by Nordic and other European aid donors (excluding Germany and Austria) and Canada. But the United States and Japan—with only 14 and 12 percent respectively of their aid going to Africa—are probably the keys to any further shift in aid distribution toward the region.

Some simple arithmetic

Forecasting aid levels is neither an exact nor an encouraging science. The current parame-ters—overall DAC aid growth in line with DAC GNP growth, with an ODA/GNP ratio apparently stable at around 0.35 percent—may be considered inadequate in the light of the challenges ahead in developing countries. Indeed, some DAC members hold that view strongly. The Policy Statement on Development Cooperation in the 1990s, adopted by the DAC in December 1989, recognized the "huge task ahead" and sought further substantial increases in aggregate aid. It also said that the new needs for assistance in Central and Eastern Europe would not diminish DAC members' determination to give priority to their development cooperation with the developing countries. These are necessarily loose undertakings. While there seems to be increasing awareness in OECD countries of the great need for development assistance in Africa, it is not clear that this will translate into faster growth of aid.

The common perception in the early and mid-1980s that ODA volume was stagnant or declining resulted from the sharp fall in OPEC aid. This lowered the growth of global ODA, while DAC ODA continued to increase strongly. DAC ODA has grown at 3 percent a year over the past two decades, and such growth (despite recent signs of a slowdown) is not impossible over the next 10 years.

How feasible is the "requirement" in the World Bank's study for 4 percent growth in ODA to Sub-Saharan Africa in 1990-2000? It is assumed that this applies to bilateral and multilateral ODA equally, although a faster growth rate in multilateral ODA could compensate for slower growth in bilateral ODA. The examples here are based on OECD growth of 3 percent and a DAC ODA/GNP ratio of 0.35 percent.

Example A in table 4.2 represents a continuation of the trends of the 1980's in DAC aid growth overall and in the growth of DAC aid to Africa. It implies a further increase in the share of total ODA going to Africa. In example B, DAC ODA to all other recipients continues to grow at 3 per cent a year, in line with OECD GNP growth. It shows that, if aid to Africa were to grow at 4 percent a year, DAC ODA would have to increase at a rate above OECD GNP growth. This has not been achieved in any previous decade. Example C shows the effect of a fall in DAC ODA growth to 2 percent a year in the 1990s, below the historical norm. Maintaining aid growth at 4 percent a year would then mean a drastic fall in the share of aid to other regions. Example D shows the consequences of maintaining aid shares for all other regions at the 1988-89 level, assuming 2 percent annual growth in aid volume. ODA to Sub-Saharan Africa would also have to be constrained to 2 percent growth each year—or half the "requirement" specified in the Bank's study.

Example A is a feasible outcome and, on this basis, the "requirement" is achievable. Examples C and D, however, illustrate that less favorable conditions (in overall aid growth or donors' priority for the region) would have big implications. For A, B or (especially) C to be tolerable or sustainable by donors or the world community, there must be more

Table 4.2 *Examples of possible aid growth in the 1990s*

	ECD GNP growth 1990-2000	*ODA* to SSA	ODA to all others	in total DAC ODA	*DAC* ODA/GNP ratio (1988/89)	*SSA ODA share of total* DAC ODA in year 2000[a] (1988/89=30.9)
	(annual percentage growth)					
Example A	3.0	4.0	2.5	3.0	0.35	34.4
Example B	3.0	4.0	3.0	3.3	0.36	33.3
Example C	3.0	4.0	1.0	2.0	0.31	38.3
Example D	3.0	2.0	2.0	2.0	0.31	30.9

a. Percentage of net ODA disbursements.

evidence of the effective use of aid—and of sustainable growth with equity in Sub-Saharan Africa. It must be shown, too, that aid reliance is not a permanent condition—that the emergence of a flourishing private sector and attention to "good governance" will generate autonomous financial flows through an expanding domestic financial system.

Attitudes, issues, and policies

Prospects for the volume of aid cannot be divorced from success or failure in revolutionizing the productivity of investment and of aid in the aid-dependent countries of Africa. This means more than simply striving for greater efficiency. On the recipient side it means radical change in institutional capacities, development models, and political cultures. Bilateral donors are now conscious of the issues on the "supply side" of the aid equation. Can they adjust their "cultures" and capacities to meet the need for more coherent aid geared to recipient-defined strategies? And can they ensure that the imperatives that drive the orientation and quality of aid are governed by developmental concerns more than by their domestic political and economic interests? These remain fundamental questions.

The policy perspectives for the 1990s set out by the DAC in December 1989 are almost identical to those of the World Bank's study. They advocate a shift:

- To a new development paradigm, based on broad participation of the population in market-based economic activity, the strengthening of human resources, demographic and environmental sustainability, and harnessing science and technology to widen the options open to the economy and to the people.
- To a new political paradigm, with democratization, decentralization, real accountability, and respect for human rights.
- In the role (and an increase in the effectiveness of) the state. This implies a strengthened capacity to set and implement policy and institutional frameworks of an enabling kind, as well as a need to formulate and conduct programs in areas where the private sector cannot function adequately, in particular in social and human resources.

These shifts began emerging in the 1980s, but events in Eastern Europe have sharpened attitudes of DAC donor governments and their public opinions. There has been an increase in the criticism of political regimes and economic performance in Africa, magnified by the burst for freedom and market economies in Eastern Europe. Aid donors are often accused of underwriting abuses of human rights, lack of freedom, economic waste, and corruption. In the absence of real political reform, respect for human rights, and a reduction in excessive military spending, some countries in Africa that have relied on sustained aid support may find donors turning away.

The implications of the new development program in Africa for donor operations are of major proportions.

- With "governance" at the heart of the problems in Africa, aid donors have to take a radical look at how they are interacting with the state and its agencies in recipient countries. An uncoordinated project-seeking aid community with a multitude of missions and procedures undermines the responsibility, accountability, and efficiency of the domestic machinery of government.
- The quality of much technical assistance is also a negative factor. Approaches to technical assistance which durably build local capacity are essential. This is an area for major increases in the productivity of aid. Moreover, the "new areas," such as private sector development and participatory development, are not finance-intensive; they require extremely skillful and considered approaches often in association with NGOs.

- Major infrastructure investments will not (or should not) become a dynamic sector of donor activity until the political, economic, administrative, and institutional reforms are under way. Otherwise the misallocation of resources and the failure of maintenance systems that have plagued the region will recure.

The donor community has been thinking hard about all these issues. The DAC has principles for aid coordination, principles for project appraisal, and best practices for procurement. More recently, the coordinated effort under the World Bank—led Special Program for Africa (SPA) has produced a new level of collective action on financing and some progress on procedures. The DAC is now compiling principles for program assistance—drawing on the donor community's experiences in supporting adjustment and policy reform programs and in providing general economic support and other forms of program lending. A set of DAC principles for new orientations in technical assistance is also near completion.

These challenges are profound, involving habits of thinking and doing, and the interactions between donor agencies and their administrative, political, and wider domestic environments. "Doing things differently" for donor agencies means a challenge like that facing African governments in implementing comprehensive structural adjustment programs. As the Bank's study shows, the reforms needed in donors' and recipients' practices are one.

As the Special Program for Africa moves into its second phase, the discussion should move beyond financial programming to wider issues of development management. It is crucial that aid should flow into recipient-defined and recipient-administered programs. The desires of donors to move past fast-disbursing balance of payments assistance should not mean a shift back to fragmented donor projects and programs. Instead, donors should buy into well-defined sector and subsector programs that form part of the recipient government's long-term development strategy. They should radically simplify administrative procedures. And their technical assistance programs should build long-term national capacity.

A more profound issue for donors is what a strategic emphasis on participatory and private sector development means for aid and the aid system. How can the situation in many Sub-Saharan African countries be changed if most of the aid and total investment effort passes through the public sector? These issues are being discussed by the DAC and by others. Still missing, however, is awareness and concern at the highest political level in the donor countries that the supply side of aid is deeply in question. The changes needed among donors will require strong political support and statesmanship. The recent formation of a Coalition for Africa under Robert McNamara, President Mesire of Botswana, and Minister Jan Pronk of the Netherlands is therefore a most timely initiative toward making these issues a key part of the world's agenda for the 1990s. support and statesmanship. The recent formation of a Coalition for Africa under Robert McNamara, President Mesire of Botswana, and Minister Jan Pronk of the Netherlands is therefore a most timely initiative toward making these issues a key part of the world's agenda for the 1990s.

Notes

1. The Development Assistance Committee of the OECD was formed in 1960 as a forum for OECD donors to work for the expansion of aid volume and the improvement of aid effectiveness. Its members are Australia, Austria, Belgium, Canada, CEC, Denmark, Finland, France, Germany, Ireland, Italy, Japan, Netherlands, New Zealand, Norway, Sweden, Switzerland, United Kingdom, United States, The IMF and the World Bank are permanent observers.

References

OECD. 1989a. *Development Co-operation in the 1990s*. DAC Chairman's Report for 1989. Paris.

OECD. 1989b. "Policy Statement on Development Cooperation in the 1990s." Adopted by OECD's Development Assistance Committee Meeting of Aid Ministers and Heads of Aid Agencies, Paris, 4-5 December 1989.

World Bank. 1989. *Sub-Saharan Africa: From Crisis to Sustainable Growth. A Long-term Perspective Study*. Washington D.C.

Comment

Stephen Denning

The world has changed more than this chapter may indicate. I think when we look at what happened in African financing in the last three years, there has been a shift from a major struggle to see whether one had funds available to adjustment (with SPA) in getting the funds used correctly. There has also been the geopolitical shift. The world looks very different today from a year ago, the Cold War being over. One of the major factors underlying bilateral aid is simply less important than before, and this has led in part to the interest in governance. Bilateral donors now feel able to raise issues that perhaps they had not raised before. This is a change not simply related to an assessment of the effectiveness of their and programs.

I like the river metaphor system. Richard Carey says he is amazed that such a complex system could work, I guess I would be amazed if a very simple system could work; because given the multiplicity of recipients and tasks and issues, I do not think any single agency or even a small number of agencies could really cope with such a complex problem. In fact, when I was in Tanzania at a huge meeting of bilateral donors, one of them asked me why we have so many agencies, and he was wondering what is the right number. I guess I had the feeling that, yes, there were too many people in this room for coordination. On the other hand, reducing it to one or two, would not be the solution. I agree that productivity of aid is a critical issue. I wouldn't put the whole emphasis on governance, however; it seems to me there are other factors that are equally important.

I am not sure that all bilateral aid is aimed at development objectives. If development is not the objective in the first place, then one shouldn't be surprised that grain silos or industrial projects that were essentially done for commercial purposes do not yield development results. And in terms of the results of the aid, it does often seem that in the aid business, for multilaterals as well as bilaterals, there is sometimes more of an emphasis on making new commitments as opposed to actually getting results from the investments. Many bilateral agencies do not formally evaluate their programs. And if you don't evaluate what you have done, it is difficult to have an adequate emphasis on results. Where evaluations do take place, it is not always obvious that this information is disseminated either within the aid community or to the public, which is ultimately financing the assistance. One does wonder, whether there is a governance issue for bilaterals in the sense that the openness to criticism waged on the recipients might also be applied to their programs.

Coordination, is an important factor, and I think there is a set of arrangements that is being put in place, not only in the SPA program but in the global coalition of the individual sector issues, to have groups of donors that can get a consensus on objectives. Will aid be available in adequate quantities? The growth in OECD countries is important, but the historical factors that drive aid programs and the changes in the ideological situation in the world now put some of those in question.

Governance is an important issue and does bear on the political support that aid programs receive, but one has to wonder how much political support there has been for bilateral programs in the past. A few months ago I saw a poll of readers in one major bilateral donor country. It asked them what they thought of the bilateral aid program and whether money was being well spent in Africa. Only fifteen percent of the people in this poll thought that aid money was being well spent. It would not surprise me if that was a result common to many bilateral donor countries, and that may not even have changed despite the new interest in governance. There is also a question of how long one can keep bilateral aid going without having greater political support for it. The alternative is that if you ask any taxpayer whether the money of the government is well spent, fifteen percent is probably quite a good result. I think it also bears on the question of whether aid is a big organization (the river system is a big organization, $10 billion a year). It is not a single organization, but collectively it is a very large organization. The question facing big organizations today is that they are very strong and can raise large amounts of money, but are they agile enough to survive in a world in which there is a global competition, radical political change across the globe, a second industrial revolution making technological change a major factor, and changes in the way the whole world of finances is being run? The question for bilateral aid is, can they survive in this kind of organization, in this kind of world where agility and change are necessary for survival? I would say the jury is still out on the aid agencies, and that is the challenge we all have.

External Development Financing for Sub-Saharan Africa: Multilateral Concessional Assistance

Kathryn Larrecq

In their assessment of the longer-term outlook for the economies of Sub-Saharan Africa, the authors of *Sub-Saharan Africa: From Crisis to Sustainable Growth* propose that, in order to meet targeted growth of 4-5 percent a year in the 1990s coupled with financial stability, Africa would require a net transfer of external resources equivalent to about 9 percent of the region's projected GDP in the year 2000. Attaining that level of resource transfer means an increase in concessional external financing for Africa by about 4 percent annually in real terms over the decade.

This chapter discusses prospects for concessional financing (ODA) for Sub-Saharan Africa in the 1990s from multilateral agencies. Following a brief review of the role of multilateral ODA in the 1980s (section one), prospects for the 1990s are considered in terms of two sets of factors. The first is a series of initiatives undertaken by multilateral agencies in the second half of the 1980s in response to a new focus on the needs of Sub-Saharan Africa and, in particular, the adoption of adjustment programs by a wide number of countries in the region (section two). These initiatives were reflected in a strong rise in resource transfer to the region in the latter 1980s and will continue to be major determinants of resource flows through at least the early 1990s.

The second set of factors consists of developments emerging in the 1990s: recent agreements for replenishing the funding of the multilateral agencies and, secondly, prospects for new funding in the course of the decade (section three). Finally, the overall prospects for multilateral ODA to Sub-Saharan Africa over the course of the 1990s are measured against the projected 4 percent growth in concessional financing required to sustain the targeted rate of economic growth in the 1990s (section four).

The role of multilateral ODA in the 1980s

The evolution of ODA funding

Over the course of the 1980s, Sub-Saharan Africa realized a moderate rise in receipts from multilateral agencies in spite of the fact that the funding of these agencies' activities by their respective national members remained highly constrained throughout the decade. Indeed, the funding environment of the 1980s was such as to yield virtually no growth in concessional resources extended by governments to the developing world as a whole through multilateral and bilateral channels alike. Overall, concessional development assistance (ODA), averaging some US$39 billion annually in the early 1980s, had risen to a level of about US$54 billion a year by the end of the decade, but in real terms had tended to remain constant (table 5.1).[1]

This record was the product of a moderate rise in aggregate contributions from DAC Member governments by a yearly average of close to 3 percent and, at the same time, an offsetting decline in support from sources of ODA funding outside the DAC—higher income petroleum-producing states and the centrally planned economies of the CMEA. Resources deployed through multilateral channels, at a fairly steady one-quarter share of total ODA, paralleled the trend of negligible change over the decade.

Africa's ODA receipts[2]

Despite the generally constrained funding of ODA by its national government donors, the actual ODA receipts of Sub-Saharan Africa showed a rise in real terms by more than 30 percent over the 1980s. For their part, the multilaterals expanded their resource transfer to the region by close to 45 percent over the period, or an average of about 4 percent annually, slightly faster than the bilaterals. At an estimated US$5.1 billion as of 1989, transfers from the multilaterals accounted for nearly one-third of *Sub-Saharan Africa*'s total receipts from all sources (table 5.2).

The rise in transfers to Africa by the multilaterals was led by IDA and the European Economic Community (EEC).[3] Net disbursements to the region by IDA tripled in real terms over the course of the 1980s, and those by the EEC rose by 70 percent. By 1988-89, IDA's disbursements had reached a level of US$1.65 billion annually, while the EEC was in close second position with disbursements averaging close to US$1.60 million a year. Both had surpassed the UN agencies, which as a group had been Africa's largest source of multilateral concessional assistance at the beginning of the decade. IDA and the EEC together accounted for fully two-thirds of Africa's receipts from the multilaterals by the late 1980s, and the UN agencies, despite a late rally, had slipped to third place, accounting for about 25 percent of the region's multilateral receipts[4]. The African Development Fund (AfDF) expanded its transfers in real terms more than three-fold over the 1980s, though its share of the region's receipts from the multilaterals remained comparatively modest, just 8 percent as of 1988-89.

Table 5.1 ***The funding of multilateral ODA, 1980-89 (annual averages)***

	1980-82	*1983-85*	*1986-87*	*1988-89*[a]
Total ODA (billions of U.S. dollars)				
at current prices and exchange rates	37.9	36.4	48.2	53.9
Of which from DAC member governments	26.0 (68.6%)	28.2 (77.5%)	38.8 (80.5%)	47.0 (87.2%)
Of which through multilaterals	9.0 (23.8%)	9.2 (25.4%)	11.5 (23.8%)	13.7 (25.4%)
Annual growth (%; in constant 1987 dollars)				
Global ODA funding	-2.0	1.5	-0.6	-2.4
Multilateral agencies' funding	-1.2	6.6	-5.7	4.1

a. Estimated.
Source: OECD, World Bank.

Table 5.2 ***ODA to Sub-Saharan Africa, 1980-89***

Average annual net disbursements (current US$ millions)

	1980-84		1985-87		1988		1989[a]	
Total ODA to SS Africa	8,024		11,337		15,205		15,836	
Of which: Multilaterals	2,373	(29.6%)	3,564	(31.4%)	4,798	(31.6%)	5,081	(32.1%)
Of which								
IDA	555		1,294		1,657		1,655	
EEC	641		843		1,591		1,585	

Average Annual Growth of ODA to SSA (in constant US$)

	1981-84	*1985-89*	*1980-89*
Total ODA	2.4%	3.9%	3.2%
Multilateral ODA	3.4%	4.5%	4.0%

A. Estimated.
Source: OECD, World Bank.

Initiatives of the 1980s: response of the multilaterals to a new focus on Africa

The growth in transfers by the multilaterals occurred largely in the second half of the 1980s, shifting from an average of 3.4 percent a year in the first half of the decade to 4.5 percent in the second half. This expansion arose with a new focus on the part of the donor community on the consequences of the difficult international environment of the 1980s for the low-income, heavily indebted countries of the region. Throughout the latter 1980s, the attention of both bilateral and multilateral sources of ODA turned increasingly to the need for accelerated resource transfer to the region and, in particular, for external support of the structural adjustment programs on which a wide number of low income African countries were embarking in that period. The multilateral agencies, like the bilaterals, stepped up their financing of investment projects and, at the same time, employed non-project, or "program" assistance in support of the emerging structural adjustment programs. It was the latter which gave principal impetus to Africa's receipts in the second half of the 1980s.

Adjustment financing, mobilized and coordinated through the IDA-sponsored Special Program of Assistance for Africa (SPA), was extended by all of the region's major sources of bilateral assistance as well as by the multilateral agencies, with the exception of the UN group. In the SPA's initial three-year phase, 1988-90, such financing was accorded to more than twenty countries of the region eligible for SPA support by virtue of their low levels of per capita income, heavy external indebtedness and progress in implementing their structural adjustment programs, and it represented some 35 percent of their total ODA receipts in that period.

In order to effect their response to Africa's adjustment financing requirements, IDA, the EEC and, on a more modest plane, the African Development Fund undertook special initiatives to expand and accelerate their resource transfers to the region. These initiatives were of three types: the mobilization of supplementary funding and/or revision of the regional distribution of regularly funded resources, and the use of quick-disbursing forms of assistance conditioned on recipients' adoption of macroeconomic and sectoral policy reforms. Each of the agencies undertook such initiatives in varying degrees—IDA beginning 1986, followed by the AfDF, and, finally, the EEC in 1988. By contrast, the diverse and specialized functions of the UN agencies, largely of a technical assistance nature, did not place them in position to respond operationally in a similar manner.

For IDA, resources supplementary to its regular funding were mobilized in mid-1986 through a new Special Facility for Sub-Saharan Africa (SFA), which was created specifically to meet the need for increased support for adjustment programs in the region. These incremental resources, committed largely in 1986-87, amounted to some US$1 billion, or close to 10 percent of IDA's regular funding agreement prevailing at the time, its Seventh Replenishment (IDA 7).[5]

Second, IDA modified the regional distribution of its lending resources, not only through the addition of the SFA, but also by effecting through the mid-1980s a steady rise in the share of its regularly funded resources which it committed to Sub-Saharan Africa for both investment and adjustment support. By 1987, in the context of the Eighth Replenishment of the agency's regular funding (IDA 8), which governed the volume and deployment of its lending over its fiscal 1988-90 period, it was established that Africa's share of all commitments made by IDA out of the newly funded resources would be permitted to rise to about 50 percent. IDA 8 thus marked the full incorporation in the agency's regular funding process of the regional allocation of its resources, which was formerly effected by introducing the supplementary Special Facility for Africa and by intermittent modifications in the allocation of IDA's regularly funded resources. Thirdly, in support of African adjustment, IDA made increased use of the "quick-disbursing" form of lending, this out of both the SFA resources and a 25 percent share of the regular IDA 8 funding, which enabled it to transform its new commitments into disbursements at an accelerated pace.

The European Economic Community took similar action in early 1988 when its Council of Ministers approved a special ECU 500 million (US$590 million) facility for quick-disbursing support of adjustment programs in Sub-Saharan Africa. These resources, for commitment in 1988-90, were mobilized both outside and within the EEC's regular ODA funding agreement prevailing at the time, the Lome III Convention, which otherwise governed the bulk of its new commitments to the region over the five-year period 1986-90.[6] The new package was equivalent to only 7 percent of the ECU 7.4 billion (US$8.5 billion) in concessional resources funded under Lome III. But, similar to IDA's Special Facility for Africa in its effect, the new EEC facility contributed significantly to an increase in Africa's share of global EEC operations and, by introducing for the EEC the instrument of "quick-disbursing" assistance, similarly contributed to the earlier-cited surge in EEC transfers to the region to the US$1.6 billion level in 1988-89.[7]

The African Development Fund (AfDF) initiated its support of structural adjustment programs in the region as early as 1986 and has since become an important source of financing of this type. Although the AFDF did not mobilize resources supplementary to its regular funding for this purpose, its governing Deputies directed that 20 percent of all new lending commitments out of the AfDF's Fifth (funding) Replenishment, covering commitments made over the three-year period 1988-90, take quick-disbursing form, thus permitting as much as US$540 million to be so deployed over the period.

The initiatives taken by these three multilaterals in the second half of the 1980s in response to the new focus on Africa's financing requirements were by no means uniquely responsible for the growth of their ODA transfers to the region, but they played a major role to that effect by raising the level of the agencies' new commitments to the region and, in turn, translating those commitments into disbursements at an accelerated rate.

Whereas IDA's commitments to Africa as of 1985 had amounted to some US$1 billion, or a little more than 30 percent of its global operations, IDA was committing by the late 1980s close to US$2.5 billion annually to the region, nearly 50 percent of its total commitments on a global basis, and 40 percent of these new commitments to Africa were in quick-disbursing form. The EEC, which in the mid-1980s had committed to Africa US$750-800 million a year, or about 50 percent of the global total, had by the late 1980s expanded its new commitments to the region to an annual level of US$2.8 billion, close to 60 percent of its global total, and 10 percent of its new commitments to the region were of the quick-disbursing type. For its part, the AfDF had raised its commitments from about US$500 million annually in the mid-1980s to about US$800 million as of the late 1980s, 20 percent of this in quick-disbursing form.

At the level of disbursements, or actual transfers to the region, the upturn in activity on the part of each of the agencies corresponded to the timing of its initiatives. IDA's disbursements climbed to a new plateau beginning in 1986 and remained through 1989 at a level double that of the preceding four-year period in nominal terms. The actions taken by the EEC and AfDF, having applied largely in the period beginning in 1988, were reflected in increases in disbursements in 1988-89 by 75 and 30 percent, respectively, over those of the preceding two years.

Closely associated with the new emphasis on concessional financing for adjustment in Africa was the establishment by the IMF of its Structural Adjustment Facility (SAF) in 1986 and Enhanced Structural Adjustment Facility (ESAF), in January 1988. Incorporating a substantial grant element of 48 percent, some 65 percent of these new resources, all in quick-disbursing form, has been directed to countries in Africa in support of their macroeconomic adjustment programs. As of 1989, SAF/ESAF disbursements to Sub-Saharan Africa had reached an annual level of close to US$800 million, equivalent to about 7 percent of the combined transfers of the region's traditional sources of multilateral ODA.[8]

Recent and prospective developments in the 1990s

The upward shift in the multilateral agencies' resource allocations to Sub-Saharan Africa in the late 1980s, a significant share in quick-disbursing form, will continue to exert its favorable impact on the region's receipts in the early 1990s as the new commitments signed in the late 1980s are further disbursed. But will the multilaterals be in a position to sustain the 4 percent a year growth in transfers that they realized in the 1980s and therefore achieve their share of the expansion in overall ODA to the region which is targeted for the 1990s? The answer further rests with the implications of recent and proposed agreements to replenish the funding of three of the multilaterals, prospects for new ODA funding over the course of the 1990s and, thirdly, the likely provisions of future funding agreements for the agencies' deployment of those resources to Africa and in quick-disbursing form for adjustment support.

Recent funding agreements

Important funding agreements for IDA and the EEC have been concluded recently and a third, for the AfDF, is currently in negotiation. These agreements represent new commitment authority of the respective agencies, outlining the volume and deployment of resources which they can commit to Africa over the next 3 to 5 years. The volume of new fund- ding in question for each of the agencies varies considerably relative to that available in the late 1980s. In all cases, however, the new agreements make provision, or are expected to make provision, for continued quick-disbursing assistance in substantial amounts, and those of IDA and the EEC indicate the maintenance of commitments to Sub-Saharan Africa representing, respectively, 50 and 60 percent of their global commitments. These new funding agreements can thus be expected to extend the momentum in resource transfer to Africa begun in the latter 1980s, though they cannot be expected to have the same pronounced impact on the agencies' commitments and disbursements to the region which the initiatives of the late 1980s exerted when they were newly introduced.

In the case of IDA, as noted earlier, the recently completed Ninth Replenishment (IDA 9), which provides SDR 11.7 billion (US$15.1 billion) in funding for IDA's operational commitments in its fiscal years 1991-93, represents no growth in resources in real terms over those mobilized for the 1988-90 period under the predecessor IDA 8 exercise. However, commitments to Africa will continue to account for as much as 50 percent of the total in global commitments, and quick-disbursing assistance is expected to account for 25-30 percent of total commitments, the bulk of which is expected to continue to be directed to countries in Africa.

As for the European Economic Community, Africa should benefit strongly from the new Lome IV Convention, signed in December 1989, which provides for the funding of new commitments to be made over the five-year period 1991-95. The new Convention provides concessional resources to the EDF for onward commitment in that period of ECU 10.8 billion (US$11.9 billion), representing an increase in real terms of 25 percent over those available in the 1986-90 period under Lome III. Ten percent of the new funding is designated for continued quick-disbursing support of structural adjustment in Africa. Again, the provisions of the Lome IV Convention mark the formal incorporation in the EEC's regular funding process of its *ad hoc* initiatives of the second half of the 1980s to support adjustment programs in Africa.[9]

The African Development Fund is currently concluding negotiations for its Sixth Replenishment, ADF VI, which will fund new commitments to be made in 1991-93. Alternative funding proposals range widely but suggest at least a moderate increase in real terms over the FUA 2.25 billion (US$2.71 billion) in resources which were available under ADF V for commitment in 1988-90. It is furthermore likely that the share of total commitments to be deployed in quick-disbursing form will be raised to 25 percent under ADF VI from their 20 percent share under ADF V.

The UN agencies, though in cases gearing their operations to indicative five-year programming cycles, are in fact funded on an annual basis, unlike the other three of Africa's principal sources of multilateral ODA. The resources available to the UN agencies for onward transfer to the region will consequently be determined annually by prevailing prospects for new funding throughout the 1990s.

Before turning to prospects for further ODA funding of the multilateral agencies in the 1990s, it is important to note the very heavy extent to which the volume of multilateral ODA to Sub-Saharan Africa in the 1990s is already indicated by the forward, multi-year funding agreements of IDA and the EEC and, including the agreement to be finalized shortly, the AfDF. The new funding agreements of these three of Africa's four principal sources of multilateral ODA will broadly fix the volume and deployment of their new commitments up to at least mid-1993, and in the case of the EEC up through 1995. Disbursement of these commitments, together with disbursement of balances yet outstanding under commitments made in previous years, i.e. in the context of earlier funding agreements, will in turn define the actual rate of transfer which these agencies are able to make through the first half of the 1990s and, on a declining scale, through the remainder of the decade. The subsequent funding agreements of these agencies will govern the volume and deployment of their new commitments as of mid-1994 at the earliest; they will consequently exert an impact on disbursements, thus Africa's receipts, only in the second half of the 1990s.

The extent to which ODA transfers to SSA in the 1990s are already indicated at this time is illustrated by the case of IDA in tables 5.3 and 5.4. As table 5.4 indicates, disbursements by IDA through 1993 will be made all but exclusively out of resources mobilized under funding agreements already in place at this time. The next addition to IDA's resources, its Tenth (funding) Replenishment, IDA 10, will not be negotiated until 1992-93, and its impact will be significant at the level of developing countries' receipts only beginning about calendar years 1995-96 given observed time lags between funding, commitment and disbursement.[10]

Prospects for new funding.

For the UN agencies, and similarly for IDA, the EEC,and the AfDF beyond the expiration of their existing funding agreements, the outlook for the 1990s will be determined by the prevailing funding "environment", that is, the ability and willingness of donor governments to make concessional resources available to these agencies as well as to meet the demands of their own bilateral programs. Funding prospects inevitably bear a high degree of uncertainty, but on present indications the funding environment could remain highly constrained in the 1990s as it was throughout the 1980s. Additionally, it must be noted that the availability of ODA for current developing country recipients could be eroded in the 1990s by new and competing demands, whether for concessional or non-concessional resources, to meet the expanding requirements of Eastern Europe, including those of the European Bank for Reconstruction and Development (EBRD), the funding of which is expected to amount to some US$3.6 billion, equivalent to about 7 percent of all ODA resources presently mobilized.[11]

Table 5.3 ***ODA targets for Sub-Saharan Africa* in the 1990s**

	1990 (1990 US$billion)	% Growth per annum	2000 (1990 US$billion)
Gross ODA [a]	15.1	4.0 ?	22.0
Of which			
by Multilaterals	4.4	4.0 ?	6.6 ?

a. Gross disbursements excluding technical assistance.

Table 5.4 ***The funding of IDA's disbursements to Sub-Saharan Africa in the 1990s***

	1991-93	*1994-96*	*1997-99*	*2000*
	(calendar years)			
	(Share of gross disbursements provided by Funding Agreement)			
Funding Source				
Existing agreements [a]	98 %	70 %	29 %	23 %
Future agreements				
IDA 10 (FY1994-96)	2 %	29 %	45 %	30 %
IDA 11 (FY1997-99)		1 %	25 %	45 %
IDA 12 (FY2000-2002)			1 %	7 %

Total gross disbursements 1991-2000 out of funding agreements

Existing agreements	58 %
New agreements	
IDA 10	27 %
IDA 11	14 %
IDA 12	1 %

a. As of September 1990, including IDA9 and undisbursed balances of all previous funding exercises dating back to IDA6, plus IDA Reflows (advance commitments and annual allocations).

The level of ODA funding in the 1990s will be determined chiefly by DAC member governments, which currently account for close to 90 percent of all ODA; others such as non-DAC petroleum producers and the CMEA countries can be expected to stagnate or decline further in importance. Country-by-country analysis of the outlook for the foreign assistance programs of the DAC countries suggests that overall ODA can be expected to rise annually in real terms in the range of 2-3 percent on average over the 1990s, and probably at rates towards the lower end of that range through at least the first half of the decade.

This very limited outlook is forecast despite the fact that DAC governments in the aggregate are far from targeted level of ODA funding—0.7 percent of their GNP. Their funding of ODA has stagnated at only half that targeted level, and the outlook for the 1990s suggests that, in the aggregate, they could slip downward from that target rather than progressing upward. An important number of DAC member countries can be expected to increase their funding of ODA at a rate somewhat below the rate of growth of their economies. Among these could be three of the largest DAC countries—the U.S., Germany and the U.K., which have in fact been on a declining course in terms of ODA/GNP in recent years. On the other hand, two of the larger DAC countries—Japan and France, which together presently account for about 35 percent of DAC's total ODA—have announced intentions of increasing their ODA relative to GNP and could consequently achieve an average rate of growth in ODA funding on the order of 4 a year in the 1990s.

As for the volume of resources to be channeled through the multilateral agencies, it cannot be assumed that the one-quarter share of total ODA funding registered throughout the 1980s will necessarily be maintained throughout the 1990s. Some variation in that share could arise depending on a mix of factors such as donor governments' own aid programming capacity for bilateral operations and their views as to the effectiveness of multilateral instruments in addressing their priority concerns.

Provisions of future funding agreements.

The funding environment of the 1990s will clearly determine the volume of new resources available to the UN agencies from year to year throughout the decade, but for IDA, the EEC and the AfDF only as they enter negotiations with their national government members for their successive multi year funding periods, which for IDA will next begin in mid-1993, for the AfDF in 1994, and for the EEC in 1996. The principal issue foreseeable at this time is one confronting the UN network: a need to realign resources in accordance with changing priorities among the agencies' respective areas of activity. This issue was initially raised by the UN General Assembly in late 1987 and has yet to be fully addressed. There does however appear to be sustained support for many of the larger agencies—UNDP and those specialized in the social sectors—and presumably for UNEP, which (along with UNDP) is taking on an important role in the area of environmental conservation.

For IDA, the EEC, and the AfDF, new funding agreements concluded in the 1990s will additionally set out guidelines for the deployment of these resources in terms of regional allocation and/or quick-disbursing form for adjustment support.

As for *regional allocations*, the increased share of Africa in total commitments by IDA and the EEC as of the late 1980s may be the maximum that can be foreseen for the 1990s. For IDA in particular, any further increase in the allocation of its resources in favor of Africa would raise very difficult issues for the agency as a global institution. It is recalled that the shift in IDA's regional allocations in favor of Africa in the 1980s was effected as a result not only of the supplemental Special Facility for Africa, but also in part by reallocating to Africa a portion of IDA's regular resources. Because these regular resources were expanding at only a very modest pace, new commitments to all other regions were reduced not only as shares of IDA's total lending but, in fact, in absolute amounts. In view of the concessional financing requirements of IDA-eligible countries outside of Africa, as well as those of countries which could become eligible for IDA resources in the immediate years, IDA's regional allocations are not likely to be revised further to the benefit of Africa, especially given the very constrained funding outlook for the 1990s.

The EEC as well as the UN agencies would likely confront similar constraints to further increases in the share of Africa in their total operations of 40 and 60 percent, respectively. Although the EEC's Lome Conventions do not specify the allocation of their resources among ACP recipients, individually or by region, the maintenance of a 50-60 percent share for Africa as registered through the 1980s can be assumed given the preponderance of African states among the ACP and the built-in provision, beginning with Lome IV, for EEC adjustment support in Africa.

The second element in the deployment of resources by IDA, the EEC and the AfDF in favor of Africa's receipts in the 1990s will be the extent of their use of the *quick-disbursing* form of assistance. Whereas the introduction of adjustment programs in numerous African countries in the second half of the 1980s prompted the sharply increased use of quick-disbursing instruments, the number of countries under going such programs (presently 22) has grown only gradually over the past 2-3 years and is not likely to be increased abruptly in the foreseeable future. The demand for quick-disbursing support in Africa is in fact likely to subside over the 1990s as present recipients approach the end of their adjustment cycles and turn to relatively heavier investment spending.

The outlook for the 1990s

The foregoing discussion of the factors governing prospects for multilateral ODA to Sub-Saharan Africa in the 1990s suggest its growth will remain moderately strong, at an annual rate approaching 4 percent, through the first half of the decade. In this period, Africa will benefit from continuing disbursement of the pipeline of heavy commitments of the late 1980s and, secondly, the provisions of the recent and pending funding agreements of IDA, the EEC, and the AfDF for deployment of an important share of the new resources both to Africa and in quick-disbursing form.

For the second half of the decade, while prospects are far less defined at this stage, present indications suggest that the rate of growth of Africa's receipts from the multilaterals could taper off to less than 3 percent a year. Disbursements by the agencies could tend to level out corresponding to a flatter trend in the volume of new commitments made in the earlier years, new funding is likely to remain constrained, and the share of quick-disbursing assistance in funding agreements concluded through the latter half of the 1990s can be expected to decline gradually.
provisions for their future deployment are currently under consideration.

Prospects for otherwise narrowing the gap which are within the control of the multilaterals are extremely limited. As emphasized earlier in this paper
ing requirements and likely availability of ODA as

Table 5.5 ***Sub-Saharan Africa: projected receipts of multilateral ODA***

	1990 US$billion			*Annual percentage growth*		
	1990	*1995*	*2000*	*1991-95*	*1996-2000*	*1991-2000*
Gross disbursements excluding TA						
Targeted	4.4	5.4	6.6	4.0	4.0	4.0
Projected	4.4	5.3	6.0-6.2	3.8	2.5-3.0	3.2-3.4
N.B. net disbursements including TA	*5.5*					

Note: Receipts expressed in terms of gross disbursements excluding technical assistance per "ODA" as employed in LTPS. Estimated 1990 disbursements on a net basis, including technical assistance, as "ODA" is defined throughout this paper, is shown for reference.

The quantitative dimensions of the outlook for multilateral ODA in the 1990s should not be overemphasized. They serve only to illustrate trends which can reasonably be expected on the basis of recent developments in ODA funding and the operations of the respective agencies. They nonetheless indicate that the level of multilateral ODA to Sub-Saharan Africa could fall significantly short of financing requirements implied by the 4 percent per annum rate of growth targeted for the African economies throughout the 1990s.

One unknown, though potentially important, factor towards narrowing the gap between projected finance defined here is the future role of the IMF's ESAF. authority to commit ESAF resources has recently been extended up through late 1992, and specific , the likely rate of resource transfer to the region by these agencies is already broadly defined by their pipelines of commitments yet undisbursed and by the scale and provisions of respective funding agreements governing their new commitments well into the 1990s.[12]

The principal option for better aligning available concessional resources with Africa's financing requirements is probably that of raising the efficiency in the use of these scarce resources. On the side of the multilateral agencies, indeed of all sources of ODA, possibilities for greater selectivity among recipient countries should be continually re-examined with the aim of sharpening the effectiveness of this assistance. Increased selectivity in concessional resource use is an important contribution of the Special Program for Africa, which has demonstrated a strongly catalytic effect on resource transfer to the region in terms of both its volume and its quality. Donor selectivity in line with recipient performance must continue to be made prominent on the agenda for the 1990s.

Notes

1. ODA includes all bilateral and multilateral concessional assistance provided with a grant element of at least 25 percent and with the economic development and welfare of developing countries as its main objective. The terms "ODA' and "concessional assistance" are used interchangeably throughout this paper. Historical data cited are based on OECD statistics, which include technical assistance, but not assistance extended under the IMF's Structural Adjustment Facility (SAF) and Enhanced Structural Adjustment Facility (ESAF).

2. Whereas the preceding paragraphs traced levels of funding, including resources transferred *to* multilateral agencies, ODA transfers discussed in the remainder of the paper refer to receipts of developing countries, including resources extended to them *from* the multilaterals. Throughout this paper, the terms "transfer" and "net disbursement" of ODA are used interchangeably.

3. The EEC is associated with the African, Caribbean and Pacific (ACP) States, currently 68 in number, through a series of Lome Conventions which establish the funding of the European Development Fund (EDF), the principal instrument of EEC concessional assistance. Some 90 percent or more of the EEC's ODA to Sub-Saharan Africa in a typical year is made through the EDF. Additionally, the EEC extends substantial ODA out of the General Community Budget to countries both within and outside the ACP sphere, mainly in the form of food aid.

4. The UN agencies are treated as a group and include among others: UNDP, UNFPA, WFP, UNHCR, UNICEF, UNWRA, and various technical assistance programs (UNTA).

5. Since 1988, IDA has also provided for supplemental credits for IDA-eligible countries undertaking adjustment programs and having outstanding IBRD

debt incurred in previous periods. Such credits amounted to SDR 151 million (IS$195 million) in IDA's FY 1989-90, close to 80 percent of this amount having been extended in Africa.

6. The structural adjustment facility established by the EEC in 1988 was mobilized principally out of resources not programmed under previous Lome Conventions, reflows from ACP states, and accelerated deployment of Lome III funding.

7. In addition to the resources of its special adjustment support fund, the EEC extends rapidly disbursing assistance to Africa through its food aid, STABEX and SYSMIN programs in amounts which vary widely from year to year. Exceptional transfers of this type in 1988 were largely responsible for the sharp rise in EEC disbursements to the region in that year, while those made out of the new adjustment facility came into play chiefly in 1989.

8. Aside from its SAF/ESAF, which will be included in the OECD's accounting of ODA beginning 1991, the IMF is not a source of ODA inasmuch as its resources are otherwise extended for purposes of securing balance of payments stability, rather than longer-term development, and they do not carry a grant element of at least 25 percent. An exception 1976-81.

9. ODA extended through the General Budget of the Community is programmed to rise in parallel with that of the Lome IV resources for the EDF, although it is expected that virtually all of the increment will be designated for Eastern Europe.

10. For purposes of this illustration, IDA's gross disbursements beginning mid-1993 are projected on the assumption that future funding agreements (IDA 10,11,12) will yield and increase in volume corresponding to the expected rise in real terms of ODA funding over the three-year period in question, that 50 percent of the new commitments funded will be allocated to Africa, and that the quick-disbursing component of total commitments to Africa will decline progressively to 20 percent.

11. EBRD funding of US$3.6 billion: representing paid-in capital of 30 percent of an ECU 10 billion (US$12 billion) total.

12. The multilaterals' very limited room for maneuver is suggested by a modest step which may be taken by the AFDF to relax the constrained availability of new ODA funding for ADF VI, as was taken with respect to ADF V: that of blending with the new resources a small amount of the non-concessional resources of its sister agency, the African Development Bank.

Comment

Robert Ayres

The paper suggests that there probably will be a gap between the volume of official development assistance (ODA) likely to be supplied to Sub-Saharan Africa during the 1990s and the volume required to sustain the target growth rate for the region contained in the Bank's study, *From Crisis to Sustainable Growth*. Specifically, the growth rate of multilateral ODA in the 1980s is unlikely to be repeated in the decade ahead.

The concessional resource gap is in fact likely to go unfilled by either bilateral or multilateral donors for a number of reasons. These include the competition for resources represented by the emergence of E Eastern European countries, the rapid disappearance of "peace dividend" (if indeed it ever existed), the impossibility of further regional shifts in the allocation of aid to low-income Africa, and so forth.

This only serves to underscore the emphasis placed in a number of papers, but especially in the paper by Richard Carey, on the need for a radical improvement in the quality, productivity, and effectiveness of aid—as well as, obviously, the importance of required changes in the policies and procedures of recipients. Much has been said about the latter in recent years. We have had a thorough recitation concerning what the developing countries receiving aid must do to improve their performance. This is not the place to go into detail about whether the new conventional wisdom—notably concerning the role of the private sector, market-oriented reforms, nongovernmental organizations, and the like—does not itself represent an ideology as uncritical as the statist and aid-reliant ideology of the past. That would be the subject of quite another, perhaps very interesting, seminar. But I shall not pursue this topic here.

So much for the recipients. What about the donors? What would they have to do? Are they prepared to do it? (Complete answers to these questions would require further distinctions between bilateral and multilateral donors, but these are not made here).

Reduce the pressure to lend. This could make an important contribution, but it would require enormous changes in the incentive systems of donor agencies and, indeed, the whole political economy of the

Donor community. Ironically, it would reduce the external resource constraint, at least as narrowly construed, to the extent that such agencies drive up the estimate of the gap through their own self-interest in committing funds.

Relatedly, effect important changes in the allocation and composition of aid, including multilateral aid. (Although this point is clearly more relevant to bilateral aid). Aid should be increased to countries seriously committed to reforms and reduced to those which are not. Moreover, the reforms in question should not only be those discussed in conjunction with the Special Program of Assistance for Africa. They should, in addition, be more explicitly poverty-related.

Avoid duplication and overlap; coordinate better. This has become a virtual platitude which has gained ascendancy at the rhetorical level. The real question is how to translate it into actual practice, something on which there has been far too little action.

In a resource-constrained environment, the need for priority-setting becomes even more crucial. But who is to set such priorities? In what fora? According to what criteria? Obviously, these are exceedingly difficult questions to answer. But unless they are faced head-on, we will continue with the incremental accretion of activities reflecting the particular priorities, often politically determined, of each individual donor. As a result the total impact of the aid system, including the multilateral aid system, will continue to be considerably less than it could be.

In short, unless serious and systematic reforms take place on the donor side, aid will fail to complement effectively the reforms undertaken by the recipients—leaving aside for the moment the perhaps herculean assumption that such reforms will actually take place. The relevance of this point to the seminar's focus on financing requirement is clear. A case for a greater volume of concessional assistance to Sub-Saharan Africa can certainly be made—but only as *World Development Report 1990* on poverty argues, if recipients undertake requisite policy reforms, especially those designed to reduce poverty, and donors learn better the lessons of past experience and mend their ways in the future. In my view, the likelihood that all this will occur probably ranges somewhere between minimal and moderate.

6

The Role of the IMF

Paul A. Acquah
Michael E. Edo

The International Monetary Fund has had a long association with Africa. Indeed, four African countries (Egypt, Ethiopia, Liberia, and South Africa) were among the initial members of the Fund. Ghana and Sudan became members in 1957, and Libya, Morocco, and Tunisia joined in 1958. The large expansion in African membership took place in the early 1960s, following the accession of most of the African countries to independence. The latest addition to membership from Africa was Namibia in 1990. The Fund has during this past association built up a record of close cooperation with African countries, and African countries have contributed to the formulation of policies of the Fund through their full participation in discussions in the Executive Board, the Interim and Development Committees, and the Joint Annual Meetings of the Fund and the Bank.

An important part of the Fund's work in Africa from the early years has been the development of the statistical base, the adoption of the economic policy instruments, and the development of institutions and skilled manpower needed for the effective formulation and implementation of economic policies. These aims have been pursued through the Fund's technical assistance programs, through training provided by the IMF Institute, and through work by Fund staff and country officials in the compilation, analysis, and publication of economic data, as well as through discussions of economic policies in periodic Fund consultations with its member countries. This work will continue to be of great importance in the 1990s as members seek to continue to enhance economic policy implementation capacity, and as institutions and instruments are continually adapted to meet new economic challenges as they arise.

The aspect of the Fund's role that is most frequently mentioned is the provision of financial assistance. The Fund as a cooperative institution has been at the center of the collaborative process of promoting adjustment and financing, supporting the efforts of its members who have sought to address their economic problems, often under difficult domestic and external circumstances. Specifically, the Fund has been assisting members in formulating and implementing adjustment programs, providing its own financial resources, and serving as catalyst for mobilizing the required support from other external sources. In doing so, the Fund has had to adapt its instruments and policies on the use of its resources in light of changes in the international environment.

This aspect of the Fund's work in Africa became more prominent during the 1970s, with the substantial increases in world oil prices and the declines in some primary commodity prices at the end of the decade, after high levels in the middle of the decade. In 1974, the Extended Fund Facility (EFF) was established in recognition of the need to extend the adjustment period. The Trust Fund was created in 1976 to extend low-interest loans to low-income members out of the profits from the sale of gold. The supplementary financing facility was established in February 1979 to provide assistance to members facing payments difficulties considered to be large in relation to their economies and their Fund quotas. The policy on enlarged access to the Fund's resources became operational in May 1981, permitting the Fund to use borrowed funds to augment resources available under stand-by and extended arrangements. Also, the maximum entitlement under the compensatory financing facility (CFF) was enlarged in 1979, and this was followed in 1981 by the introduction of the cereal facility.

At the begining of the 1980s, the economic situation and prospects were difficult for many African countries. Large financial imbalances had accumulated in the late 1970s as countries maintained fiscal programs and incurred increasing levels of external debt at a time of significant reductions in the terms of trade. In the early 1980s, high real international interest rates and depressed conditions in world markets for the exports of most African countries exacerbated the already weak financial condition of many countries. The Fund responded by creating new financing facilities, expanding disbursements under existing facilities, and working closely with members to devise the appropriate policy response to the difficult economic circumstances.

In the ten years from 1980 to 1989, the Fund's assistance in the form of quick-disbursing financing to African countries totaled SDR 11.3 billion, averaging some SDR 1.1 billion annually, and at end-July 1990 total obligations of African countries outstanding to the Fund amounted to SDR 5.6 billion (equivalent to 134 percent of Africa's quota in the Fund; this excludes Nigeria which chose not to draw under its stand-by arrangement from the Fund) (table 6.1). The extent of this support compares with total financing of SDR 48.3 billion, averaging some SDR 4.9 billion annually, provided to other developing countries over the same period, whose obligations outstanding to the Fund at end-July 1990 amounted to SDR 21.9 billion (80 percent of their total quota). There was a large increase in the Fund's financial assistance to African countries during 1980-84, which reflected not only the balance of payments difficulties but also the modifications to the financing facilities and policies introduced in 1979-81 regarding access to the Fund's resources.

The number of African countries for which the Fund approved financing arrangements each year (excluding assistance under the CFF) rose from 8 in 1979 to 15 in 1981, and since then no less than 11 countries have entered into such arrangements each year. Since 1980, 36 of the 44 Sub-Saharan African countries have had at least one arrangement from the Fund, and several have had more than six.

The SAF and ESAF facilities introduced by the Fund during the 1980s constitute a special financing window that is important in Fund assistance to eligible countries. The total resources available to all eligible countries under these two facilities amount to SDR 8.7 billion, at an interest rate currently at 0.5 percent, with a maturity period of 10 years and a grace period of 5 1/2 years. Sixty-two countries are eligible for access to these facilities, including 34 Sub-Saharan African countries. Under the SAF, countries may obtain a maximum of 70 percent of quota in loans in three annual installments, each in support of a one-year program and disbursed at the beginning of the arrangement. SAF resources amount to about SDR 2.7 billion. Access under the ESAF is considerably larger. It is normally expected to average about 150 percent of quota over a three--year period, with provision for up to 350 percent in exceptional circumstances. In practice, the amount an eligible member can borrow depends on the strength of its adjustment effort and the size of its overall balance of payments need, and disbursements under each one-year program are made semiannually. In July 1990, the Fund's Executive Board agreed in principle to extend the date by which a member may request a three-year arrangement under the ESAF from November 1990 to November 1992.

At end-July 1990, the total amount committed under the SAF for all countries was SDR 1.8 billion, of which SDR 1.6 billion had been disbursed. The amount committed for African countries was SDR 999 million, of which SDR 961 million had been disbursed, representing 60 percent of the total disbursements of SAF resources. As of end-July 1990, 11 African countries had programs supported by ESAF arrangements. Total ESAF resources committed to these countries amounted to SDR 1.3 billion, of which SDR 724 million had been disbursed, compared with total commitments of SDR 1.5 billion and disbursements of SDR 830 million under all ESAF arrangements as of end-July 1990.

The SAF and ESAF facilities are particularly suited to the individual circumstances of most of the African countries. They have several important features. First, apart from their significant concessionality, a SAF/ESAF arrangement is based on the policy framework paper (PFP), which is the result of close technical collaboration between the authorities of the country and the staffs of the Fund and the World Bank. The PFP process helps define the appropriate medium-term development strategy and focuses on priority economic and financial objectives and policy measures, as well as on financing requirements. The PFP provides a framework for the coordination of technical and other assistance from donors in specific areas critical to reform, and, for the authorities, the consistent set of policies contained in the PFP may be used to help mobilize a domestic consensus for the adjustment effort. Second, the World Bank has increasingly relied on the PFP in IDA lending operations and for its assistance under the Bank's Special Program of Assistance for Debt-Distressed Countries in Sub-Saharan Africa (SPA). The SPA provides a mechanism for multilateral coordination of the amounts, forms, and timing of aid to the 23 eligible countries. IDA and Bank commitments for policy-based lending to SAF-eligible countries that had entered into SAF or

Table 6.1 ***New stand-by arrangements, arrangements under extended fund facility, structural adjustment facility, enhanced structural adjustment facility, and compensatory financing facility (during Period 1980-1990)[a] (millions of SDRs)***

	1980	*1981*	*1982*	*1983*	*1984*	*1985*	*1986*	*1987*	*1988*	*1989*	*1990* Jan.-July
					During period						
Amount agreed											
SBA	686	590	1,050	1,984	767	779	1,336	834	511	966	100
EFF	1,028	3,200		100				245	207		
SAF							172	635	168	25	
ESAF									640	595	85
CFF	113	258	353	157	86	200	240	70	184	315	
Total	1,827	4,048	1,403	2,241	853	979	1,703	1,785	1,709	1,900	185
Cumulative amount agreed since 1980	1,827	5,875	7,278	9,519	10,372	11,351	13,098	14,883	16,593	18,493	18,678
Amount purchased											
SBA	173	297	526	790	283	410	335	45	188	264	24
EFF	188	823		10				23			
SAF							54	200	53	7	
ESAF									147	172	9
CFF	113	258	353	157	86	200	240	70	184	315	
Total	474	1,378	880	957	369	610	629	338	571	759	33
Cumulative amount purchased since 1980	474	1,852	2,732	3,689	4,058	4,668	5,296	5,633	6,205	6,963	6,996
					End of period						
Undrawn balance											
SBA	513	293	524	1,194	484	369	1,001	789	323	702	76
EFF	840	2,377		90				223	207		
SAF							118	435	115	18	76
ESAF									493	422	
Total	1,353	2,670	524	1,284	484	369	1,119	1,447	1,138	1,142	152
Memorandum items:											
Number of arrangements[b/]		13	15	12	16	11	14	24	19	19	122
Number of CFF purchases		7	10	4	3	3	5	5	2	4	1
Total purchases[3/]	874	1,876	1,719	1,940	1,226	955	777	483	662	742	98
Total repurchases[3/]	343	358	273	376	553	767	1,124	1,034	953	1,122	529

a/ Excluding South Africa.

b/ A combination of SBA and SAF or SBA and ESAF is considered one arrangement.

c/ Under prior and new arrangements, including CFF drawings.

Source: IMF, Treasurer's Department and Research Department.

ESAF arrangements rose from US$0.4 billion in1985 to US$1.5 billion in 1989, and, over the same period, disbursements increased from US$0-.2 billion to US$1.1 billion. These resources have been augmented by additional official financing in the context of Consultative Groups and other donor meetings. Third, SAF/ESAF programs have, as is the case for other Fund arrangements, served as a basis for Paris Club rescheduling agreements for a number of countries.

To avail themselves of SAF/ESAF arrangements, eligible countries undertake to implement far-reaching reforms with a view to increasing growth and achieving substantial progress toward balance of payments viability. Programs are designed to fit the special characteristics of individual economies, and have generally involved macroeconomic policy corrections and structural reforms requiring careful preparation, sequencing, implementation, and monitoring. Usually, the broad objectives are to improve the regulatory environment, reduce administrative controls, encourage private sector activity, strengthen public sector resource management, promote domestic savings necessary for self-sustaining development, induce reflows of flight capital, and improve the operations of markets and the flexibility of the economic system, thereby lessening its vulnerability to internal and external shocks.

The pursuit of such broad objectives often necessitates reform of the exchange and trade system, including corrections of overvalued currencies, liberalization of domestic pricing and marketing policies, reform of public enterprises, reduction of labor market rigidities, reordering of public sector expenditure priorities and programs, restructuring of the tax system, and reform of the financial sector, and the development of effective instruments for monetary control. Moreover, safety nets—appropriate compensatory measures, income-support programs, targeted subsidies—are devised to cushion the most disadvantaged and vulnerable groups of society against the distributional effects and burdens of the adjustment process. Environmental concerns are addressed, without undermining the overall adjustment effort. Success in the above areas will determine the effective demand for the Fund's resources by Africa in the 1990s and is needed for the achievement of the important objectives of sustainable rapid growth and high employment.

Fund support for Africa is not restricted to operations under SAF/ESAF arrangements. Several countries that are not eligible for these facilities have in place or are negotiating Fund-supported programs under the Fund's other facilities (Cameroon, the Congo, Morocco, Nigeria, Tunisia, and Côte d'Ivoire). Moreover, some of the SAF/ESAF eligible countries have combined an arrangement under the ESAF or SAF with a stand-by arrangement (Burundi, the Central African Republic, The Gambia, Guinea, Kenya, Malawi, Mali, Mauritania, Niger, Senegal, Sierra Leone, Somalia, Togo, and Zaire).

In this context, it is important to note that on June 28, 1990, the Fund's Board of Governors adopted a resolution proposing increases in members' quotas. The proposed increases in quotas will expand the size of the Fund by 50 percent and augment considerably the amount of normal Fund resources available for stand-by and EFF arrangements. Additionally, countries could benefit from the compensatory and contingency financing facility (CCFF), which was established in 1988 and integrates a contingency financing mechanism into the existing compensatory financing facility. The CCFF allows the Fund to provide financing to cushion a member's adjustment effort against adverse exogenous shocks, such as interest rate fluctuations or unanticipated significant terms of trade movements, in addition to that provided to compensate for temporary export shortfalls and excesses in cereal import costs. Also, in response to the Brady Initiative, the Fund has started to support debt- and debt-service reduction operations, whereby some 25 percent of the financing that the Fund provides in support of a member's adjustment program can be set aside for these purposes. Moreover, the Fund can provide additional resources of up to 40 percent of the member's quota for further reductions in debt service. The few countries in Africa classified among the market borrowers with heavy debt-service burdens (e.g., Nigeria, Côte d'Ivoire, and Morocco) could benefit from this policy.

A development of major importance for member countries (among which are five African members—Liberia, Sierra Leone, Somalia, Sudan, and Zambia) that were in prolonged arrears to the Fund at the end of 1989 has been the recent introduction of the "rights" approach. The central elements are the adoption and implementation by such members of a recovery program monitored by the Fund and the formation of support groups to help mobilize external assistance in support of the required strong policies and to help restore normal financial relations with multilateral institutions and other creditors, including the clearance of arrears to the Fund so as to re-establish the member's eligibility to use Fund resources. A member accumulates "rights" based on sustained economic performance under the Fund-monitored program toward future financing of the adjustment process, once its arrears to the Fund have been settled. Under the Fund's cooperative strategy, Guyana and Honduras cleared their arrears to the Fund in June 1990. Two African countries—Sierra Leone and Zambia—along with Panama have in place or are actively seeking to implement Fund-monitored programs.

The Fund, therefore, has developed the framework and instruments for assistance to Africa in the 1990s, both for providing its own financial resources, policy advice, and technical assistance, and for catalyzing expanded external flows in support of economic recovery and sustained growth.

In the next few years, the Fund can continue to increase its financial support for African countries as more SAF/ESAF-eligible countries avail themselves of these facilities. The Fund's resources will also increase when quota increases under the Ninth Review come into effect. The level of net transfers to Africa is likely to rise, although it is difficult to indicate specific levels since use of Fund resources depends on a number of factors including balance of payments need, strength of economic policy programs, and the degree to which resources can be mobilized from other sources. Many African countries are unlikely to achieve external payments viability for years, and they will continue to need external support on terms that do not add to their debt-servicing burden and thus complicate their macroeconomic management. Thus, much of the assistance they need must necessarily be on concessional terms over a prolonged period, and on a scale adequate to raise growth rates sufficiently to reverse the decline in per capita incomes. Given the relatively expensive nature of the Fund's general resources and the extent of the past use of these resources by African countries that are still in need of adjustment and financing, the Fund's role as a catalyst will remain of central importance in mobilizing concessional resources to support Africa's economic programs.

Comment

Robert Armstrong

I don't really have much to comment upon—much less to quarrel with—regarding the paper or Mr. Acquah's presentation. I will focus my remarks more upon the questions *not* addressed.

The main theme of the paper and presentation is that "the Fund has had to adapt its instruments and policies on the use of its resources, in light of changes in the international environment, in order to better serve the needs of its members." True enough. But the key questions now are: How will it adapt in future, not only in terms of the instruments available, but also in terms of how those instruments are used? And what can we envisage regarding the types, terms and volumes of finance that will be provided to Africa in the 1990s. How do our Fund colleagues see the role of the Fund in Africa evolving in the coming years?

The paper states that the Fund "expects to continue to be active in Africa." But it doesn't shed much light on the volume of direct financial disbursements, gross or net, that one might foresee the Fund providing to Africa in the coming years, or on the prospective terms of Fund assistance. To be sure, the very nature of the institution and its historical mandate make these matters especially problematic. There is in fact an inherent contradiction in prfojecting, at least over a near term, the use of resources that are in essence designated for facilitating adjustments to largely unforseeable shocks and events as distinguished, say, from "normal" foreign aid that is geared to meet more predictable and hence more "projectable" development finance requirements.

As the paper states: "Each multilateral agency will function within the constraints imposed by its mandate as one institution...and the principles governing the use of those resources." To be sure, the Fund has a special mandate that distinguishes it from the Bank and other development financing agencies. As we have seen it in the past, however, that mandate has been an evolving one.

So the most fundamental questions that may warrant addressing here are, I would propose, those relating to how flexibly or inflexibly the aforementioned mandate and principles are to be interpreted and adjusted. And will the impetus for this kind of adjustment come from above or below? From within or without? I am reminded here of Gerry Helleiner's apt remark, made here at another conference last week, that: "One man's constraint is another man's objective function." This observation applies as well to the issue at hand.

I believe that a lot of fog tends to fall over debates about the role of the Fund precisely because of this differing percveption regarding objectives and constraints. But today's immutable constraints have a way of becoming tomorrow's variables.

I also believe that a lot of fog falls over this debate because so many things are meant by the word "adjustment." It used to be that the Bank financed projects while the Fund financed adjustment to shocks that created temporary liquidity problems in a country's balance of payments. Now, the Bank and Fund are both in the business of financing adjustment. But we certainly don't always mean the same thing by adjustment or structural adjustment, or what the ECA calls structural transformation. And this tends to make it harder to ascertain how much our instruments (our lending and advisory instruments) are truly geared to meet our objectives.

Thus, as we discuss the role of the Fund in Africa in the 1980s and 1990s, the underlying question, it seems to me, has to do with the consistency or congruence—or the lack there of—between the Fund's objectives—(or the objectives the Fund's critics would have it pursue)—and the instruments at its disposal.

Against the background of these considerations, I would pose the following more specific questions which I hope may serve to provoke some lively discussion.

Isn't there perhaps a basic mismatch between the Fund's desire to finance structural (and I emphasize the word structural) adjustment in Farica (where adjustment is inherently and inevitably a medium-to-long term matter) and the Fund's financial instruments (even including the SAF and ESAF) which range from short term to only medium-term? The structures that need adjustment are in production, consumption, imports, exports, investment, employment, income distribution, skills, and technologies. And these structures all take time to adjust. But the Fund's instruments, it may be argued don't match these time needs.

A related question. Isn't the time horizon of the policy framework papers at three years, far too short? Isn't it counterproductive to try to force some key performance ratios to move in the "right direction" within a year or two or three? Doesn't this time frame tend to force the Fund into making unrealistically optimistic projections of export, savings, and GDP growth rates, and too low estimates of ICORs and import elasticities?

Are the Fund's lending terms, even on the SAF and ESAF, not too hard for most African countries? Can Africa afford to borrow from the Fund? What happens when the relatively short grace periods on the SAF and ESAF run out?

What is the prospect that the IMF will be a netprovider of external finance to Africa in the 1990s? According to our World Debt Tables, in the period 1980-84 the Fund provided a positive net transfer to Sub-Saharan Africa in the amount of $3.6 billion. In the period 1985-89, the negative net transfer was $3.4 billion—about a wash. What's likely in the years ahead? What's the schedule of interest and repurchases for the coming years?

Is there a case to be made for the Fund to be concentrating more on shadow programs, as for Nigeria, Zambia, Sierra Leone, and other countries, where the Fund could play all the roles it now plays except that of providing finance?

How can the Fund reconcile its objective to respond quickly to African requests for quick-disbursing finance with the joint Bank-Fund objective to foster maximum possible government ownership of structural adjustment programs? What can be done differently and better to foster the internalization of these programs, and so increase the prospect of their sustainability?

What role does the Fund see for itself in capacity building in training and otherwise helping Africans and African institutions to develop their own capacities for policy analysis and design? What are the Fund's lessons of experience with its own technical assistance in Africa? What role for Fund technical assistance is envisaged in the 1990s.

What is the prospective role for the Fund in the 1990s in terms of mobilizing additional aid and debt relief for Africa from other donors and creditors? What does it propose to do differently in the 1990s? What role does the Fund envisage playing in aid coordination? And how to ensure that Fund activities in these areas are complementary to those of the ank, rather than competing or duplicative?

The Bretton Woods Agencies and Sub-Saharan Africa in the 1990s: Facing the Tough Questions

Richard E. Feinberg

The IMF and the World Bank will play major roles in Sub-Saharan Africa's economies in the 1990s, so their performance will be critically important for Africa's future. Yet both Bretton Woods agencies themselves face difficult institutional issues that, if not properly handled, could seriously impede their ability to assist the region.

To help overcome the region's severe foreign exchange constraints, the Bretton Woods agencies should reconsider their planned net capital contribution. For the first half of the 1990s the International Development Association (IDA) plans to provide significant resources, but the International Bank for Reconstruction and Development (IBRD) and the IMF could remove more financial reflows than they provide in new money if they do not change. A negative resource transfer could weaken the influence of the multilateral agencies and tighten the financial straightjackets already cramping many countries in Sub-Saharan Africa.

The Brady proposals were a major step forward in easing the private debt overhang that is a serious burden for a dozen or so African countries. So far, however, no Brady-style deals have been done. Nor have the Bretton Woods agencies been able to normalize Africa's external financial relations with commercial creditors. A partial response is the recent creation of a World Bank facility to reduce the private debts of low-income countries, but there will have to be more funds if its laudable aims are to be met.

The World Bank has correctly recognized that policy-based lending programs should be more selective in key policy targets and its radical analysis of the problems facing Africa suggest a more comprehensive and rapid reform program. Moreover, in the 1990s the Bretton Woods agencies will face pressures to give more weight to social equity and political variables, such as the quality of economic governance, administrative probity, and fundamental human rights. Conditionality, therefore, could become more ambitious and broader rather than more realistic and narrower. If the Bank and the Fund are to maximize their effectiveness in the 1990s, they will have to improve cooperation and synchronize their policies on all issues—resource transfers and arrears, commercial debts of the middle and low-income countries, and economic and political conditionality. Such collaboration should occur in the context of long-term strategic planning exercises for Africa.

Resource transfers

In the first half of the 1990s the Bretton Woods institutions intend to provide a positive net resource transfer to Sub-Saharan Africa. But this masks sharp differences among the agencies. IDA is planning a positive net transfer of over $3 billion a year in 1991-94 (table 7.1).

Under current policy plans, the IBRD will make disbursements roughly equal to anticipated principal and interest repayments, thus yielding little if any net transfer. It is hard to predict future IMF flows because the number of future standbys is inevitably unknown, and the IMF refuses to release repayment schedules by country or even by region. But in the second half of the 1980s, purchases declined and repurchases rose sharply. Consequently, the Fund drained money from Sub-Saharan Africa, the average annual negative transfer reaching nearly $700 million in 1985-89 (table 7.2).

The World Bank's projections of disbursement schedules may be optimistic. Countries may be

Table 7.1 ***Projected World Bank resource flows to Sub-Saharan Africa, 1991-94 (in millions of dollars)***

	1991	*1992*	*1993*	*1994*
IBRD				
Commitments	3,297	3,700	3,300	2,617
Disbursements	1,493	2,064	2,013	1,957
Principal payments	800	879	894	944
Interest payments	808	898	980	1,056
Net resource transfer	-115	287	139	-43
IDA				
Commitments	995	3,700	3,300	2,617
Disbursements	3,201	3,721	3,748	3,563
Principal payments	71	95	123	158
Interest payments	142	170	197	225
Net resource transfer	2,988	3,456	3,428	3,180
IBRD and IDA				
Commitments	8,292	7,400	6,600	5,234
Disbursements	4,694	5,785	5,761	5,520
Principal payments	871	974	1,017	1,102
Interest payments	950	1,068	1,177	1,281
Net resource transfer	2,873	3,743	3,567	3,137

Source: Author estimates based on World Bank OPMIS Database and projections.

Table 7.2 ***IMF Resource flows to Sub-Saharan Africa, 1980-89 (in millions of dollars)***

	1980	*1982*	*1983*	*1984*	*1985*	*1986*	*1987*	*1988*	*1989*
Purchases	1,217	1,152	1,618	952	738	735	650	990	772
Repurchases	384	266	401	591	769	1,217	1,216	1,215	1,190
IMF Charges	103	296	338	402	402	472	326	267	255
Net Transfers	730	590	879	-41	-433	-954	-892	-492	-673

Source: World Bank (1989, 82) and IMF (1990b, 18, 30, 32).

unable to meet conditions attached to quick-disbursing structural adjustment loans, and fiscal stringency may prevent governments from moving ahead with Bank-supported investment projects. Indeed, four African countries—Botswana, Côte d'Ivoire, Liberia, and Mauritius—are projected to encounter negative resource transfers to the World Bank (IBRD plus IDA) of $50 million or more in the 1991-94. Seven other countries (Ghana, Kenya, Malawi, Mauritania, Senegal, Tanzania, and Zambia) estimated to have positive overall flows from the World Bank will suffer negative transfers to the IBRD of more than $50 million.

To augment the financial contribution of the IBRD, why not reconsider the amortization schedule of new and old loans? If granted to all low-income countries, a retroactive terms adjustment of principal repayment on old IBRD loans could improve the debtors' cash flow without involving the World Bank in Paris Club or other formal debt rescheduling. That could be done without impairing the present value of IBRD loan assets or damaging its credit rating on world capital markets any more than have previous adjustments in repayment terms.[1]

The World Bank should continue to resist calls to give up its preferred creditor status and reduce its assets. So long as the World Bank (IBRD plus IDA) is providing net flows, it should be under no financial or moral obligation to grant its own debt reduction. Nor would such a move necessarily be equitable, since it would be at the expense of other developing-country borrowers, unless the industrial countries were willing to offset losses through additional contributions.

The IMF has sought to improve its resource transfer, and to reduce the cost of its credits to low-income countries, through the SAF/ESAF mechanism. Yet most African countries have used the ESAF—up to December 31, 1990, only 11—and only SDR 1.4 billion of the total SDR 4.6 billion available had been committed (table 7.3).

The sticking point has been conditionality: many countries with SAF agreements have been unwilling to enter into stringent three-year commitments. When the ESAF was founded, Fund management emphasized that it would be used only to support strong adjustment programs.

The dilemma with the ESAF arises from its two conflicting objectives: to catalyze tough adjustment programs and to transfer concessional resources to low-income nations, a tension that runs throughout Fund (and many Bank) programs. For the ESAF it is especially acute because the program was designed to provide enhanced resources to very poor nations. Indeed, if ESAF funds continue to lie fallow, IDA supporters may argue that the scarce ODA resources should be transferred to the World Bank.

The conflict could be resolved by a two-tier conditionality system. The lower-tier program might focus on macroeconomic management and a narrower range of structural reforms, and yield a lower percentage of quota than would be available under a comprehensive ESAF reform package.[2] As Joan Nelson argues, such a system does not imply softer conditionality. "Indeed, it is the existing pattern that erodes the credibility of conditionality by setting often unrealistically ambitious conditions.... Reserving more demanding conditions for the higher tier of more vigorous and capable reformers would similarly restore the integrity of the process" (p. 21).

Table 7.3: ***Enhanced Structural Facility, status of loan arrangements on December 31, 1990 (millions of SDRs)***

Member	*Date of Arrangement*	*Amount agreed*	*Undrawn balance*
Bangladesh	August 10, 1990	258.8	215.7
Bolivia	July 27, 1988	90.7	45.3
Gambia, The	November 23, 1988	17.1	3.4
Ghana	November 9, 1988	265.9	96.0
Guyana	July 13, 1990	47.1	14.7
Kenya	May 15, 1989	170.4	60.5
Madagascar	May 15, 1989	43.7	31.9
Malawi	July 15, 1988	29.8	5.6
Mauritania	May 24, 1989	44.1	30.5
Mozambique	June 1, 1990	85.4	76.3
Niger	December 12, 1988	43.9	27.0
Senegal	November 21, 1988	127.7	37.1
Togo	May 31, 1989	26.9	15.4
Uganda	April 17, 1989	159.4	77.2
Total		1,410.5	736.3

Note: Resources under Enhanced Structural Adjustment Facility Arrangements may be provided from the Adjustment Facility within the Special Disbursement Account and from the Enhanced Structural Adjustment Facility Trust.
Source: IMF (1990a, 60).

Above all, the availability of Fund resources for Africa will be a function of access policy, which determines the amounts of money members are permitted to borrow. This policy issue will be reviewed in the wake of the recent 50 percent quota increase, but access policy should not take away with one hand what the quota increase is offering with the other. The net affect of the quota increase and access-policy decisions should be to increase the availability of resources to countries with reform programs.

Arrears and the Fund

For countries without acceptable reform programs, arrears have been a way to reduce the resource transfer to the Fund. Even countries with reform programs face a negative transfer to the IMF so long as they must make payments to the Fund before becoming eligible for fresh IMF resources, unless the Fund immediately allows an offsetting stream of credit. Of the nine countries in arrears to the IMF at the end of 1990, five—Liberia, Sierra Leone, Somalia, Sudan, and Zambia—were in Sub-Saharan Africa (table 7.4). In three cases (Sudan, Zambia, and Liberia) the arrears are large and have been outstanding since 1984-86.

Initially, the IMF asked bilateral donors to provide "support" funds to allow debtors to clear arrears and proceed with stabilization programs. Helped by other western countries, Guyana and Honduras cleared their arrears in June 1990, but the nine other cases of protracted arrears, including all in Sub-Saharan Africa, are unresolved. Bilateral donors were reluctant to take out another creditor that seemed unwilling to risk fresh resources. By excluding itself from arranging stand-bys, the Fund deprived potential donors of the comfort of a well-designed and monitored adjustment program in the debtor country.

In April 1990 the IMF decided to apply a new "rights" approach to arrears. The International Monetary Fund will help construct and monitor a medium-term adjustment program, with the debtor nation only having to clear its arrears at the end of the program. It will be assisted in doing so by being eligible (pending approval of the IMF of the adjustment program) to cash in the purchase "rights" accumulated during the "shadow" program. ESAF funds will also be available for eligible members. (The IMF agreed to pledge up to 3 million ounces of gold as additional security for use of ESAF resources in connection with financing of accumulated rights.) However, countries will be expected to make payments to the IMF falling due during the probationary period.

This "rights" strategy allows the Fund to recommence dealings with estranged members and, instead of expecting other donors to clear arrears to the Fund, it realistically calls on the Fund to use its own resources. Even so, this approach has weaknesses. It

Table 7.4 ***Country arrears to the IMF, January 31, 1990 (millions of SDRs)***

Member	*Total*	*Longest overdue obligation*
Kampuchea, Democratic	30.1	March 1975
Liberia	305.2	January 1985
Panama	181.2	December 1987
Peru	624.9	December 1985
Sierra Leone	69.0	January 1987
Somalia	111.7	July 1987
Sudan	895.3	July 1984
Viet Nam	46.4	February 1984
Zambia	882.4	June 1986

Source: IMF (1990a, 16).

excludes writedowns or other IMF-financed relief (from resources generated through SDR issuance or gold sales, other than the concessional rescheduling inherent in the substitution of ESAF money for ordinary resources). Thus, it is unclear how countries with large arrears in relation to export capacity will be able to regain membership rights. Moreover, the recent decision to build a SDR 1 billion contingency reserve gives scope for future leniency, should the IMF decide that it would be better to grant some relief than to permanently marginalize members from the international monetary system.

Another problem is that the member state must not only agree to a three-year program, but must complete it successfully, and enter into a successor arrangement, before gaining access to IMF resources. Such heavy front-loading would seem to establish conditions more demanding than those that have limited the effectiveness of the ESAF.

Most important, while performance requirements are front-loaded, the funding schedule is back-loaded. During the program the member country receives no new IMF resources but is expected to make payments on old debts—so the resource transfer to the Fund will be negative during the reform years. This is the opposite of the fundamental theory underlying all Fund standbys: that purchases are released during the program to facilitate adjustment. The International Monetary Fund might hope that other donors will provide resources to support the adjustment program, but this is normal in any stand-by. Paradoxically, the Fund is breaking with its policy of linking financing and adjustment in countries in the most desperate straits. While the Fund understandably might seek tighter assurances from countries with poor track records, this approach could be counterproductive. So, although the "rights" approach is a step forward, and could, like the "support group" strategy, respond to the needs of some debtors, it is unlikely to meet those of others. In that case, more flexible and innovative arrangements should be considered.

The Bretton Woods agencies and private debt

While much progress has been made in dealing with debts to official bilateral agencies, less has been made with those owed to private creditors.[3] These account for a lesser percentage of the region's total debts (28 percent of long-term debt) than for Latin America but the burden is more significant than is assumed. Including short-term debts, the percentage rises to about 34 percent. (Short-term private credits are derived as the difference between short-term debt and interest arrears on long-term debt outstanding (World Bank 1989, 82-85). Private debts account for more than 20 percent of the long-term debt of 12 Sub-Saharan African countries (Benin, Cameroon, Congo, Guinea-Bissau, Côte d'Ivoire, Gabon, Kenya, Mauritius, Mozambique, Niger, Nigeria, and Zimbabwe), and for over 30 percent for six (Benin, Congo, Côte d'Ivoire, Gabon, Nigeria, and Zimbabwe; see table 7.5). Moreover, interest on these loans averages more than twice the official debt.

Many African countries are not servicing private debt and are accumulating arrears. This weakens domestic confidence, makes macroeconomic management difficult, increases the cost of trade finance, and discourages alternative sources of external capital. For all these reasons, an organized restructuring of private arrears would be beneficial.

Some African countries are eligible for a Brady-style reduction of debts to commercial banks, but so far no deals have been concluded. Discussions between the Côte d'Ivoire and Nigeria and creditor banks are still dragging on. Other countries are in limbo, as banks either give them low priority or prefer to avoid precedent-setting deals involving deep discounts on the face value of loans.

The World Bank has a partial answer for low-income countries (per capita income under $580) eligible to receive only IDA money. In June 1989 it sanctioned up to $100 million in IBRD profits for the reduction of commercial debts of these countries. The scheme is expected to involve cash buybacks, although it might also collateralize debt exchanges. To qualify for the scheme, which should enhance growth and development prospects, a country must have an approved medium-term adjustment program and be the recipient of substantial debt relief from bilateral creditors. (As of August 1990 no such deals had been concluded, but three countries—Bolivia, Mozambique and Niger—were negotiating World Bank-financed buy backs.)

So far, the commercial debts of most IDA-only countries have not been actively traded on secondary markets. Those inter-bank swaps that have been made have been at deep discounts, varying from 50 up to 95 percent. Thus, even assuming a favorable average discount of 80 percent, the new facility's $100 million could retire only $500 million of debt. If the Bank succeeds in persuading other donors to match dollar for dollar, up to $1 billion in private debts might be erased. However, public and publicly guaranteed medium- and long-term commercial debt owed by IDA-only countries is more than $11 billion

Table 7.5 *Debt structure of Sub-Saharan Africa, 1988 (in millions of dollars)*

Country	*All Debt*	*Private*	*Private as percentage of all*
Benin	1,055	362	34.31
Botswana	499	28	5.57
Burkina Faso	866	34	3.93
Burundi	793	20	2.52
Cameroon	4,229	1,032	24.40
Cape Verde	133	3	2.11
Central African Republic	673	24	3.57
Chad	346	38	11.06
Comoros	199	0	0.10
Congo, People's Republic	4,763	2,086	43.80
Côte d'Ivoire	14,125	6,980	49.42
Djibouti	183	1	0.71
Equatorial Guinea	200	9	4.25
Ethiopia	2,978	461	15.48
Gabon	2,663	798	29.97
The Gambia	327	26	7.95
Ghana	3,099	260	8.39
Guinea	2,563	213	8.31
Guinea-Bissau	423	88	20.69
Kenya	5,888	1,294	21.98
Lesotho	281	22	7.82
Liberia	1,632	201	12.32
Madagascar	3,602	312	8.66
Malawi	1,349	52	3.85
Mali	2,067	27	1.31
Mauritania	2,076	111	5.35
Mauritius	861	176	20.44
Mozambique	4,406	984	22.33
Niger	1,742	356	20.44
Nigeria	30,718	17,982	58.54
Rwanda	632	7	1.17
Sao Tome & Principe	99	1	0.61
Senegal	3,617	209	5.78
Seychelles	159	30	18.86
Sierra Leone	727	95	13.07
Somalia	2,035	34	1.67
Sudan	11,853	1,804	15.22
Swaziland	265	10	3.81
Tanzania	4,729	276	5.84
Togo	1,210	54	4.46
Uganda	1,925	107	5.56
Zaire	8,475	700	8.26
Zambia	6,498	523	8.05
Zimbabwe	2,659	1,060	39.86
Total	139,622	38,890	27.85

Source: World Bank (1988, vol. II).

(World Bank 1989). Excluding suppliers' credits, debt to financial markets is nearly $9 billion, although a large chunk of this may be eventually absorbed by official insurance agencies. Even so, the remaining commercial exposure of IDA-only countries will exceed $1 billion.

A deeper pool of resources (by IBRD supplementary financing) would permit relaxation of the $10 million per country ceiling. Future contributions will depend on IBRD profitability. If there is a tradeoff between reducing IBRD lending margins and the availability of funds to replenish this debt reduction facility, the pressing financial needs of the world's poorest nations argue in favor of maintaining this modest tax on middle-income countries.

A more comprehensive solution to Africa's commercial debt problems remains elusive. The March 1989 proposals of U.S. Secretary of the Treasury Nicholas Brady legitimized the concept of debt reduction and the use of the resources of the Bretton Woods institutions to reduce commercial debts. But progress has been slow: only four deals—Mexico, the Philippines, Costa Rica, and Venezuela (all were non-African) were negotiated by August 1990. Two key problems: the uncertainty of criteria for the amount of debt reduction, and the absence of a strong coordinating mechanism to push deals through.

The IMF and the World Bank should be empowered by the major creditor nations to inject more order into developing country finance—specifically toward making each country's debt service conform to a payment stream consistent with sustained adjustment and growth. They would calculate a nation's financial requirements in the medium term, an exercise that the Bretton Woods agencies already perform for many borrowers. These estimates would have to be objective, free from political interference and endorsed by key industrial-country governments. Then, the agencies working with creditor governments would work on commercial banks for support. Banks would have the right to choose from a menu of options, but not nonparticipation.[4]

Such "guided voluntarism" will be possible only if the major shareholders of the Bretton Woods agencies agree. Until then the IMF and World Bank should continue to lend into arrears. Anything else would be to augment unduly the leverage of commercial banks who have largely lost interest in developing countries—and to deprive those countries of badly needed advice and finance.

Conditionality

Policy-based lending was central to the operations of the Bank and Fund in the 1980s. The Bank devoted about a quarter of its loan commitments to this effort to persuade governments to alter fundamental economic policies. The IMF has always provided balance-of-payments loans in support of policy reforms, but in the 1980s gave more emphasis to structural reforms embedded in longer term programs. Both agencies pressed such loans particularly in Africa. In the 1990s the Bank and Fund plan to continue their broad-based attack on Sub-Saharan Africa's economic policies, especially the comprehensiveness and speed of reforms. They also want to place greater emphasis on equity, which could further complicate the politics and economics of policy-based lending. Moreover, pressure is growing in donor nations to add political conditions to the financial assistance from the agencies.

Pace of economic reforms

In the 1980s policy-based lending produced mixed results in Africa, as elsewhere. Programs were frequently overambitious, encompassing too many objectives in too brief a time. Projections were often based on overoptimistic assumptions about the availability of external finance or the response of domestic investors. Moreover, financially strapped governments too often felt compelled to sign loan agreements even though they were not fully committed to them.

The World Bank agrees that it should reduce the number of issues addressed in policy-based loans.[5] The civil service in most African nations has proved unable to coordinate and implement wide reforms simultaneously. Governments with narrow political bases also hesitate to tackle numerous reforms at once for fear of stirring up a hornets' nest of offended interests that could swarm into a powerful opposition. Although public opinion may be willing to accept or even enthusiastically endorse select reforms (lower tariffs that benefit consumers or privatizations that promise better services), it may draw the line at liberalization which threatens key concepts in the role of the nation state or the distribution of power and wealth among social classes.

So, sector loans rather than structural adjustment loans (SALs) will often be more in keeping with the ability or intentions of African governments. Even sector loans can strain political and administrative capacities, given the energies required to revamp, e.g, agriculture, industry, the fiscal budget, or education. That is one reason why the World Bank has been (and should continue) placing greater emphasis on the more narrowly focused sector adjustment loans (SECALs) rather than comprehensive SALs.

Reducing and streamlining the reform package is not enough, however. It must be allowed to unfold in a realistic time. Africa's notion of short to medium term (as well as the IMF's and the World Bank's) has often resulted in reforms compressed into an unrealistically brief timetable. The pressure for putting fires out quickly is one reason for overoptimistic assumptions about the likely availability of external finance and the domestic supply response. Hardly surprising then when domestic investment remains depressed in the face of sharp, prolonged contractions of domestic demand and a seemingly endless foreign exchange crisis. Take the ill-fated Zambia program in the mid-1980s. It harbored excessively optimistic assumptions about the response of foreign investment—and was blind to the ramifications of the overwhelming debt overhang. Understandably, the incompleted reform package was eventually junked by the Zambian government. The sobering experiences of Sub-Saharan Africa in the 1980s would suggest modesty, rather than haste, in reform proposals. Yet, the World Bank's major blueprint for African development, Sub-Saharan Africa: From Crisis to Sustainable Growth: A Long-Term Perspective Study, appears to point in the opposite direction—toward more radical, comprehensive, and rapid reform. This important report, which offers devastating critiques of African policies and all-encompassing solutions to a wide range of problems, is not a document of caution. Indeed, its basic thrust suggests even more ambitious conditionality.

Ideally, governments would reach agreement on a comprehensive radical reform program and then proceed to implement it step-by-step. Initially, they might tackle the most destructive distortions, including major fiscal imbalances, and combine measures that provoke little political opposition but promise to please some sectors. Administratively complex or politically difficult measures, including institution-building and human capital development, could be undertaken gradually.

All this assumes a government that has a long-term strategic vision and is unified enough to avoid the inevitable efforts by those whose interests are damaged by the reform process to regroup and organize opposition. It also assumes political stability. Some new Eastern Europe democracies may enjoy such unity of vision and mass backing, but most African states have not experienced such a sharp break with the past.

In most African countries, donors and governments must choose among the many reforms proposed in the Bank's report. Priorities should be politically feasible and based on realistic assumptions regarding the administrative capacity and the likely response of producers and investors. Above all, for any reform agenda to succeed, the African government must feel that it owns the program. The design of adjustment programs should be by dialogue, not dictate, as actions taken because of externally imposed conditions rather than domestic convictions are unlikely to be sustained.

Economists are in agreement on critical matters, such as the need for responsible fiscal and monetary policies, expanded savings and investment, and supply-side restructuring toward tradable goods through realignment of prices and other incentives. But much less is known about the dynamics of economic adjustment, the timing and phasing of reforms—how to get from here to there. Economists are even less prepared to advise individual nations as to what political roads to follow and what institutions to build. Furthermore, decisions on, say, the distribution of income, the role of government, the composition of taxes, and the structure of the educational system are political and must be carefully thought out for each country.

Social equity

The Bank and the Fund have frequently stated that their programs should take into account the social costs of adjustment. As IMF Managing Director Michel Camdessus says:

> Macroeconomic policies can have strong effects on the distribution of incomes and thus on social equity and welfare. A responsible adjustment program must take these effects into account, particularly as they impinge on the most vulnerable or disadvantaged groups of society. (p. 108)

Equity and relieving poverty are thus official objectives. Many adjustment programs include measures aimed at improving the distributional impact of government interventions (for example, by reducing subsidies to the middle classes and more carefully targeting social programs) and at compensating those who must inevitably suffer during the adjustment process (by providing severance payments, public-works employment, and nutrition programs). Yet these welfare aims remain secondary to efficiency objectives in the policy-based lending programs of the Bretton Woods agencies.

Should equity (or poverty alleviation) be a key condition of policy-based lending and a determinant of tranche disbursement?

Should enough weight be given to equity objectives so that if a government's policies are grossly unjust (however defined), its access to policy-based loans would suffer?

The authors of *World Development Report 1990* on poverty, say yes. They argue that "external assistance should be more tightly linked to an assessment of the efforts that would-be recipients are making to reduce poverty" (World Bank 1990, 4). Countries where policies are inconsistent with efforts to reduce poverty, they say, should receive only "moderate" aid targeted at highly vulnerable groups. The authors go on to suggest that poverty alleviation should be measured economywide (rather than in the project-based fashion favored by the World Bank). The most recent replenishment of IDA stressed the importance of poverty criteria in allocating IDA resources (World Bank 1990, 134). Poverty alleviation in Africa will not be easy. To hold the number of poor at the 1985 level will require a massive effort, which (says the World Bank) must involve not only more effective foreign assistance, but also comprehensive domestic reforms in industry, agriculture, infrastructure, and social services—virtually the whole political economy (World Bank 1990, 5).

Political conditionality

The political conditionality being written into the charter of the European Bank for Reconstruction and Development will open a pandora's box. Sooner or later, its commitment to "the fundamental principles of multiparty democracy, the rule of law, [and] respect for human rights" will spill over to other multilateral lending institutions. Moreover, the increasing pressures for political change in Africa and the distress among donors with government in many African countries will force the Bretton Woods agencies to consider more directly the political milieu in which they operate.

Several factors have inhibited donors from pressing political conditionality in Sub-Saharan Africa. East-West geopolitical rivalries often took precedence over the niceties of human rights and domestic governance. Underlying ethnic tensions in Africa lent credence to the argument that only a strong, single-party state could preserve national unity and prevent tribal bloodshed (which, it was feared, the Soviets would exploit). And economic efficiency was associated with centralized political power.

These factors are now less compelling. With the dramatic shift in Soviet domestic and foreign policies and the sudden decline in Soviet interest in the developing countries, the West is less worried that African regimes may align with a hostile global rival. And while ethnic, regional, or religious cleavages remain, they may be less virulent than in the early days of independence. Finally, there is a growing feeling among donors that democracy need not conflict with responsible macroeconomic management and market-oriented economic reform, as many had assumed during the *realpolitik* 1960s and 1970s. Indeed, Eastern Europe has enthralled the world with speedy, simultaneous leaps toward multiparty democracy and liberal economy.

Economic governance

In future, the Bretton Woods agencies should develop minimal conditions on economic governance which, if not met, would result in cuts in lending. So as not to contradict the "nonpolitical" clauses in the institutions' founding charters, such conditions could be justified on grounds of a borrower's prospective efficiency and credibility.[6] That would also be consistent with concerns raised in Africa about the links between governance style and economic performance.

Rampant official corruption is an area likely to be targeted in this new list of "unacceptable behaviors." Among donors, there is mounting concern that foreign assistance is wasted on self-interested governments whose behavior is antithetical to their own values. Vocal, well organized, and often well informed private voluntary organizations are among those most critical of official assistance to kleptocratic regimes in the developing world.

Widespread corruption often makes it more difficult for governments to implement agreed policies and decreases the efficiency of resource allocation. For private investors, arbitrary and capricious implementation of government regulations adds to the uncertainties and headaches of doing business in Sub-Saharan Africa. Indeed, one serious obstacle to private investment and growth in Africa is that everything is "open to negotiation" with government officials.

Reforms targeted at economic governance could include: more transparent government budgeting, open and competitive bidding for large public contract; accountability of state-owned enterprises, and greater consistency in the implementation of regulations governing investment.

These might raise questions regarding programs in countries such as Ethiopia and Zaire—where the 1989 World Bank annual report boasted of positive net transfers of $211 million and $340 million, respectively, during fiscal 1985-89—but they are a necessary remedy.

Even where there is gross misgovernance, lending agencies may want to sustain modest core programs to maintain continuity and presence. In the long run, it would be perverse and even counterproductive to punish poor people in a country because of the practices of a government already victimizing them. In particular, Bank support for basic education and human capital-building efforts could help prepare a population to better hold its government accountable to the masses. The Bank should therefore proceed with sound basic-needs projects, unless it feels that skulduggery is so rife in those sectors as to preclude efficient expenditure of funds.

There is also pressure for political matters, such as popular participation and multiparty democracy, to be taken into account. That could further complicate conditionality and possibly contradict the mandates of the Bretton Woods institutions. Other official agencies and nongovernmental organizations will often be better equipped to promote these laudable goals but there are ways for the Bank and Fund to address these issues. Again, education—whether primary or the training of economists—lays the foundation for intelligent political participation. Public debate can also be stimulated by funding local social science research institutes and by the release of certain Bank and Fund documents that discuss country economic conditions. Furthermore, Fund missions can seek the opinions of an array of nongovernmental organizations, and the Bank can involve NGOs in the design and implementation of projects. By doing this, the Bretton Woods agencies would be better able to deflect pressures for a sanctions approach to promoting political reform.

Political objectives carry a danger of partisanship, cultural arrogance, and hubris. There is also tension between the well-founded desire to reduce the complexity of conditionality and the emerging interest in adding conditions regarding equity and economic governance. The quandaries will be multiplied by cases where regimes pass one or two but not all key tests—such as a regime with efficient economic policies, generally good governance but little concern for equity. Nevertheless, the Bretton Woods agencies cannot escape these dilemmas in the 1990s. They should confront them directly—however conceptually difficult and politically sensitive—and devise clear policy guidelines, rather than be caught in a defensive position.

Bank-Fund relations

Both agencies are likely to remain involved in policy-based lending in Sub-Saharan Africa for the near future. The World Bank is deeply committed to fostering structural reform. The 10-year repayment period of the ESAF/SAF is an indication that the Fund will also remain in Africa for the long haul. Furthermore, in light of the region's unstable macroeconomics, increasingly volatile politics, and the present inhospitable external environment, Fund advice and financing are likely to be in demand in the 1990s.[7] Given the strong probability of this mutually extended presence, the Fund and the Bank will want to collaborate closely in Sub-Saharan Africa. They will need to synchronize policies and organize efforts to increase their effectiveness. Policies need to be sufficiently coordinated so as not to send contradictory signals to African officials.

In Africa as elsewhere, the IMF's extended facilities and the World Bank's policy-based lending have often resulted in overlap in jurisdictions. The policy framework papers are an effort to address this issue by assuring coherence between Bank and Fund programs in a multiyear framework. Bank and Fund staff do work well together in some countries, and recent efforts by country teams to compare findings and projections and to reconcile differences are encouraging. Still, much remains to be done to assure that the papers are more than a cut-and-paste job. Medium-term country programs should be designed by joint Bank-Fund missions. The current practices of including "across the street" representatives in mission teams and "parallel missions" that are in-country at the same time, are positive steps in this direction, though even these depend too much on individual personalities to guarantee coherent programs.

Such collaboration will proceed more smoothly if one institution leads. In Sub-Saharan Africa, it makes sense for the World Bank, not the IMF, to take the lead in organizing external assistance efforts and policy reform programs. This approach would be consistent with the 1989 decision to give the World Bank primacy over structural matters, though it ought not to prevent the IMF from continuing to assist on macroeconomic problems. Ideally, the result of this division of labor should be more consistent policy advice and more efficient, less time-consuming dialogues with member governments.

In resource transfers, it is desirable that IDA increase its exposure in low-income Africa vis-a-vis the less concessional IBRD and IMF. But IDA monies should not be recycled to the IMF at a time when many African countries are in dire financial straits. It is therefore in the interest of the World Bank, as well as Africa, for the IMF to cease to be a financial drain on Sub-Saharan Africa.

The Bank and Fund have worked closely together to follow the outline of the Brady debt proposals but they could play a more dynamic role if their management could join forces in proposing amendments to the Brady proposals that would speed their implementation. And since the Fund is as interested as the Bank in erasing the commercial debts and arrears of many low-income countries, it might want to match the IBRD's contribution to the new debt reduction facility. Close collaboration will be especially important in the newly emerging areas of policy conditionality: economic governance and social equity. Both the Fund and the Bank can take economic governance into account when considering stand-bys and policy-based loans, since the commitment and credibility of corrupt regimes may be in question. It would be embarrassing for the Fund to be lending to a regime where the World Bank had curtailed lending because of repeated jiggery-pokery. The International Monetary Fund cannot, however, be expected to deny credit to a member because its stabilization plans are regressive. But Michel Camdessus has given Fund staff the mandate to address the social costs of stabilization programs and therefore to analyze the composition of expenditures and incidence of taxation as they affect different social groups. As the Fund develops these capabilities, it will be better able to assist receptive governments to design equitable programs—and to share its analysis and recommendations with Bank staff.

Finally, it is time for the Bank and Fund to engage in long-term planning for Sub-Saharan Africa. Policy framework papers should go beyond the three-year horizon dictated by the timetable of Bank and Fund country programs, and look five and even 10 years ahead on some issues. The Bank and Fund should also join forces to produce regionwide strategic plans for this decade to guide their own work as well as to give clear signals and realistic expectations to the region. Needless to say, the countries of Sub-Saharan Africa should play major roles in designing these programs that would so vitally affect their interests.

Notes

1. The relative weight of the variables that influence the IBRD's credit rating is a matter of some dispute. For an argument that emphasizes capital subscription and retained earnings, see Blitzer (1989).

2. Mistry (1988, 46) suggests using ESAF monies to assure a zero net transfer to such debt-distressed countries. Two-tier conditionally has also been proposed, in broader contexts, by Nelson (1989, 18-22) and Finch (1989, 89-91).

3. For an analysis of the "Totonto terms" for official bilateral reschedulings, see World Bank (1989, 47-48).

4. For a fuller treatment, see Gwin and Feinberg (1989).

5. For example, see World Bank (1988). The conventional wisdom also holds that the "integrated rural development" strategies of the 1970s were too complex and demanding.

6. In the past, Fund and Bank lending decisions occasionally were influenced by the political motives of major shareholders, and their economic advice can also be seen as ideologically based. But these "political" motives are distinct from concern for the domestic political practices of borrowing states. I am indebted to me colleague, Joan Nelson, for clarifying for me this and other points regarding political conditionality.

7. Fund staffing patterns have been sticky, however, and have not adjusted to this institutional commitment to Africa. Staff in the African bureau are spread very thin, suggesting that their numbers ought to be augmented.

References

Blitzer, Charles R. 1989. "Financing the World Bank." In Richard E. Feinberg, ed., *Between Two Worlds: The World Bank's Next Decade*. Washington, D.C.: Transaction Books and the Overseas Development Council 1989.

Camdessus, Michel. 1990. "The IMF Support for Growth-Oriented Adjustment in Africa." Remarks made before the U.S. Chamber of Commerce, Washington, D.C., March 26, 1990. Reprinted in *IMF Survey*, April 2.

Finch, David. 1989. "An IMF Debt Plan." *The International Economy* 3 (March-April): 89-91.

Gwin, Catherine, and Richard E. Feinberg. 1989. *Pulling Together: The International Monetary Fund in a Multipolar World.* Washington, D.C.: Transaction Books and the Overseas Development Council.

International Monetary Fund. 1990a. *Financial Statements of the General Department of the SDR Department and Accounts Administered by the IMF.* Washington, D.C.

—. 1990b. *International Financial Statistics.* August. Washington, D.C.

Mistry, Percy S. 1988. *African Debt: The Case for Relief of Sub-Suharan Africa.* Oxford: Oxford International Associates.

Nelson, Jon. 1989. *Fragile Coalitions: The Politics of Economic Adjustment.* Washington, D.C.: Transaction Books and the Overseas Development Council.

World Bank. 1988. *World Debt Tables, 1988-89 Edition.* Washington, D.C.

—. 1989. *World Debt Tables, 1989-90 Edition.* Washington, D.C.

Comment

Joshua Greene

This thoughtful and provocative paper has many useful observations and intriguing policy proposals. At the same time, however, the paper has omitted a number of important qualifications and extensions that deserve mention, particularly as regards the International Monetary Fund.

The International Monetary Fund as a net creditor from Sub-Saharan Africa. Perhaps the most important caution to apply to this paper involves the perceived role of the Fund as an institution. The International Monetary Fund has traditionally viewed its financial assistance activities as those consistent with a monetary institution whose resources have a revolving character. Thus, the general resources of the Fund have been made available to member countries on a temporary basis, for the purpose of helping them correct external payment imbalances, with the understanding that these resources should be repaid over the medium term as their economies improve. Countries such as those in Sub-Saharan Africa that have made extensive use of Fund resources over a period of years would accordingly be expected to make net repayments to the Fund during a subsequent period. The International Monetary Fund has periodically expressed its concern about countries that are "prolonged users of Fund resources," and guidelines for the level of access to Fund resources take into account a country's past use of Fund resources and the likelihood that the country will be able to attain a sustainable balance of payments over the medium term without need for exceptional financing. Although the Fund has during the last several years used the repayments from its concessional Trust Fund loan program of the late 1970s, together with other borrowed resources, to establish new sources of concessional assistance for these countries under its Structural Adjustment Facility (SAF) and Enhanced Structural Adjustment Facility (ESAF), these moves have not been taken as a way of altering the more fundamental interpretation that Fund resources are considered temporary. To alter this longstanding view of the Fund's financial assistance activities would require a major change in Fund policy, something unlikely to occur without considerable discussion.

The arrears issue. In much the same way, the proposals in this paper regarding the treatment of Fund arrears are likely to require a major rethinking of Fund policy by its members. Considerable effort has gone into the development of various approaches to the arrears problem, including the development of the present "rights" approach, whereby members with overdue obligations to the Fund can build up rights towards a subsequent arrangement by performing well under a "shadow" adjustment program supervised by the Fund that leads to a clearing of these arrears. As with the idea of the revolving character of the Fund's resources, the Fund has taken the view that members with overdue obligations cannot draw on Fund resources, and that requests for the use of Fund resources will not be considered from members in arrears. This is not to say that the Fund's members could not reverse their views on this issue. However, allowing members in arrears to enter into new Fund arrangements, or to use purchases as setoffs to past arrears, would again require a sea change in thinking among Fund members.

Conditionality policy. Another caveat to raise regarding this paper involves its discussion of conditionality. On the one hand, the author contends that Fund-supported and, arguably, Bank-supported adjustment programs involve too much conditionality, insofar as disbursements are tied not only to attaining macroeconomic objectives, but also a number of structural policy goals. On the other hand, the author suggests there is a place for even more conditionality, insofar as the linking of adjustment programs to reducing poverty and improving economic governance are concerned. Thus, it seems that the author is really objecting more to the nature of structural conditionality in these arrangements, rather than to its degree.

In considering these objectives, one should note that both institutions, and particularly the Fund, have in recent years tried to prioritize reforms and limit structural conditions to the most important policy measures. However, both institutions have observed that in many countries it is difficult to rectify macroeconomic imbalances without addressing certain structural problems that seem the major cause of these imbalances. Accordingly, it would be seriously detrimental to try to eliminate structural conditionality from the macroeconomic adjustment programs, as opposed to prioritizing reforms and restricting conditionality to genuinely essential measures.

As regards conditionality for poverty orientation and economic governance, both institutions have increasingly devoted attention to addressing the social consequences of adjustment and to helping countries devise adjustment programs that mitigate the effects of adjustment on the lowest-income segments of their populations. One consequence is that greater attention is now paid to the composition of public expenditure and to the timing of changes in certain administered prices for goods of particular importance to the poor. Developing conditionality for economic governance is likely to be a more delicate matter, however, in view of the long-standing commitment at both institutions to take into account the domestic social and political objectives of member countries.

Traditionally the Fund has steered clear of developing explicit conditionality to limit drawing rights for countries with nondemocratic governments or perceived widespread corruption. Nevertheless, the history of adjustment programs provides indirect ways of dealing at least with this last issue. For example, a country's past performance in carrying out adjustment programs can be used in framing the conditionality and drawing rights under subsequent arrangements. Countries with poorer track records can be given more prior conditions as a prerequisite for making the initial drawing under an arrangement. Similarly, where corruption is alleged to be a problem, it may be possible to frame conditions so as to make performance of a specific policy objective, such as eliminating budget arrears or accounting-related deficits in a major public enterprise, a condition for subsequent purchases under a Fund arrangement. But all this does involve greater intervention in a country's economic decision-making, something not to be viewed lightly.

A two-tiered ESAF. Although a number of countries that are potentially eligible for support under the Fund's ESAF facility have thus far declined to request an ESAF arrangement, the Fund's experience with the simultaneous existence of the SAF and ESAF facilities does not offer much encouragement for a two-tiered ESAF. Since the inception of the ESAF in 1987, a number of countries have opted for support under the SAF, despite the smaller amount of resources provided. Although some of this may have resulted from the front-loaded nature of SAF drawings, which has made it difficult to ensure implementation of policies agreed under SAF-supported adjustment programs, there is also a perception that some countries have used the SAF in place of the ESAF as a way of avoiding the more far-reaching economic adjustment typically required for ESAF arrangements. To the extent this is true, establishing a two-tiered ESAF might simply enable countries to avoid taking more substantial adjustment measures. This is particularly troublesome from the standpoint of Africa, because most low-income Sub-Saharan African countries face the major economic problems that require serious and wide-ranging structural reform. These are not the sorts of changes that can easily be grouped into more and less-essential measures, as might be the case for countries considering milder reforms, such as how quickly to implement trade liberalization. Thus, a two-tiered ESAF might not provide much benefit to many Sub-Saharan countries.

Bank-Fund relations. As for Bank-Fund relations, experience has been that Bank and Fund staffs work closely on most countries, and the cases in which the two institutions do not comment constructively on each others' areas of major policy specialization are few. At the same time, there will always be areas, such as the balance of payments outlook and estimating external financing requirements, where it will be important for the two institutions to develop independent views. Accordingly, while the quality of Bank-Fund collaboration remains an important concern, the problems may not be so great as is suggested in this paper.

The Developmental Effectiveness of Aid to Africa

Anthony Killick

Evidence on effectiveness

Cross-country evidence

The most important task of this paper is to explicate the factors reducing the developmental value of aid to sub-Saharan Africa but we must start by reviewing the evidence on the effectiveness of aid. Consider first the evidence summarized in table 8.1 We see there that Sub-Saharan Africa received far more aid than other developing countries in the 1980s: per capita, as a proportion of income, and relative to investment and imports. Despite this, Africa had a much worse economic performance than the rest of the developing world taken together. Does this not indicate that aid has failed in Africa?

Not necessarily. For one thing, comparisons of economic performance for the 1970s would be substantially less unfavorable to Africa than they are shown to be for the 1980s. Also, more aid has been flowing to Africa precisely because its economic performance has been so weak. In any case, there are so many other influences on growth that to infer aid failure from weak growth performance would be a large over-simplification. And yet with such large aid receipts one might reasonably have looked for better economic results. In fact, in the 1970s and 1980s the amount and share of aid to Africa increased as the region's relative performance worsened. At the very least, one must conclude that aid has not been strikingly effective in economic terms—or that factors reducing aid effectiveness have more than offset any positive returns from aid.

Now consider some additional comparisons of Sub-Saharan Africa with other aid recipients:

- The World Bank's (1989d) survey of 15 years of ex post project evaluations obtained results for Africa which were substantially the weakest of all regions, with a 70% "satisfactory" score against an overall 81% average, and a deteriorating trend.
- An econometric cross-country study by Mosley (1987) found particularly weak statistical relationships between aid and GNP growth in Africa, by comparison with Asia and Latin America. This was notwithstanding a much greater amount of aid relative to economic activity.
- Gupta and Islam (1983) found similarly, with a far weaker "total effect" coefficient between aid and growth for Africa than for Asia and Latin America.
- On the basis of his country case studies, Cassen (1987, p. 295) arrived at the conclusion that aid works less well in Africa than in Asia.
- The World Bank's (1989a) evaluation of adjustment lending found the association of adjustment programs with improved economic performance weaker for Africa than for their total sample. It also found that all except one of six indicators bearing upon the sustainability of the adjustment process had deteriorated in the African case: investment ratios, GDP growth, budget deficits, balance of payments deficits, and debt—servicing ratios. The sixth—per capita private consumption growth—remained unchanged.

A second Bank assessment of its adjustment experiences, confined to Sub-Saharan African countries (World Bank 1989b), is perhaps alone in painting a brighter picture. This too uses a control group method, but simply compares countries with "strong" and "weak" or no reform programs, with no other attempt to ensure comparability. This found faster GDP and agricultural growth in the strongly reforming countries, superior export and investment records, and faster growth of private consumption. Savings performance, however, was better in the non-reforming group.

Table 8.1 *Comparative statistics on aid and economic performance, 1980-88*

	Sub-Saharan Africa	*Other developing countries*[a]
Aid indicators[b]		
1. Aid *per capita* ($)	21.85	.5
2. Aid as % of *per capita* income	4.90	.8
3. Aid as % of gross domestic investment	33.53	.3
4. Aid as % of imports	25.75	.2
Performance indicators (annual rates of change)		
5. *Per capita* income	-6.4	+0.8
6. *Per capita* private consumption	-1.1	+0.8
7. Daily calorie supply *per capita*	-0.6	+0.8
8. Gross investment	-4.1	+1.8
9. Export volumes	-5.1	+7.3

a. defined as all reporting low- and middle-income countries;
b. figures relate to net disbursements of overseas development assistance from all sources.
Source: World Bank.

These findings met with considerable skepticism, however, and riled the UN Economic Commission for Africa (UNECA, 1989b). The study raised in particularly acute form several methodological difficulties, particularly as regards the choice of control group, the difficulty of differentiating between the effects of program finance and program policies, and the absence of testings for statistical significance in the results obtained. There was also considerable subjectivism in it.

Given the pervasive influence of the policy environment on the economic performance and the growth of conditionality, we can ask whether the donors have succeeded in working with African governments towards the adoption of sound policies, or have selected for preferential treatment those governments which chose well-founded policies. This is the question asked by Lele and Jain (1989) in their assessment of the results of aid to African agriculture, from which they concluded that, although they made important contributions to agricultural and rural development, "neither the donors' project-by-project approach of the 1970s, nor their concern for policy reform in the 1980s to date has helped African governments face the inescapable hard work on constructing long-term, country-specific development strategies . . ."; that it "is difficult . . . to find much connection between where donor assistance has gone and where growth has occurred . . ." (p. 236); and that its contribution has generally been "far from satisfactory" (p. 247). At an economy-wide level, the condemnation in the Bank's 1989 report on Sub-Saharan Africa of the top-down modernization development strategies of the past (and the economic crisis it describes) can also be read as a criticism of donors' the past policy stances (or ineffectiveness). The ECA is similarly dissatisfied with the wastefulness and inefficiency of past policies and the aid dependency it has created.

Of course, the picture is not uniform. Some African country studies have reported favorably on aid's impact and there have doubtless been many excellent projects. It is also surely the case that Bank and other support has helped to improve policies and economic performance in several countries. Nonetheless, the overall picture is unsatisfactory.

A country comparison

Much the same conclusion emerges when we look at the position at the individual country level. We can, for example, compare Côte d'Ivoire and Ghana, as neighboring states which have had startlingly different post-Independence economic histories. Starting with a considerable advantage over its neighbor, in terms of skilled manpower, infrastructure and general economic development, Ghana suffered a calamitous economic deterioration during the first 25 years of independence, which only began to be reversed during the 1980s. By contrast, by the early 1980s the Côte d'Ivoire had achieved one of the best infrastructures in Africa, per capita incomes had grown at nearly three percent a year, there had been much social progress, and the country was commonly

Figure 8.1 ***Net disbursements of aid from DAC countries and multilateral agencies to Côte d'Ivoire and Ghana, 1971-88***

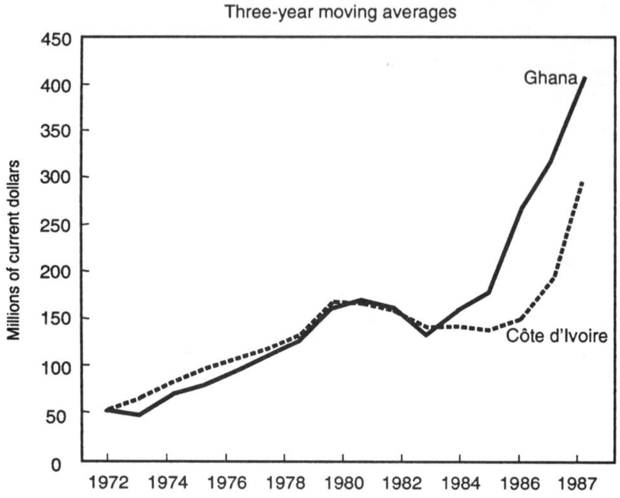

cited as a model for the rest of Africa. Since then things have deteriorated markedly, however. By the beginning of the 1990s the Ivoirian economy was in crisis, with declining incomes, large debt servicing difficulties and a deteriorating infrastructure—a position that would have been even worse were it not for large infusions of aid from France and elsewhere.

Figure 8.1 charts trends in aid to these countries in 1971-88. Although they deviate from time to time, it is striking how closely the two series move together "despite the enormously differing economic records of these two countries during this period". Aid cannot have made any very decisive impact here. Aid allocations to these countries seem to have paid scarce regard to ability to use it well. With the partial exception of the final years, the similarity of the trends is so striking as to suggest that aid trends were determined by extraneous forces unrelated to recipient economic performance. Witness the sustained level of aid to Ghana during the 1970s even though the economy was then manifestly falling apart and grossly mismanaged during much of the period. Similarly in Côte d'Ivoire, the big increase occurred in the late 1980s, just when the economy—and the standard of economic management—was deteriorating. More positively, however, there was a sharp rise in aid to Ghana after 1983, when improved economic policies were introduced.

On this and earlier evidence, then, it appears there is much scope for strengthening aid effectiveness in Africa. The next step is to examine the factors which diminish effectiveness. What follows is organized around a distinction between determinants primarily located within recipient countries, breaking these down into (a) the policy environment and (b) institutional, or absorptive capacity, questions; and those relating primarily to the policies and practices of aid agencies.

Recipient-country influences on effectiveness

The policy environment

The conclusion of a recent study of aid and development (Krueger, Michalopoulos, and Ruttan 1989) provides our starting point:

> The most important lesson learned about economic development, and therefore about the role of assistance, is the significance of the overall macroeconomic environment for economic growth. Over the past thirty years appreciation of the importance of appropriate trade and exchange rate policies, of fiscal and monetary policies, and of the overall incentive structure provided by government policies has increased continuously . . . Experience indicates that the macroeconomic setting is an important determinant of the success of sectoral and project assistance. In countries where the macroeconomic framework is appropriate, real rates of return to investment projects tend to be high . . . (p. 306).

Contrasting performances between otherwise similar economies seem largely explicable in terms of differing policy environments. Reynolds' (1985) survey of long-run development experiences concludes that "political organization and the administrative competence of governments" is the single most important explanation of variations in developing countries' growth records. And Riddell's authoritative 1987 reexamination of the case for aid (p. 198) supports the consensus that the policy environment is a major determinant of aid effectiveness.

With the shift within mainstream macroeconomics in the 1980s towards supply-side issues and to the microfoundations of macro actions, there is now wide recognition of the intimate connections between the macroeconomic environment and the performance of agriculture, industry and other key sectors of the economy. The modern approach to exchange rate management, with its emphasis on the real exchange rate, has drawn added attention to the quality of overall macro management (particularly the avoidance of inflation) as conditioning what can be done with the exchange rate instrument. Much the same is true of discussions of financial policy, with the literature on financial repression drawing attention to the influence of the macro environment on financial system development and to the avoidance of rapid inflation seen as necessary if positive real interest rates are to play their role in stimulating the financialization of saving and raising the productivity of investment. The policy environment is also seen as potentially influential on the supply of entrepreneurship, through tax and other policies affecting profits, the extent and nature of regulation of business, the influence of the public finances and other policies on the availability of business finance, and the provision of infrastructure and training. More generally, macroeconomic stability is seen as raising supply responsiveness and encouraging long-term investment.

The macro environment also strongly affects the developmental returns that can be obtained from aided projects. "Some of the most frequently cited determinants of [project] performance," states the World Bank (1989b), ". . . were in principle within the control of governments." Or again, "The experience evaluated for this review emphasizes the great extent to which the fate of projects depends on sectoral and macroeconomic policies . . ." (p. 21 and 30). Indeed, it was partly because it saw ill-chosen policies as causing increasing numbers of its past projects to fail that the World Bank moved into "policy-related lending" from the end of the 1970s.

Relating the above to Sub-Saharan Africa, there is fairly general acceptance that past policy environments have often been far from conducive to good economic performance and, therefore, to aid effectiveness. Thus, a document endorsed by a meeting of African Ministers of Finance and Planning and Development states, "government interventions in Africa have so far become discredited, not because there is an effective alternative in the form of an efficient market mechanism but because of inefficient management, poor results and misallocation of resources" (ECA 1989a, p. 47). Or Ndulu (1986):

> The current economic deterioration in Sub-Saharan Africa has partly been caused by internal economic mismanagement. Wide state intervention in the productive spheres and in markets for resources and products has led to an inefficient use of scarce resources not only in the "Pareto efficiency" sense, but also in relation to the development goals adopted by those countries. Serious biases against the development of the export and agricultural sectors have produced stagnant economic growth, arrested social development, increased dependence on food imports, and debt burdens requiring frequent reschedulings (p. 102). In its most recent report on Africa (1989d, p. 26) the World Bank showed the rate of return on investment in Africa to have declined drastically to negligible levels in the 1980s and to be far lower than in South Asian countries. Among the chief reasons it identified for this result were poor public sector management, price distortions, often created by policy interventions; and high cost structures, also much influenced by government policies. It also stressed the very heavy costs imposed by Africa's loss of export market shares. These, it suggests, are considerably larger than losses caused by deteriorating terms of trade and can be linked to past policy mistakes, notably on exchange rates (although large aid inflows may have contributed to over-valuation in some countries).

The parlous state of the public finances in many Sub-Saharan African countries is a further illustration. Budgets are often heavily in deficit, so much so that governments even have to borrow to finance part of their "current" expenditures. One consequence is that the public sector has become a large dissaver and the chief reason for the serious decline in overall saving rates, absorbing resources that could be devoted to investment (see table 8.2).

There is also evidence that the large claims of the public sector on bank credit to finance budget deficits crowds out the private sector's needs for credit; and that the expansionary effects of deficit financing are an important source of inflationary and balance of payments pressure.

These budgetary difficulties are also related to a suspicion that the fungibility of aid resources may have allowed some governments to avoid taking hard but desirable decisions to raise taxes and/or that aid has really financed marginal additions to spending with a low developmental content. The possible displacement of tax effort by aid is difficult to demonstrate but there are straws in the wind. World Bank evaluations find that tax reforms in structural adjustment programs have had among the lowest implementation rates (1989a, p. 60); and that "...cost recovery, whether directly from customers or beneficiaries, or indirectly out of allocations from government budgets, has often been much lower than called for in project designs" (1989c, p. 39).

Table 8.2 ***Gross domestic saving in SSA (as percentage of GDP)***

	1972	*1981*	*1987*
Gross domestic saving	17.8	15.3	12.6
Fiscal current a/c deficit	-3.3	-5.9	-7.2
Private and other saving (residual)	21.1	21.2	19.8

Source: World Bank 1989d, table 8.1, p. 165.

Similarly, an unpublished study of aid to Kenya by Duncan and Mosley (1985), suggests that aid may have served as a substitute for local taxes and argues that there is scope for an improved tax effort.

Fundability on the expenditure side is equally elusive and the danger is reduced by the large scale of aid receipts relative to many governments' development budgets. There nonetheless remains doubt about the developmental content of some governments' expenditure priorities. Thus, the ECA refers to a "need for expenditure-switching in the form of curtailment of government expenditures on defence and non-productive activities, [and] removal of subsidies to parastatals . . ." (1989d, p. 44). And while the Bank estimates average African military spending at the comparatively moderate level of about 10% of total government spending, it draws attention to much higher military expenditures by a number of governments. But the biggest waste in government spending is the maintenance of inflated payrolls in civil services and public enterprises—an inefficient and inequitable form of employment creation—with the probability that aid has partly been used to sustain larger numbers in public employment. (However, we point out later that aid donors have added to fiscal weaknesses by undertaking projects without thought to their subsequent budgetary implications and have sometimes eroded expenditure discipline by conducting transactions outside regular budgetary processes.)

That the quality of the policy environment is the key determinant of the developmental effectiveness of aid is also the central thesis of Stryker and Tuluy's 1989 comparison of the Côte d'Ivoire and Ghana. They point out that "all" forms of aid are affected, not just program aid, and show how aid to Ghana's agricultural sector was undermined by rapid inflation, gross exchange rate overvaluation, and other price distortions. They also point out that donor attempts to insulate "their" projects from the overall state of the economy were largely unsuccessful and gave rise to unintended adverse effects. They conclude that:

> Foreign aid is unlikely to be effective inachieving either host country or donor goals in the absence of an economic policy environment that is conducive to long-term development. This is true regardless of whether aid is seen as a transfer of resources or as a means of implementing project packages involving a combination of capital, technology, and managerial know-how. When the policy environment is seriously distorted, as it was in Ghana, it is difficult to find any type of foreign assistance that can be successfully implemented, except possibly some training and investment in human capital that may prove valuable in the future (p. 301).

However, they are also critical of the slowness of donor agencies to use their aid as a vehicle for strengthening policies, and we noted earlier how aid to Ghana and Côte d'Ivoire seemed largely unrelated to policy performance.

The position has been changing, however. Recognition of the importance of the domestic policy environment for aid effectiveness provided a rationale for the considerable expansion of donor policy conditionality during the 1980s. This "conditionality explosion" has increasingly given the donor community, especially the World Bank and IMF (the international financial institutions, IFIs), a major influence over economy-wide policies and has given particular importance to the design of IFI policy packages. The appropriateness of IFI structural adjustment policies is far too big an issue to take up here. We merely note the absence of strong evidence that these policies were effective in Sub-Saharan African in the 1980s and that there are important intrinsic difficulties in the way of using aid as a lever improving recipients' policy environments. There are conflicts between the objectives of the IFIs and recipient governments; there are mismatches between the complexities of program design and the amount of knowledge that IFIs have of domestic conditions; conditionality itself may erode governments' identification with the programs they agree to and undermine the legitimacy of both; and the forces acting upon, and within, the IFIs sometimes undermine their ability to ensure that apparently tough policy conditions are adhered to.

In any case, policy deficiencies do not occur in a vacuum. They are the products of social, political and institutional forces which themselves can be formidable obstacles to aid-effectiveness. We therefore turn to consider such factors, and others bearing upon countries' absorptive capacity for aid.

Absorptive capacity

We can view absorptive capacity as the ability of the economic system to put additional aid to productive use. When this is a major constraint it shows in a number of ways. There is likely to be much unspent aid because ministries are unable to execute agreed projects and/or programs. Partly as a response, the composition of aid-financed programs and other activities may become largely donor -driven—another symptom. There are likely to be systematically large discrepancies between ex ante and ex post project rates of return (which the Bank (1989a) found to be characteristic of its projects in Africa), and the developmental benefits of projects are not sustained.

Many African countries display such symptoms of limited absorptive capacity. In examining the sources of the problem we can differentiate between proximate and fundamental causes.

Proximate sources of difficulty. First, many African countries remain acutely short of well-trained and experienced project personnel. There are similarly drastic shortages of officials able to prepare policy reform programs acceptable to donors. This is not only a matter of numbers. Often their work setting does not reward the employment of professional skills. In some countries senior officials' salaries are well below levels in the private sector, contributing further to low morale, weak motivation, moonlighting, and high turnover.

There is a strong connection between such problems and a second proximate cause of inadequate absorptive capacity: institutional weaknesses. Almost everyone agrees on the seriousness of such weaknesses but also on the difficulties of doing much about them. In addition to the factors just mentioned, such weaknesses show up in ineffectual leadership pursuing conflicting or poorly defined objectives, and unclear and diffused responsibilities—reasons for failure of rural development projects in Malawi (Hewitt and Kydd, 1984) and Kenya (Duncan and Mosley, 1985). Lele (1989, p. 32) similarly identifies fragmentation of policy-planning as a major problem with aid to agriculture in several African countries, with decision-making responsibility scattered among government departments, parastatal bodies, and autonomous project units.

Budget constraints further restrict absorptive capacity. Sometimes governments have difficulties in finding the local counterpart funds to meet the local-currency costs of externally aided projects. This constraint has been described as a "recurrent costs problem": an inadequacy of government funds to meet the intended standards of operation and maintenance of externally-aided (and other) government services. With salaries (often on an inflated payroll) a first call on resources, other recurrent items bear the brunt of financial stringency, leading to under-use of human and physical capital: extension workers without petrol for their vehicles, schools without books, hospitals without drugs, and a decaying infrastructure.

To a substantial extent, the recurrent costs situation is a product of more general weaknesses: a narrow tax base, inadequate tax and cost-recovery efforts, and an overall economic stagnation that depresses tax revenues. Large external debt servicing obligations, sometimes exacerbated in local-currency terms by major currency devaluations, have also emerged as a major contributory factor, being a prior claim on revenues which otherwise could be devoted to relieving shortages of recurrent financing.

However, the recurrent costs situation also has more specific causes—inefficient revenue allocation systems, weak financial and project management systems, a separation of "recurrent" and "development" budgets (often the responsibility of separate departments) which hinders the integration of investment and recurrent-cost planning. Lele and Jain (1989, p. 247) argue that this has led to a capital formation bias in public expenditures, which has accelerated the growth of the aid-financed capital stock well beyond the country's revenue-earning capacity, citing Kenya and Tanzania as examples.

A final proximate cause of limited absorptive capacity, recalling that we have defined this as the ability to put additional aid to productive use, is the unwillingness or inability of some governments to create a policy environment which is conducive to such productivity, as we have already discussed.

Fundamental problems. By definition, proximate causes do not go to the heart of the matter. Of more fundamental importance are basic structural weaknesses which unavoidably limit the absorptive capacity of many African economies, and major weaknesses in political systems and processes.

The first is not controversial. The chief structural flaws include heavy dependence on primary production for the generation of incomes and export earnings, very small domestic markets, technological backwardness, weak infrastructure, rapid population growth, acute shortages of skills and other human resources, dualistic and inefficient markets, and weak institutions. These weaknesses, and the low income levels that result, reduce the ability of African countries to create a more favorable environment for aid.

Sub-Saharan Africa has little of the industrial base which gives more advanced economies greater responsiveness to changing conditions and more versatile skills. The responsiveness of the productive system to changing price relativities is weaker because of poor information flow, highly imperfect markets, and probably a stronger influence of non-market traditional values. Because of poverty and the smallness of the modern economy, savings capacity and the tax base are severely constricted. Economies tend to be unattractive to foreign investors.

The small size of the economy makes it trade-dependent and vulnerable to external shocks. Smallness also spells an undiversified output and difficulty in switching demand and output between tradeables and non-tradeables and between domestic and foreign markets. Finally, the policy instruments available to governments are fewer and weaker relative to the gravity of the problems faced. Governments and public administrations may also be less willing or able to enforce policy decisions.

These structural weaknesses are deep-rooted and can only give way gradually. While limited absorptive capacity can be interpreted as a reason for withholding aid, it can more sensibly be viewed as an additional reason why aid is needed, but targeted at addressing these weaknesses, providing support for adjustment efforts, and ameliorating the social costs that result.

Identification of political weaknesses within Sub-Saharan Africa as a second fundamental source of limited absorptive capacity is more controversial. The World Bank (1989d, pp. 60-61) caused a stir by raising this issue, but the ECA is in general agreement. Thus, the ECA's "Khartoum Declaration":

> The political context for promoting healthy human development [in Africa] has been marred, for more than two decades, by instability, war, intolerance, restrictions on the freedom and human rights of individuals and groups as well as over-concentration of power with attendant restrictions on popular participation in decision-making.

Both these organizations see a connection between the prospects for development (and hence aid effectiveness) and the nature of political systems, with the ECA calling for greater political accountability and a more grass-roots approach. More prosaic support comes from the Bank's OED evaluation (1989c, p. 33) which in its examination of agricultural projects found that "beneficiaries' participation in decision-making and in implementation increases the efficient use of [resources]." The Bank's 1989 report on Africa similarly drew a connection between political systems which foster corruption and aid effectiveness.

Political scientists have similarly noted the connection, with personal rule based on communal or ethnic ties seen as inimical to economic efficiency and development. Such "patrimonial" states are seen as penetrated by personal relations operating to satisfy individual and communal aspirations and not as the guardian of the national interest. Profits accrue to those close to the state, rather than through production, creating a self-reinforcing spiral of political and economic decay. Development, and the economic adaptation on which it depends, are frustrated.

Going back to comparisons of Côte d'Ivoire and Ghana, it would be rather easy to relate the economic deterioration in Ghana during the 1960s and 1970s to political conditions. Likewise, the superior performance of the Côte d'Ivoire could be linked to the stability and wisdom of its political leadership during the same period, just as the recent deterioration in that country could be related to the deteriorating political situation there.

At the same time, all is not gloom. There is much political diversity on the continent and economic hardship does often set corrective forces in motion, albeit belatedly. In some countries it is difficult to see a way forward without a revolution. In most the position is less desperate. In many it has been possible to make progress. Even in the lean years of 1980-87, 13 out of 41 Sub-Saharan African countries for which data are available experienced per capita income growth. Furthermore, the evidence does not support the view that the benefits of this are invariably concentrated on a small ruling group. Ultimately, bad governments that run down the economy are apt to be removed; the worst policies and practices tend eventually to generate counteracting forces. Meanwhile, however, it would be difficult to justify on developmental grounds continuing flows of aid to some of the governments of Africa. The ECA, the Bank and others are right to call for political reforms.

Although the above discussion has been about recipient-country influences on aid effectiveness, it has been suggested at a number of points that donor-country actions have contributed difficulties. We now consider the influence of donors more systematically, concentrating on the policies and practices of donor agencies.

Donor influences on effectiveness

Since Africa's economies are so open to influences and shocks from the outside world, the policies of donor-country governments have a large impact on the continent's ability to achieve development and to use aid to that end. The choices which OECD governments make between the control of inflation and expansion of their economies impacts strongly on the growth of trading opportunities. So do their policies towards protectionism. Their fiscal and financial policies affect the size and direction of capital movements and of world interest rates. Donor governments largely determine the policies of the IFIs and the extent to which cooperative solutions are sought for world economic problems.

These facts are, however, thoroughly familiar. For this reason we merely place them on the record and proceed to matters more directly related to aid donor agencies.

Problems of aid quality

Problems under this heading include: the pursuit of multiple objectives, weaknesses with aid agencies, and proliferation problems.

Problems from multiple objectives. Much difficulty arises from donor governments' multiple motives for maintaining aid programs. In addition to the promotion of long-term development, aid is used to promote foreign- and military-policy objectives, as covert protectionism, and for short-term humanitarian relief. A single instrument is being used to promote not merely multiple but often conflicting objectives. The results can only be detrimental to developmental effectiveness. McGuire and Ruttan (1989) paint a vivid picture of the US position early in the Bush administration:

> The mix of foreign policy objectives in Africa could hardly be more confusing and contradictory. The objectives include promoting the US global strategic position, supporting US positions in multilateral forums and elsewhere, ensuring access of US diplomats to the many governments in Southern Africa, fostering economic development through financing projects or balance of payments support conditional on policy reforms, and providing humanitarian relief. If any administration policy could be classified as lacking design, the Africa policy would be it (p. 30).

As a result of such situations aid can be erratic in volume or content, as Lele and Jain (1989, p. 243) complain in relation to aid to African agriculture.

A further consequence—particularly the influence of foreign policy and commercial considerations—is that it can distort country aid allocations in anti-developmental directions. There are several notorious examples of disproportionate aid allocation: French aid to Reunion and Martinique, British aid to the Falkland Islands, German to Turkey, Japanese aid to Indonesia and US aid to Israel and Egypt (more than a fifth of total US aid). It works negatively too, with "unfriendly" countries receiving little. It also exerts an influence on the World Bank and IMF, through interference with country lending decisions—a problem which worsened in the 1980s. The position is not uniform across donors, however. Gulharti and Nallari (1988) studied the influences on country aid allocations within Africa and concluded that:

> Major donors have distinctive aid profiles. Political variables are important for the United States (and to a somewhat lesser extent for the United Kingdom) but of scarcely any significance for other donors such as the Netherlands and Sweden. The trade variable is significant for Japan and Italy but it plays hardly any role in the case of other donors. Developmental motivations are strong in the case of West Germany and to some extent in the United Kingdom . . . [Moreover] donor aid objectives are not rigid. They have changed over time and the weights assigned to individual goals have varied (p. 1177).

In fact, Mosley (1987, p. 60) suggests that OECD aid has become gradually more need-related; certainly it would be difficult to explain the large proportionate shift in total aid allocations towards Africa that has occurred over the last 30 years in terms of geopolitics or trade promotion.

A further dilution of aid quality occurs through procurement-tying. Although this is sometimes defended as a way of increasing public support for aid or as a tactical weapon to use in persuading other donors to reduce their tying, the principal motive is protectionism. The precise extent of tying is difficult to measure because of informal as well as formal arrangements and because of the possibilities for recipients to use tied aid for items they would have purchased anyway. Including informal as well as formal arrangements, probably 40-50% of total OECD aid is procurement-tied, with no clear downward trend (Jepma, 1991).

Tying imposes costs on recipients, transferring some of the value of aid to beneficiaries in the donor country. The direct cost is the extra which the recipient has to pay through being unable to buy on world markets at the lowest price. Most estimates place the surcharge in the 15-30% range, although there are horror stories involving far larger proportions.

There are also indirect costs. Tying, and the commercial objectives which underlie it, introduce biases in donor project selections in favor of capital and import intensity. Tied aid is liable to incorporate inappropriate technologies or to foster a proliferation of technologies. It places more demands on recipients' scarce administrative resources, introducing more complicated procurement procedures and thus an additional source of delay in aid utilization. Tying is liable to bias bilateral donors against coordination because they see themselves as in competition with each other.

There is also a connection between tying and the recurrent costs issue. The desire to tie helps to explain past donor reluctance to contribute to recurrent and other local project costs because such assistance, by definition, could not be tied (although there are also legitimate reasons why donors should be wary of recurrent cost financing, particularly the exit problem of how to avoid taking on commitments of indefinite duration).

In developmental terms, therefore, procurement-tying is thoroughly pernicious, imposing costs on recipients which, relative to economic activity, are disproportionate to any gains to donor-country interest groups. Indeed, at the country-wide level tying is most unlikely to bring any benefits to donors at all. This partly follows from general arguments against protectionism but is also because tying appears in practice to be an inefficient form of protectionism, with benefits tending to be concentrated on a small number of economically strong exporting firms (Jepma, 1991).

One possible qualification to this general condemnation is that tying is necessary to secure public support for aid and thus permits larger transfers than would otherwise be politically feasible. The key issue here is the elasticity of the amount of aid with respect to tying. Given the substantial costs to recipients described above, the elasticity would have to be large if the volume effect were to dominate the quality effect. This would probably only happen in exceptional cases.

Problems from agency weaknesses. The complaints here are familiar enough to need only brief mention:

- That donor agencies are inadequately staffed to undertake their responsibilities. At the same time staff are under pressure to spend their budgets. This combination reduces the level of professionalism which they can bring to the design and execution of programs.
- Relatedly, that shortages of the right kinds of expertise, as well as constituency and political pressures, cause donors to take a short-term view, executing numerous projects which may not add up to a coherent whole, and being excessively influenced by swings of fashion. Lele and Jain (1989, p. 243) identify this as seriously detracting from the value of past aid to African agriculture.
- There is also what the same writers call "overextension of comparative advantage": that sometimes under popular or political pressure, agencies take on a range of aided activities that is beyond their areas of expertise. Howell (1989) argues a similar case in his examination of British aid to agriculture in three African countries.
- There are long-standing complaints of donor biases towards large, capital- and import-intensive projects, and inappropriate production and management technologies. Hewitt and Kydd's examination of sources of difficulty with rural development projects in Malawi refers to misplaced donor confidence in the superiority of improved seed-fertilizer-chemical packages and in extension recommendations about cultivation techniques; and to their promotion of an over-ambitious management concept (1984, p. #153, 155). Duncan and Mosley (1985, p. 62) have similar criticisms of the management systems sponsored by donors for rural development projects in Kenya. This tendency toward capital and import intensity is related to the existence of multiple objectives, as expressed in tying, but that is only part of the story. Mosley (1987, Chapter 3), in particular, argues that such biases are intrinsic to the incentive systems operating within agencies (which is why it is so persistent a defect) and that recipient-government officials may well share these biases.
- There is also evidence that donor practices have sometimes undermined budgetary control and discipline in recipient countries, because of agency desires to spend. Sometimes donors pursue the tactic of deliberately selecting for assistance sectors they believe to be neglected in the expectation that this will force the government to spend more because of the recurrent costs of the aided projects (Howell, 1985, p. 13). More generally, past neglect of the recurrent cost implications of projects has added to the difficulties of budgetary planning. Most seriously of all, agencies sometimes undertake activities outside the normal government budget altogether, setting up quasi-autonomous project administrations or paying suppliers direct; seriously undermining the fiscal authority of the Treasury. Take Adams' (1989) description of the situation in the Sudan:

> Sudan's total dependence on foreign assistance constrains its ability to control the free-wheeling activities of donors. The hold of the Ministry of Finance and Economic Planning over the donor agencies is tenuous. Even some of the long-established bilateral donors . . . are disbursing outside the government budget, in

> some instances without any formal agreement with the central authorities. For most intents and purposes, the government system of annual budgeting of development and recurrent expenditure has collapsed. In the circumstances, bilateral agencies tend to become a law unto themselves, preferring to retain their freedom to disburse funds in the most opportune manner and to provide the authorities with just sufficient information to justify their continued presence. Projects are often funded through informal, ad hoc channels. For example, to ensure the loyalty and commitment of government staff attached to projects, donors find it necessary to make incentive payments and to pay retainers to senior government personnel to act as "consultants". (p. #187-88)

Proliferation problems. Various forms of proliferation impair recipient countries' abilities to take advantage of aid. One is the number of "donors". According to Cassen (1986, p. 219), an average of 25-30 official agencies operate in a country at any one time, to which should be added a probably larger number of non-government agencies. The activities of this multiplicity is unlikely to add up to a coherent whole in the absence of strong coordination, to say nothing of the administrative demands created.

A proliferation of "projects" is a further aspect. Riddell (1987, p. 210) cites estimates of 600 projects from 60 donors in Kenya, 188 projects from 50 donors in Malawi, 321 projects from 61 donors in tiny Lesotho, and 614 projects from 69 donors in Zambia. An inevitable consequence is that "technologies" also proliferate, with each donor seeking to supply equipment from its own country. Thus Cassen (1986, p. 221) cites 18 different types of pump supplied by donors for rural water supply projects in Kenya. Aid for rural water in Kenya also illustrates the dangers of another form of proliferation: of "policy conditions". In this case the World Bank required a system of flat user charges based on marginal costs while the Swedish agency SIDA urged a system based on ability to pay.

Problems with coordination. Each of the forms of proliferation mentioned above calls for coordination of donors. Coordination takes place at international, regional, country, sector and project levels, usually involving meetings of staff members from donor and recipient agencies. In addition, it occurs in meetings of donors without recipients, and among different agencies of recipient governments. The World Bank and UNDP have been particularly active in promoting coordination, through meetings of Consultative Groups (CGs) and Roundtables.

Nonetheless, the record on donor coordination is at best patchy. The Development Assistance Committee (DAC) of the OECD has striven over many years to reduce the problem of donor competition in such matters as procurement-tying and mixed credits but the continuation of these practices, and the absence of any clear declining trend, attests to the difficulties encountered. There has probably been greater success at the country economy- and sector-wide levels, e.g. through the work of CGs. At the same time, there remains much room for better coordination of donor-country decisions on aid, debt relief, export credits and related matters, which have often contradicted one another.

The position is bleaker at microeconomic levels and in relation to the various proliferations mentioned above, at least according to the testimony of several would-be coordinators. Thus Whittington and Calhoun (1988) have recorded how their efforts to establish a register of aid commitments and disbursements in Sudan's Ministry of Finance and Planning was frustrated by donor refusal to supply necessary information. Writing about coordination in Kenya, Clift (1988) has recorded how agreements arrived at between donors at a CG broke down in practice and how too much attention was paid to the process of coordination rather than its content. Others have observed that monitoring and implementation of decisions of coordination meetings is generally weak, and Cassen's (1986, p. 318) study found donor coordination "sadly wanting".

Whittington and Calhoun (1988) use stronger words. They draw a sharp distinction between donor rhetoric and reality, describing the apparent campaign for better coordination as an exercise in "the ritual of planned development" and suggesting that, "few donor coordination efforts have proceeded beyond the level of general discussion because the donors place data management demands upon the ministries of finance and planning which even the donors do not know how to address" (p. 306). Even the DAC allows itself some relatively strong language:

> Close coordination both among aid institutions and between them and the recipient countries, has long been prescribed as an indispensable condition for enhancing the development effectiveness of each participant in the development process. Rarely, until recently, has such country-centered coordination been fully or consistently attempted. (cited by Riddell, p. 210)

Why should coordination be so lacking? Some point at recipient governments, arguing that there is no substitute for strong recipient leadership in this matter (e.g. Clift 1988, p. 132). Making sure that aided activities conform to government priorities and avoiding excessive proliferation is certainly best thought of as a primary responsibility of the home government. However, a government in Africa may be ambivalent about the desirability of donor coordination, fearing that it will lose freedom of action to play one off against another, or that the machinery of coordination will be used by donors to gangup against it. Whether many African governments could effectively provide such leadership, even when they wished to, must in any case be doubted. Their administrations are overwhelmed by the magnitude of the task—one which would stretch even more handsomely endowed bureaucracies. As Adams (1989, p. 189) observed about disbursement delays in Kenya, the root of the problem was in managing commitments from 15 multilateral and 20 bilateral donors, each with its own spending priorities, accounting and administrative procedures, agreement periods and financial years, and disbursement conditions.

Donors also have reasons for ambivalence. Effective coordination reduces their freedom of action too. Coordination places additional demands on sometimes already very busy staff. Cassen and others (1986, p. 230-31) suggest further that they may want to avoid the conflicts with other donors which attempts at coordination would generate. There are also basic questions about whether agencies are structured so as to encourage coordination. Many of them are highly centralized, with all significant decisions taken in donor capitals, while effective coordination would require greater delegation of authority. And Adams observes (1989, p. 187) that field staff have few real incentives to work with other donors. Their main task is to administer their budgets and, in practice, success in working with other donors is given little value in agency personnel assessments.

At the heart of the matter is authority, however. Given the conflicting interests of the various donors, as well as of the recipient government, it is most unlikely that effective coordination could be achieved by persuasion and the exercise of sweet reason alone. Ultimately, one party—preferably the government—must be in a position to knock heads together, to exert authority. Coordination implies power. As Whittington and Calhoun have put it, "all donors want to co-ordinate, but no-one wants to be co-ordinated (p. 307). In particular, do donors really want to be coordinated by recipient governments? Is that the aid relationship that in reality they seek?

Towards a fresh start

The conclusion from the above must be that, taking the region as a whole, large amounts of aid received by Sub-Saharan Africa have been ineffective in developmental terms, both for program and project assistance. At the same time, Africa's share of total aid has continued to rise, and there are frequent calls for yet further assistance. There are sound macroeconomic reasons for these, relating to the need to adequately fund adjustment programs and to help countries cope with debt difficulties—but more of the same would not necessarily produce better results than those of the past.

Can the sources of difficulty undermining aid effectiveness be resolved? There is a multitude of possible policy suggestions already on the agenda. We could, for example, suggest ways in which domestic policies could be strengthened in Africa so as to stabilize economies and raise the marginal productivity of resources. The 1989b World Bank report on Africa offers a wide range of suggestions. A shortage of advice is not a constraint upon the improvement of the policy environment. There have, moreover, been important policy improvements during the past decade. Similarly with absorptive capacity: large numbers of reports have recommended ways of strengthening fiscal and development planning and of improving the public service.

There are also many proposals for improving donor-country policies which worsen the global economic environment. In the area of debt relief, for example, there is a constant flow of analyses and suggestions. Many point to the desirability of reducing protectionism; others the need for larger aid programs. Here too progress has been made, particularly with debt relief for African countries, even though relief still falls far short of needs.

Turning to the aid agencies, many have urged that government goals be simplified, that primacy be given to developmental and humanitarian objectives, and that tying should be abolished or reduced. The desirability of contributing more to local-currency recurrent costs has been urged and mechanisms for this have been proposed. Greater use of NGOs has been suggested and implemented to overcome the difficulties official agencies have in reaching the poorest. More and better ex post evaluation has been advocated, as well as an improved learning process from the results. Everyone says they are in favor of better coordination, and here too there are improvements.

Nonetheless, the situation calls for a fresh start, a renewed effort to tackle the obstacles to effective aid. How can we break through the well-known but deep-seated obstacles to improvement? What emerges from our analysis is "the primacy of politics". The fundamental problems are not technocratic but reside in the structures of power, decision-making and execution. No fresh start will be possible unless the political constraints are addressed.

Consider first the politics of Africa discussed earlier. The World Bank is surely right (1989b, p. 60-61) that underlying the litany of Africa's development problems is a crisis of governance, as is the ECA (1989b, p. 50) in calling for "democratisation of the decision-making process at national, local and grassroots levels . . ." These, however, are matters for the peoples of Africa to resolve, and there are now important stirrings of political change in a substantial number of African countries. Aid agencies must deal with the governments of the day, however. How, then, might they respond to the primacy of governance in often ill-governed countries?

Hitherto, conditionality has been their chief weapon, using finance in order to induce governments to make improve economic. However, conditionality is unlikely to have much lasting effect on economic policies if it is forced upon a reluctant and unconvinced government. Following events in Eastern Europe, some donor governments, notably that of the United States, have begun to talk of political conditionality, or of confining aid to governments operating within, or moving toward, pluralistic, multiparty democracies. It is doubtful, however, whether aid conditionality could be effective in bringing about constitutional change in other than exceptional circumstances. For if conditionality relating to economic policy is not very effective when a government is unconvinced of the desirability of the change, what prospects are there of using aid to induce governments to adopt constitutional changes that will likely result in their being voted out of office?

The logic of this situation is for donors to be more selective and flexible in their country aid allocations, to confine most of it to those countries which have a framework of governance and policies and an absorptive capacity which permits aid to be used effectively.

However, there are difficulties with this. First, backing governments that can use aid effectively may well result in a return movement of aid proportions in favor of Asia at the expense of Africa—a shift that may well be desirable in any case, on developmental and anti-poverty grounds. Relatedly, some of those least able to employ aid productively need it most: think of Angola, Burkina Faso, Mozambique or Sudan. It may, moreover, be very difficult to identify potential winners in advance: who in 1982 would have predicted that a populist military administration in Ghana dedicated to the ideology of Kwame Nkrumah would have turned out to be the Fund and Bank's favorite African government?

Crucially, however, a recommendation for donor governments to be more selective in their country allocations begs the question of how much importance they attach to the development objective in relation to the other motives for aid. In particular, it would create tensions with their desire to use aid as a foreign policy instrument.

Many of the weaknesses in donor agencies stem from this multiplicity of objectives or from other reasons that would require a breakthrough at the political level for their remedy: tying and the resulting project biases, under-resourcing, dysfunctional personnel incentive systems, and ambivalence about coordination. There is, in other words, no less a need for policy improvements on the part of the donors than of developing country governments. If there is to be a fresh start the log-jam will have to be broken at the political level.

A potentially attractive route for avoiding donor constraints on aid effectiveness is to increase the proportion of aid channelled through multilateral agencies, which are less beset by conflicting objectives and better able to concentrate on maximizing developmental effects. They are relatively immune from tying and some of the other practices that reduce aid quality. They probably have greater degrees of freedom in country allocation decisions, and are better placed to engage in constructive policy dialogue with recipient governments. With larger resources, and the donor-government support that would imply, they would be in a stronger position to exert the authority which we have suggested is necessary for effective coordination.

But some multilateral agencies are more professional and non-political than others. There would be obvious dangers of spawning yet larger international bureaucracies, with even greater concentrations of power vis-à-vis African governments. There is, in any case, little sign of a shift to multilaterals actually happening, with their share in total aid remaining constant at around a quarter throughout the 1980s, and such a shift would be resisted by many donor governments. Here again we come up against donors' multiple objectives, for the resulting loss of freedom to use aid for foreign policy and commercial advantages has been among donor-government reasons for resisting larger shares for multinational aid. However, with the ending of the Cold War and consequent reductions in the importance of security-cum-foreign-policy considerations, more progress might now be possible. The politics of the situation is thus the key, among both donors and recipients. If there is to be a fresh start, it is at the political level that it will have to be initiated, and now is a good time to begin. Political stirrings within Africa and the radical reevaluations of security and foreign policies under way among donor countries will create new policy priorities that can help overcome some of the old obstacles to aid effectiveness. There has now been created a "Global Coalition for Africa" intended as a new type of forum at which mutual difficulties can be frankly discussed. To engineer a new beginning in effective aid should be the priority task for this Coalition.

References

Adams, Martin E. 1989. "Aid Coordination in Africa: A Review." *Development Policy Review* 7 (2).

Cassen, Robert, and others. 1986. *Does Aid Work?* Oxford: Oxford University Press.

Clift, Charles. 1988. "Aid Coordination: Are There Lessons to Be Learned from Kenya?" *Development Policy Review* 8 (2).

Duncan, Alex, and Paul Mosley. 1985. "Aid Effectiveness: Kenya Case Study." Study commissioned by Task Force on Concessional Flows (unpublished draft).

Gulharti, Ravi, and Raj Nallari. 1988. "Reform of Foreign Aid Policies: The Issue of Inter-Country Allocation in Africa." *World Development* 16 (10).

Gupta, K., and M.A. Islam. 1983. *Foreign Capital, Savings and Growth: An International Cross-Section Study*. Dordrecht, Holland: Reidel Publishing Co.

Hewitt, Adrian, and Jonathan Kydd. 1984. "A Study of the Effectiveness of Aid to Malawi." Study commissioned by Task Force on Concessional Flows (unpublished draft).

Howell, John, ed. 1985. *Recurrent Costs and Agricultural Development*. London: Overseas Development Institute.

Howell, John. 1989. "British Aid to Agriculture in Malawi, Tanzania, and Kenya." In Uma Lele, ed., "Aid to African Agriculture: Lessons from Two Decades of Donor Experience." Washington, D.C.: World Bank (discussion draft).

Jepma, Catrinus J. 1991. *Tying of Aid*. Paris: OECD Development Centre.

Krueger, Anne O., Constantine Michalopoulos, and Vernon W. Ruttan. 1989. *Aid and Development*. Baltimore, Md.: Johns Hopkins University Press.

Lele, Uma, ed. 1989. "Aid to African Agriculture: Lessons from Two Decades of Donor Experience." Washington, D.C.: World Bank (discussion draft).

Lele, Uma, and Rahul Jain. 1989. "Synthesis: Aid to African Agriculture." In Uma Lele, ed., "Aid to African Agriculture: Lessons from Two Decades of Donor Experience." Washington, D.C.: World Bank (discussion draft).

Mcguire, Mark, and Vernon W. Ruttan. 1989. *Lost Directions: US Foreign Assistance Policy Since New Directions*. Minneapolis, Minn.: Economic Development Center, University of Minnesota.

Mosley, Paul. 1987. *Overseas Aid: Its Defence and Reform*. Brighton, UK: Wheatsheaf Books.

Ndulu, Benno J. 1989. "Governance and Economic Management." In R.J. Berg and J.S. Whittaker, eds., *Strategies for African Development*. Berkeley: University of California Press.

Reynolds, Lloyd G. 1985. *Economic Growth in the Third World, 1850-1980*. New Haven and London: Yale University Press.

Riddell, Roger C. 1987. *Foreign Aid Reconsidered*. London: Overseas Development Institute and James Currey.

Stryker, J. Dirk, and Hasan A. Tuluy. 1989. "Assistance to Ghana and the Ivory Coast." In Anne O. Krueger, Constantine Michalopoulos, and Vernon W. Ruttan. 1989. *Aid and Development*. Baltimore, Md.: Johns Hopkins University Press.

UNECA (United NAtions Economic Commission for Africa). 1989a. *African Alternative Framework*. Addis Ababa.

UNECA (United Nations Economic Commission for Africa). 1989b. *Statistics and Policies*. Addis Ababa.

Whittington, Dale, and Craig Calhoun. 1988. "Who Really Wants Donor Co-ordination?" *Development Policy Review* 6 (3).

World Bank. 1989a. *Adjustment Lending: An Evaluation of Ten Years of Experience*. Washington, D.C.

World Bank. 1989b. *Africa's Adjustment and Growth in the 1980s*. Washington, D.C.

World Bank. 1989c. *Annual Review of Evaluation Results*. Report No. 8164. Washington, D.C.

World Bank. 1989d. *Sub-Saharan Africa: From Crisis to Sustainable Growth*. Washington, D.C.

Comment

E. Tumusiime-Mutebile

The precise influence of aid is thoroughly elusive. There are so many diverse alternative influences on the variables that aid might affect that to extract the contribution of any one of the various dimensions of aid on, say, growth is not very fruitful. There is an identification problem here. The counterfactual state of affairs, what would have happened in the absence of a particular package of aid, serves to complicate matters further. Then, of course, there is the problem of defining what is developmental, the old debate about whether an increase in output can unambiguously be called development.

Professor Killick gives us what he calls an informal analytical framework which is quite useful in thinking about the effectiveness of aid. I feel, however, that the theoretical framework could have been usefully augmented if the analysis were formulated as a formal equation, so that a reduced form of the equation could be derived to show the interlinkages.

In addition to the purely methodological problems is the issue of the time frame for assessing the effectiveness of aid. Some methods for increasing economic growth in the short run are not necessarily appropriate in the long run. For many *Sub-Saharan African* countries where underutilization of existing productive capacity is rampant, foreign aid financing of recurrent imported inputs will have a much quicker impact on economic growth than foreign aid that attempts to create new productive capacity. Indeed, it may not be efficient at all to create new capacity or to expand existing capacity when available capacity is so grossly under utilized. Yet it is traditional to think of aid as being effective only if it goes into capital investment. But, of course, in the longer term as existing productive capacity is more fully utilized capacity constraints will slow down economic growth unless new capacity is created.

Professor Killick gives a number of interesting reasons why aid is sometimes not a positive force in development. I will highlight only a few of the most critical ones.

Poor governance

This is undoubtedly one of the most important reasons detracting from the effectiveness of aid. What is required is governance; particularly more transparency, more accountability, more popular participation, and less government participation in directly productive investments outside socioeconomic infrastructure. After the Maastricht Conference on Africa which created the Global Coalition for Africa, there is an emerging consensus that better governance is a prerequisite to enhanced effectiveness of economic policy and programs, including aid. In several African countries including my own, there is a growing awareness that broadly based political coalitions are necessary to guarantee democracy and widespread access of the mass of the population to remunerative productive assets. So, better governance and democratic institutions are important. But the questions regarding the form and content of democracy remain open. There is the argument that in some countries multiparty political activity could engender political instability if not outright internecine intertribal warfare.

Before leaving the question of governance, however, I want to flag a potential problem with what Professor Killick calls the "primacy of politics." In his view, "the fundamental problems are not technocratic but rest with structures of power, decisionmaking, and execution. No fresh start will bepossible unless the political constraints are addressed. I think we need to clarify what exactly is the nature of this "primacy of politics" and to clarify precisely what the political constraints are that need to be addressed so as to avoid another false start in Africa. In particular in seeking greater popular participation, because of high levels of illiteracy and widespread ignorance of the importance of economic fundamentals, there is a danger of the politics of macroeconomic populism, whereby leaders downplay the evils of inflation and hold up a fixed nominal exchange rate as some symbol of national virility.

Basic structural weakness

Professor Killick says the other problems which he identified are "proximate crises" which do not "go to the heart of the matter," and that "of more fundamental importance are (a) basic structural weaknesses which afflict many *Sub-Saharan African* economies and which unavoidably limit their absorptive capacity; and (b) major weaknesses in political systems and processes." He adds that the first of these—"basic structural weaknesses"—is not controversial! Maybe it is not. However, there is a question that needs to be asked. If this is the fundamental problem for all

Sub-Saharan African countries, how come some of these countries have been in the top league of developing country performers? I think that the answer to this question is that while structural weaknesses undoubtedly reduce the possibilities of transferring resources between sectors in response to relative price changes, substitution possibilities are also to a great extent influenced by policy. The adaptability and resilience of Sub-Saharan economies can be and has in some countries been built or created by appropriate economic policies, both macroeconomic and microeconomic, as well as by good mesoeconomic policies.

While on the theme of appropriate economic policies, I think I should also mention that this factor is important not only for ameliorating the effects of structural weaknesses, but also in determining the impact of shocks—whether foreign or domestic. Good domestic economic policies help countries to adjust in an orderly fashion to external shocks. More generally, the proper role of foreign resources is to "supplement" rather than to "supplant" domestic savings and investment. If domestic economic policies do not encourage the mobilization of savings and their productive investment, why should we expect foreign aid to be effective? There is no doubt that if macroeconomic discipline prevailed in Africa and there were appropriate incentives for the efficient use of available resources, without harmful distortions in tax regimes, exchange rates, prices, and interest rates, aid would have been as effective in Africa as it has generally been in Asia. Witness the relative success of Kenya and Cameroon. Professor Killick's paper does recognize the significance of the overall macroeconomic environment for economic growth, but he does not give it the importance it deserves. I think that the inhospitable macroeconomic environment throughout most of *Sub-Saharan Africa* is the most fundamental detriment to aid effectiveness.

Whether or not the economic policy environment is hospitable to foreign aid is determined in large measure by the characteristics of the policy within which policy is made. It seems to me that the more open and well informed the policy discussions are, the more likely it is that sound economic policy will emerge. The quality of the debate, and the quality of the resulting environment, are products of the institutio—both political and bureaucrat—through which the debate is conducted. To this extent Professor Killick is right to highlight the "primacy of politics."

The importance of the policy environment for the effectiveness of aid is the central rationale for program aid conditionality. And to the extent that conditionality can ensure a conducive policy environment, it is clearly effective. The most important determinant of the effectiveness of conditionality is the quality of the process by which stabilization and structural adjustment programs are agreed. The quality of this process is jointly determined by the recipient and the donor: in this case the Bretton Woods institutions. This interaction is crucial for the quality of outcome, the quality and sustainability, of the policy environment, and thus, the effectiveness of aid.

Policy conditionality sets an agenda for recipient governments and their domestic economic policy debate. Those who seek to affect the outcome bear some responsibility for that outcome if their influence succeeds. Professor Killick has outlined most of the institutional problems faced by *Sub-Saharan African* countries and he notes that "institutional factors are unfortunately treated as a black box, with little concrete content". This may be a part of the problem. It is often compounded by missions from the Bretton Woods organizations, under heavy pressure to deliver quickly, who are generally insensitive to these institutional factors. Unless the management of such field visits is of high quality the impact of the policies and practices of the donor agencies may have a negative impact on the institutional problems affecting the quality of the recipients contribution to policy. A well-known example is that of joint missions of the Bank and the Fund where each agency prefers to deal with different parts of the government because of different, usually conflicting aims. They eventually come to some internal compromise. But too often this compromise is at the expense of the government side of the triangle, which is left divided and confused. Perhaps this explains the remark from Lele and Jain which is cited by Professor Killick that "neither the donors' project by project approach of the 1970s, nor their concern for policy reform in the 1980s have helped African governments face the inescapable hard work on constructing long-term country-specific development strategies...."

Poor absorptive capacity

This, as Professor Killick notes, is partly due to budget constraints as well as to institutional weakness. Once again, however, poor absorptive capacity can be remedied by good policies. Lack of skilled manpower and managerial capacity in many *Sub-Saharan African* countries is due to bad policies that have undermined the governments' capacity to pay realistic salaries. The problem in countries like Uganda is that skilled personnel have left for greener pastures, or they are not in government service because of low remuneration. In response to this absorptive capacity constraint, governments have tended to seek technical assistance experts. But this response has seldom been effective because technical assistance personnel have simply displaced rather than reinforced local capacity and local staff have no incentive to work. To be effective, technical assistance projects in such situations need to include a carefully targeted package of incentives for the local staff directly engaged on projects.

There is one other reason which is sometimes given for the ineffectiveness of aid. This is the role of the state. It is true that in many *Sub-Saharan African* countries the state has been overextended, and its intervention has tended to bring out distortions in the incentive structure for savings and for investment, not least by driving a wedge between prices and marginal costs. But this issue is not an ideological one. The solution is not stopping state investment so much as improving the efficiency of all investments. And this means leaving the state to concentrate on public administration where it has a comparative advantage. But the state also needs to put investments into those areas where the social returns are high but private returns are low. We must not forget that efficient infrastructure, better roads, efficient telephones and reliable power supplies are part of the enabling environment for private sector investment. And aid can be effective in financing investment by the state to create public infrastructure.

My concluding remark is to agree with Roger Riddell's conclusion, arrived at from specific country studies, that "aid can be and frequently is a positive force in development." As long as the economic policy environment is right.

Part III

Commercial External Finance

9

Commercial Bank Lending: Outlook and Constraints

Ellen Johnson Sirleaf
Francis Nyirjesy

The record of commercial bank lending

In 1960-1970, when commodity prices were strong and per capita incomes rose rapidly, commercial bank lending to Sub-Saharan Africa was negligible. From 1970 to the early 1980s, when there were strong fluctuations in commodity prices and requirements for petrodollar recycling, commercial lending increased exponentially—from less than $500 million in 1970 to a stock of $13 billion in long-term loans, on the strength of annual net flows that peaked at almost $3 billion in 1980. Since then the stocks have moved in response to many factors—new lending as a function of perceived creditworthiness of borrowing countries or entities and the viability of various forms of security for loans, the depreciation of the U.S. dollar and its effect on debt stocks, debt reschedulings and debt service performance, and activity in the secondary debt markets.

The aggregate statistics in table 9.1 indicate that commercial bank long-term debt stocks in Sub-Saharan Africa amount to approximately $22 billion of the $118 billion in total long-term debt stocks reported in the *World Debt Tables* (World Bank 1989). However, these statistics are likely to be overstated since Côte d'Ivoire's private sector is shown to have received some $900 million a year in commercial bank medium-term loan disbursements in 1985-88—a high proportion of new lending to the region and an unlikely 10 percent of Côte d'Ivoire's GNP. By comparison, the Bank for International Settlements (BIS) and the Organization for Economic Cooperation and Development (OECD), using different definitions and data sources, reported commercial bank term debt stocks at $11 billion at end-1988.

The *World Debt Tables* also indicate that commercial lending to Sub-Saharan Africa has been highly concentrated, with some 15 countries accounting for 97 percent of total stocks, and that lending to the private sector (without host government guarantees) has exceeded sovereign lending in recent years.

Some 80 percent of the approximately $10 billion outstanding in the London Club reschedulings of 18ub-Saharan African countries are owed by Nigeria and Côte d'Ivoire, who have performed poorly or not at all under the initial agreements. This tends to obscure the fact that a number of countries have performed well on their restructured debt.

In addition to reducing their cross-border lending to Africa, a number of commercial banks who have had local presences in the region, many of them since the colonial era, began withdrawing in the mid-1980s. However, most banks continue to do selected offshore risk-free business, such as providing correspon

Table 9.1 ***Commercial bank long-term loan activity (billions of U.S. dollars)***

	Stocks	*Disburse-ments*	*Principal*	*Interest*	*Non-flows*
1970	0.4	0.1	0.07	0.02	--
1980	13.0	4.0	1.2	1.2	--
1983	18.5	3.0	2.2	1.5	--
1984	17.7	2.8	2.9	1.7	(0.07)
1985	18.5	2.2	3.1	1.4	1.7
1986	18.0	2.6	1.5	1.2	(0.9)
1987	23.0	2.0	1.6	0.8	4.6
1988	22.1	1.9	1.5	1.1	(1.3)
83-88	14.5	12.8	7.7	4.03	

Source: World Bank (1989).

dent services under donor-funded programs. Since both good and bad economic performers have been affected by this slow exodus, it seems that the banks' departure has to do partly with the changing nature of their business objectives and target markets.

Nature of commercial bank lending

In all bank cross-border lending there are four main risk categories: unsecured lending, export-secured lending, asset-based finance, and secured lending.

Unsecured lending

Unsecured bank loans are extended on the basis of the borrower's ability to service them from resources generated from its activities in the borrowing country and transferred to the lender through the country's foreign exchange allocation system. The lender assumes both the "commercial" risk (i.e., the borrower's solvency) and the "political" risk (mainly foreign exchange availability).

The most common forms of unsecured lending to Africa have been:

- Short-term revolving loans to central and commercial banks for advance settlement to offshore suppliers of goods and services, usually through letters of credit or short-term advances. As these are repaid, new advances can be drawn within the facility's limits.
- Loans to non-bank borrowers (sometimes underwritten by local banks) in the form of guarantees to offshore suppliers or through discounted purchases of suppliers' credits.
- Medium-term loans, for specific private or parastatal investment projects. These are based on the borrower's creditworthiness, the viability of the project based on cash flow projections, and the likely availability of foreign exchange.

The risk in unsecured lending tends to increase where foreign exchange availability is regulated or constrained. Thus banks have continued to provide short-and medium-term unsecured loans to profitable bank and non-bank borrowers in the CFA zone, who have automatic access to French francs. Banks are also more likely to make unsecured loans (usually short-term) in countries with adequately funded auction systems or liberal foreign exchange regimes (such as Guinea, Ghana, Madagascar, and Nigeria) and in countries that have had no payment problems (such as Zimbabwe, Kenya, Ethiopia, Mauritius, Burundi, and Rwanda).

Banks have been moving away from unsecured lending, and many now typically require some offshore security. These take such forms as offsettable cash deposits, or revolving flows of export proceeds that are ultimately available for repatriation to the borrowing country.

Export-secured lending

A variety of mechanisms are used to mitigate foreign exchange transfer risk by establishing liens on exports and/or export proceeds. Banks may require, *inter alia*, (a) assignment of title to exports, (b) irrevocable instructions to a buyer to make payment directly to a lending bank, or (c) foreign exchange escrow accounts held in the bank's or the exporter's name with the lending bank, another offshore bank, or in the borrowing country's foreign exchange system.

A classic form of export-secured lending is pre-export finance. This is used for balance-of-payments support in many countries, such as Angola, Cameroon, Tanzania, Uganda, and Zimbabwe. Facilities range from disbursements repayable in one "bullet" (typically less than a year) to multi draw/multi installment repayments, revolving on a more or less permanent basis, but typically with terms of not more than three years. In addition, control over exports or export proceeds is used by the oil and mining sectors to secure medium-term loans.

Insurance companies have played an important role in export-secured lending by covering banks and/or suppliers (who then assign their rights to the lending bank) against non-delivery and export contract frustration. Nevertheless, a significant volume of African exports is financed directly by suppliers under insurance cover, without the intervention of banks, while banks competing for large pre-export finance facilities must weigh the cost of the insurance and delays in recoveries should problems arise.

Asset-based finance

Banks have been willing to finance high-value, moveable assets, such as aircraft, vessels, and mobile equipment, based on a lien on the asset's market value (with loans normally covering 50-70 percent of the asset value). Private insurers generally support such transactions, often with loss and/or repossession cover.

Secured lending

Commercial lenders often require offshore security, which can take the form of cash deposits, cross-guarantees among suppliers, buyers and direct investors, undertakings from official external agencies, and private political risk insurance. Unless formally - guaranteed by an official agency, secured loans appear in the World Bank statistics, but are not usually included in the BIS reports.

Increasingly, commercial banks act as intermediaries of donor funds, providing correspondent banking services against cash deposits or reimbursement guarantees from donors. On occasion, these facilities allow banks to extend unsecured loans indirectly funded by the deposits. More importantly, they are replacing the unsecured short-term credit lines that the banks traditionally provided to their subsidiaries and correspondents in many countries.

Secured lending can also rely on guarantees to banks by offshore private entities, such as oil exploration and production companies. These can vary from "comfort letters" to legally-binding full or partial guarantees.

Constraints perceived by the commercial banks

In a series of informal interviews with commercial banks in Europe and the United States that have traditionally been active in Africa, little optimism was expressed about the prospects for new medium-term lending to Africa on a wide scale in the 1990s. Nor did many foresee aggregate net increases in their short-term portfolios in the near future. They raised a number of issues that underlie this pessimism, summarized below in seven broad areas.

Mandatory provisioning

Most OECD countries have imposed selective provisions (or guidelines) on bank lending to developing countries. These regulations, as well as voluntary provisions, have generated significant losses on LDC portfolios and made it difficult to justify new lending to non-performing countries. Equally important, the provisioning requirements are often applied to *new lending* as well: these policies are considered a major deterrent or even (for some banks) an absolute bar to further activity, since they can lead to immediate accounting losses. The policies are seen as signals that OECD banking authorities do not want banks to be active in affected countries.

Many of these regimes became more stringent in 1989-90: for example, the Bank of England issued a stiffer "matrix" in January 1990, and private sector/local bank risk in the CFA zone has come under closer scrutiny in other countries, including France. Some of the regulations are considered excessive, such as the 100 percent provisioning on Zairean debt imposed in the United States, which normally follows a more liberal and selective policy than other OECD countries.

Capital adequacy and risk: reward relationships

With some (undercapitalized) banks, portfolio growth is constrained generally, and high-risk lending particularly. Capital adequacy must be strengthened to comply with regulatory targets, and some banks are sensitive to bank stock analysts, who seem to view any African lending as a negative. Consequently, in the past two to three years these banks have tended to reduce aggregate exposure in LDCs (as well as in other poorly performing sectors), minimize and absorb current losses, and generally improve asset quality and streamline operations.

It is difficult, therefore, to convince analysts and bank management of the attractiveness of certain lending opportunities in Sub-Saharan Africa. A related problem is that the scope for adjusting pricing to reflect actual (or perceived) risks and to take advantage of the scarcity of long-term commercial bank financing has been declining. Decision-makers are averse to lending at any price to non-performing borrowers, while some borrowers and external public officials object to the high fees and interest margins that are proposed as being commensurate with the risks.

It may be possible to establish a more realistic "risk:reward" relationship in lending that is shifting to the private sector—perhaps more along the lines of venture capital financing and commercial profit margins—that can generate far higher returns than traditional interest margins and fees on loans. However, there was little sign of the banks' pursuing such new strategies in Africa at present.

Instead, they appear to be opting for no-risk, fee-based services, through fully secured letters of credit and other traditional trade-related facilities: intermediation and management of donor funds, representing governments in debt negotiations and reduction operations, and providing merchant banking or financial engineering services.

Export credit agency support

Aggregate statistics in the *World Debt Tables* (World Bank 1989) suggest that OECD export credit agencies have also been less active in Africa in recent years. They also face non-performing loans, budgetary discipline, more conservative borrowing practices and depressed demand in some countries. Many agencies have suspended or been slow to reopen or commit resources under credit, guarantee, and insurance programs. Since commercial banks have traditionally provided funding and/or residual risk financing for official export finance programs, this has also meant fewer opportunities for them.

The decline in export credit agency support may also be related to increased concessional financing. An increasingly critical event in country-donor relationships, Consultative Group meetings, now generate nearly all long-term financing for public investment programs, traditionally financed in large part by commercial banks and export credit agencies. Similarly, balance-of-payments support through structural adjustment facilities may have reduced the need for import financing by banks, suppliers, and export finance agencies.

Co-financing mechanisms and other security arrangements

Given the foreign exchange constraints and debt-servicing difficulties of many countries, commercial lenders are wary of projects that generate no foreign exchange revenues, or of export projects where export receipts and debt service payments have to transit through the host country's foreign exchange allocation system. There is also virtually no interest for projects involving lending to otherwise non-performing public borrowers and/or state enterprises.

Some banks have indicated that they would participate significantly in some new lending only if the security is sufficient to remove (or reduce) the "sovereign risk". Both the co-financing programs offered by the donor community and export-related security arrangements are considered promising territory for solutions. Co-financings offered by the International Finance Corporation (IFC) do generally meet the banks' concerns, since the agency acts as the lender of record, with bank syndicates taking sub-participations and sharing in all debt service payments on a *pari passu* basis. However, other co-financing methods seem to provide insufficient comfort, as they do not permit the banks to enjoy, however indirectly, the "senior creditor status" of the multilateral co-financing agencies. There is a sense that programs should be devised whereby the agencies would shoulder more of the political risk and more aggressively enforce debt- servicing obligations to the co-financing banks. Banks are also concerned about the lengthy processes involved in co-financings and the pressure put on them by sponsoring agencies to reduce their pricing. Finally, some donors and African policy-makers are perceived as opposing the assignment of export proceeds and royalties and other project-related mechanisms that reduce various political and commercial risks of lending, whether or not co-financing is involved.

There is nevertheless a trend towards more flexible and mutually satisfactory donor-bank partnerships and active marketing to banks by sponsoring agencies. However, it is still too early to say that this will mean a major surge in bank lending.

Credit experience and the debt crisis

Some banks saw a lack of political will to service debt in some countries and were concerned that donors and African governments underestimated the effect that pressure for debt forgiveness would have on future lending—"forgive (debt) and forget (new lending)," as they said.

While harsh reschedulings and market-based debt reduction schemes are not as strongly opposed as outright forgiveness, they weaken the position of pro-African lenders within the banks. Some also feel that official creditors and donors are overzealous in requiring commercial bank debt restructuring similar to Paris Club creditors and/or in advocating sweeping debt forgiveness.

Differentiating between types of commercial bank lending could, according to some banks, help mitigate their reaction to debt forgiveness or (particularly) drawn-out rescheduling terms. For example, a renewed commitment to servicing responsible trade facilities and past loans to healthy projects could yield long-term benefits in restoring Africa's links to the private financial markets.

Banks readily admit their irresponsible contribution to Africa's debt growth, making ill-advised balance-of-payments loans and supporting "white elephant" projects in the late 1970s and early 1980s. However, some argue that official agencies also financed questionable activities and ignored corruption and/or weak economic management in some borrowing countries.

Clearly, the banks' role in debt relief, and radical options such as debt forgiveness, should be carefully reviewed, with more bank involvement.

Project quality

All banks seem willing to back important "corporate customers" doing business in Africa, and many would at least consider financing profitable and economically justified investment projects by African enterprises. However, transactions of the scale, quality, or strategic importance to warrant the banks' attention are few—partly because of lower-cost alternative finance from official agencies. While there is no shortage of speculative proposals involving short-term trade activities, the banks also point out that most private borrowers are unable (or unwilling) to take much project risk, even when they have significant assets outside of their home countries.

Focus on other markets

A handful of banks say they no longer view Africa as a market for new lending, no matter how well-secured or potentially profitable, and they have reduced their personnel in Africa. Instead, they are allocating a larger share of resources to new domestic lending and to other regions.

The banks also claim that the prospects for commercial lending to Sub-Saharan Africa are poor because of:

- The weakness of African domestic banking systems and institutions, in terms of financial condition and quality of services.
- A deep-rooted view that commercial banks are ignored by the donors as significant players in Africa in the 1990s.
- The insufficient recognition given by policy-makers, designers of donor-sponsored projects, and private investors (African or non-African) to restructured or non-performing bank debt as a financial resource. Too little attention is given to maximizing local currency components in projects and to establishing appropriate debt conversion schemes to help finance these local costs.
- The exchange risk inherent in cross-border transactions with borrowers in countries likely to undergo progressive currency devaluations as part of reform programs.

Opportunities perceived by the commercial banks

The banks informally expressed fairly consistent views about opportunities for lending in Africa and the suitability of different forms of lending.

Mining sector

The mining sector appears the most likely to attract medium-term lending support from commercial banks. Better-known project and market variables, project size, the status of corporate investors in such projects, and the likely quality of security arrangements explain why oil, gold, and diamond-producing countries have been preferred borrowers in the recent years and likely candidates for new medium-term loans in the future.

Banks believe that these models will not be extended readily to other productive activities such as as agriculture, industry, tourism, and fishing, due to higher risks (climate, market, etc), smaller project size, and the relative lack of attention from corporate sponsors. Only improved co-financing arrangements, expanded export credit agency activity and/or major corporate sponsor guarantees and relationships will attract banks to these sectors.

Asset-based financing

Some banks are still competing for aircraft and major (e.g., mining) equipment financing in Africa, secured by the value of the underlying assets, but there is also no indication that these models could be stretched into other sectors. Assets in these sectors are less mobile and depreciate quickly and are therefore not considered adequate security, while the underlying economic activities are seen as more vulnerable to policy and market changes.

Regional development and projects

Banks believe that closer economic links and more business relationships within the African region could provide a stimulus for economic expansion, leading to high-quality investment projects, new intra-regional financial systems, and a more attractive business environment generally. South Africa and Nigeria could serve as "growth poles" in their respective sub-regions, but some banks felt that resumed lending to South Africa could come at the expense of other African countries.

Building on local presences and relationships

Banks pointed to the contributions that their African subsidiaries have made over the decades and even in recent years, including local currency financing for working and investment capital and human resource development. Many banks feel that their personal and institutional relationships (through subsidiaries or representation) in Africa are being overlooked as resources for meeting Africa's future external finance requirements. Banks have a comparative advantage in evaluating private sector risk and in responding quickly to opportunities, but few seem prepared to take advantage of this in the immediate future.

Short-term lending

Short-term lending is viewed as the principal means for maintaining continuity in banks' relationship with

Africa, while efforts are made to rebuild confidence. The banks recognize that reform efforts and donor support are improving the creditworthiness of some countries and/or their private sectors, and creating new opportunities. In particular, they are paying more attention to developing new mechanisms to support Africa's export sectors through short- and medium-term lending, due partly to minimization of risks through security arrangements.

Scope for action

Under what conditions will commercial banks resume normal lending to Sub-Saharan Africa? What might accelerate change? What are the opportunities for commercial banks and how are these opportunities constrained by the countries' borrowing capacities?

Africa's long-term debt stocks and debt service payments over the next 5 years will depend largely on current outstandings—in particular the debt performance of four sovereign borrowers (Côte d'Ivoire, Nigeria, Gabon, Congo) who hold the bulk of the region's long-term commercial bank debt. Totalling $12.5 billion, it represents 80 percent of long-term public and publicly-guaranteed debt of $16 billion, and 60 percent of the total long-term commercial bank debt of $22 billion. There may also be an impact from non-flow factors, such as more accurate debt information, exchange-rate fluctuations, reschedulings of interest arrears, market-based debt reductions (through conversions and discounted trading), and negotiated debt cancellations or buy-backs.

Without attempting to project the future profile of Africa's debt overhang, the minimum objectives for commercial bank long-term lending by the year 2000 could be to:

- Double the aggregate annual disbursements to the private sector, (as narrowly defined by the World Bank and excluding Côte d'Ivoire from the statistical base) from the current $600 million per year;
- Achieve a broader distribution of disbursements to the private sector in more countries and economic sectors;
- Bring aggregate disbursements to public and publicly guaranteed borrowers, as broadly defined, to 1986 levels of $1.2 billion.

Such a performance would bring commercial banks to over half of the peak new lending of $4 billion reached in 1980.

Opportunities and commercial borrowing capacity

African governments agree with the World Bank that development strategies must put emphasis on human resources and physical infrastructure, as well as on conventional policy reforms, to provide an enabling environment for private-sector producers. This implies a shifting of intervention in the economy from the state to private enterprises, which represents the greatest opportunity for commercial bank lending in Africa.

Many productive assets in the hands of discredited state agencies are underutilised and the introduction of new ones is stymied by the lack of physical infrastructure. These include under-exploited mineral reserves, fishing, and agriculture, where commercialization of millions of subsistence producers is a priority. Buoyant agriculture and an expanding manufacturing base represent a growth model which has succeeded in other regions. The potential for direct investment (local and foreign) and commercial bank lending to entrepreneurs is great.

The arguments for increased commercial bank lending to Africa include:

- The emphasis on private sector development means that high value-added projects, of significant profitability and often export-oriented, may begin to proliferate in Africa. Such projects would support commercial borrowing and generate incremental foreign exchange earnings and/or savings for debt service. Frequently, the cost of borrowings from abroad is lower than that in local markets, particularly if there is little exchange risk or if this risk is offset by foreign exchange retention or local currency guarantee or hedging mechanisms. There are such guarantees in some medium-term onlending to the private sector, including some of the World Bank "APEX" lines.
- Equity investors seek to leverage capital with debt financing. Commercial banks have human and financial resources that can be put to work and respond quickly to sponsors of attractive projects, given the right circumstances. Moreover, a borrowing country's outflows on debt service should amount to a fraction of the outflows on dividends and capital gains on foreign direct investment.
- Private borrowers, particularly foreign investors, can take advantage of the banks' relationships with African decision-makers and potential partners, the banks' local subsidiaries, and other sources of financing (like the private insurance industry). This will allow them to accelerate the structuring of their projects and develop various supports for project development and operation (including short-term trade finance).
- The banks' rescheduled debt is an important resource for advancing Africa's privatization,

export diversification and infrastructure development. Market-based debt reduction through conversion should be encouraged: as balance-of-payments support, for more judicious use of local currency in public and private investment, and as an incentive for banks to renew their interest in Africa.

Despite the important role that the banks could be playing, the prevailing view is that the commercial borrowing capacity of many African countries is limited. Overall external indebtedness is already too high in relation to foreign exchange earnings, and the banks' credit terms are considered onerous compared to low-cost financing from concessional sources and export credits.

Commercial bank support is likely to be concentrated in short-term trade finance and non-risk banking services in the 1990s and beyond. Even for the private sector, much hope is pinned on more *equity financing* from foreign and local investors and on longer-term, fixed rate *debt financing*, such as the APEX lines and new programs developed by International Finance Corporation, DEG, FMO, PROPARCO, and other quasi-donor agencies.

However, all external sources of financing will not necessarily provide sufficient resources to help Africa exploit its opportunities.

Countries will have to become creditworthy independently for sustained access to the international financial markets. Joakim Stymne has shown that export growth supplemented by debt relief is the key to improvement in the creditworthiness of African countries. With annual export growth of 7 percent and no debt forgiveness over 5 years, his study showed that Africa's composite debt ratio (total debt: total exports) would fall to 180 percent (from 330 percent in 1987), implying a current account surplus of $30.6 billion and imports of $178.5 billion over the period. If export growth were only 3 percent a year, debt cancellation of $5 billion would be needed for a comparable imports and current-account surplus. Commercial bank lending would then be in jeopardy, while the need for external support would also strain the international community's ability to bridge Africa's resource gaps.

Banks should be pulled closer into the dialogue on African external finance in the 1990s, despite their mild interest and the problem of Africa's commercial borrowing capacity. The challenge is to encourage all potential partners, including the commercial banks, to contribute skills and resources to developing Africa's potential.

Prospects and proposals for the alleviation of constraints

The scope of commercial banks' activities and future plans for Africa has never been narrower. They are broadly passive, especially in medium-term lending. Nor have policy-makers actively engaged them to find innovative solutions. Having witnessed the deterioration in their African portfolios over the past few years, the banks appear to be "waiting out the debt crisis", while relocating the financial and human resources once devoted to Africa.

Africa's commercial potential is vast, and commercial bank lending could be stimulated in the 1990s. However, African and OECD government communities will have to take much of the initiative for restoring bankers' interest and confidence, both by addressing the constraints perceived by the banks and by continuing with efforts to resolve the immediate debt crisis and restore economic growth.

Mandatory provisions on new lending. These imply an immediate loss on new loans to some African countries and are a powerful disincentive to new lending. Some banks already have excess provisions, or a critical mass of "revolving provisions", where the reversal of past provisions can offset provisions on new loans. In these cases, their aggregate loan loss reserve expenses would not necessarily increase.

Given the small share of African debt in most banks' portfolios, and the conservatism of banks, a strong case should be made to the regulatory agencies for the elimination of these provisioning requirements on new lending.

Banking authorities in such countries as France, the UK, and the Netherlands have already ruled that co-financings with IFC (and some other multilateral lenders) are exempt from provisioning rules. Some similarly treat other well-secured transactions (such as aircraft financings or cash-collateralized facilities).

Co-financing. The principal reason for seeking bank participation in co-financings is to leverage the official agencies' risk and funds. Until now, official co-financing agencies (excepting IFC with its "lender of record" system) finance and/or guarantee all of the risk on a portion of the principal, leaving to the other participants all risks on the balance.

It is not impossible to devise a formula in such "parallel financing" arrangements whereby the sponsoring agency would take a larger portion of the sovereign and/or transfer risk, while private participants would bear a larger share of the commercial risk. The difficulty is drawing the line between political and commercial risk, though perhaps achievable as follows:

- If the borrower has the necessary local currency funds and has applied for a foreign exchange transfer, but the transfer is not made, the sponsoring institution's transfer risk guarantee of the commercial bank funded portion of the facility would be invoked; and
- If the borrower for any reason does not have the local currency funds to apply for a foreign exchange transfer, the commercial banks' commercial risk guarantee of the donor funded portion of the facility will be invoked.

Neither agency nor bank is likely to provide such guarantees for all the principal, but the concept recognizes the advantage of the official agencies in assessing the transfer risk, providing long-term balance-of-payments support and encouraging debt service. It would also place more onus for analyzing project risk on the banks.

The formula is not a panacea. Banks are aware that changes in the economic environment, even ones that are necessary and beneficial, can be detrimental to the borrowers' local currency solvency, affecting debt servicing as surely as lack of foreign exchange.

These issues are best resolved in the long term through the improved economic health, economic management, and political performance of the borrowing country, as well as continued fine-tuning of risk-sharing mechanisms. More immediately, there could be a distinction between foreign exchange and local currency performance of a transaction, based on a reasonable "valuation" of risk, and limited to reasonable percentages of principal.

There should also be more sensitivity to banks' concerns about pricing and the time lags in completing co-financings. Under IFC's recent "agency agreement" with NMB, a Dutch bank, processing time and costs are reduced because the bank plays the lead role in appraising the projects and structuring the loans. Export credit agencies can also rely more on the banks to accelerate appraisal and commitment; witness the "agency agreement" between the U.S. Eximbank and Standard Chartered in 1987-88. A particularly promising area for banks is the intermediation of Japanese aid and official export credits. Finally, since many African projects have been too small for typical bank lending activities and co-financings, bank resources might be channeled through specially-managed co-financed loan funds, with some subsidy for development and operating costs.

Transfer risk-mitigating mechanisms for export projects. An urgent objective of African countries is to dramatically increase and diversify exports through economically rational investment projects. Banks are willing to support these efforts, *provided that* cash flows are committed to debt-servicing; this is typically accomplished through pledges of (and/or escrow accounts for) export earnings of a borrower, preferably flowing through the bank's own accounts with the right of offset. This is common and prudent in other bank lending, but difficult and costly to structure in some of Africa's foreign exchange regimes.

More objectivity towards export cash-flow commitment is needed for resumed lending, until open foreign exchange regimes or full convertibility are achieved. Concerns about distortions could be mitigated by setting a limit on the funds committed by a country or borrower, and by better appraisal of the projects. A number of countries have adopted universal or limited export retention schemes. Some are managed through centralized foreign exchange management systems and, partly for this reason, have not necessarily generated new medium-term lending. In some countries without generalized retention schemes or open foreign exchange regimes, exporters nevertheless have de facto preference in obtaining foreign exchange, whether due to their economic and political importance (such as a state petroleum company), foreign exchange retention by the local banks, such as in Zaire, or other reasons.

Some countries have moved to more open foreign exchange regimes, with varying control over the external assets as between the Central Bank and local and offshore banks. Some systems need fine-tuning to set the stage for medium-term lending: those, for example, that are restricted to current account transactions, where alternative mechanisms for private borrowers to contract and service commercial bank long-term debt are not clear or complete.

The 14 members of the CFA zone have partially convertible currencies, where local currency can be used to obtain French francs and deposits can be held in France (except commercial banks, who may only hold operating accounts). Term loans denominated in French francs can be contracted and serviced automatically, and simple procedures have long been in place for approval of loans in other currencies. These loans are indeed being serviced, according to the borrowers' and local banks' liquidity in CFA terms.

The aim is for African countries to achieve hard currency status, but complex and long-term multilateral approaches are required. There are in fact doubts about the CFA zone and its present structure, stemming from overvaluation of the CFA franc in many countries, capital flight when funds held in France are used to purchase other currencies, and the anticipated single European currency.

The exchange risk. Lenders' and borrowers' decisions are influenced by the exchange risk faced by local currency earners with cross-border loans (including exporters obliged to repatriate and convert export proceeds prior to debt service). In some donor-sponsored private-sector projects and credit facilities, the borrowing country bears the exchange risk in local currency. Such cover could be extended to private borrowers seeking support from private banks. Many donors have substantial counterpart funds in Africa that could be used.

Improved credit information. Commercial banks have difficulty in analyzing the creditworthiness of developing countries. They have little confidence in the plethora of statistics and inconsistent public information, and have little influence on economic policy or foreign exchange management.

While IMF and World Bank economic reports are the closest to an "independent audit function," they are protected unless the member government authorizes release. Why not routinely grant authorizations, with the encouragement of the institutions? Countries seeking commercial bank support could also submit relevant information to correspondent banks and other potential participants on a regular and timely basis (as some do).

The IMF does not publish statistics on outstanding debt by lender because of its confidential relationship with countries; the World Bank does not distinguish between types of short-term lenders because it simply does not have the information. However, these institutions and other public agencies do have access to some information that private financial markets do not.

Banks cannot make an informed judgement about creditworthiness without some sense of the country's short-term debt and near-term cash flow situation. This "fear of the unknown" is acute in those African countries with low reserves and a chronic need for exceptional financing to achieve positive overall balance-of-payments. Better information is again not a cure-all, but would be relevant in unsecured *short-term* lending, and would provide banks with a better understanding of the countries' longer-term economic objectives and strategies.

Improving project quality. There are a number of new private investment promotion and management assistance initiatives underway, including the IFC-sponsored Africa Project Development Facility, Africa Management Services Company and Foreign Investment Advisory Service. These provide valuable expertise to private entrepreneurs and policy-makers and are likely to expand throughout the 1990s. They should continue to draw the attention of private lenders to the higher-quality opportunities and improving environments in Africa, with their efforts supplemented from other quarters.

Special private sector initiatives. New approaches to increasing and broadening commercial bank lending to the African private sector need to be tested on an experimental basis to help develop momentum for the 1990s—especially since no bank loan disbursements were reported by the World Bank for 26 countries in 1985-88 and private borrowers received loans in only 12 countries. All African countries should be eligible for such programs, which could involve:

- Each participating country establishing a target or budget for commercial bank lending to private borrowers, to be replenished as targets are met.
- The transfer risk on loans secured by (1) zero-coupon bonds or escrow accounts financed by the borrowing country and held with a multilateral donor and (2) at least a matching guarantee by one or more multilateral donors. These guarantees would be called whenever a debt service payment is missed, provided that the borrower has lodged the local currency equivalent with a local bank.
- If at all practical, additional guarantees provided by host governments concerning critical policy conditions that must be maintained for private borrowers to remain viable. Foreseeable policy changes, such as devaluations and price liberalization, would not be covered.
- Sponsoring multilateral agencies could also cover some of the banks' marketing expenses through, say, brief technical assistance contracts or small grants modeled on the "marketing insurance" programs provided to exporters by export credit agencies.
- The efforts could also include a multiplication of project development assistance programs, including feasibility studies and market research.

While banks must necessarily bear the commercial risk, such initiatives would be providing protections similar to those granted direct investors by the Multilateral Investment Guarantee Agency (MIGA).

Debt conversion initiatives. Debt conversion in Africa lags behind Latin America for many reasons: countries have been slow to introduce mechanisms; banks have provided little impetus for them to do so, given the small exposures in relation to Latin America; and some larger debtor countries are in the CFA zone, where the partial convertibility of the currency presents conceptual problems to policy-makers.

Nevertheless, considerable African debt has been sold at deep discounts by the original holders to investing institutions, and large provisions have been made on much of the non-traded debt. Thus the threshold which makes debt conversion attractive has been lowered. More could be done, including:

- Special funds, created for investment of the debt. Some banks have done just that in Latin America, and have accumulated deeply discounted African debt, perhaps with such a program in mind. African governments and donors could encourage these banks through incentives and promotional measures.
- Increasing local currency components in public investment programs and/or donor-funded development projects. Commercial bank debt could be purchased with donor funds for conversion into local currency funding for such projects. The foreign exchange savings from an increased and more judicious use of local resources could justify the payment of a market premium when the debt is purchased.
- Adjusting the terms of debt conversion (such as the length of grace periods on dividend remittances or borrowers' central bank fees) to be more generous for banks providing new foreign exchange financing for conversion.

Potential impact on commercial bank lending

Given the passivity of the banks, the borrowing countries and donors should make a concerted effort to draw attention to improvements in the lending environment.

Some of the areas where increased lending may take place are co-financing, special private sector initiatives, new partnerships, new trade patterns, and export processing zones.

Co-financing. The opportunities here are primarily in large-scale production and infrastructure projects, such as IFC's package for Ashanti Goldfields in Ghana or the as-yet-unexplored rebuilding of the Benguela Railway. IFC's recent syndication of a major onlending facility for banks in Zimbabwe could be extended to other countries. Donors and export credit agencies may step up co-financing programs for private ventures. Co-financing agencies and banks are likely to seek out revenue-earning projects with secure repayment mechanisms, such as petroleum production and marketing projects. However, co-financing could help attract commercial banks into non-commercial projects, even in countries with chronic balance-of-payments problems, provided long-term multilateral support is assured and the projects are strategically important.

Private sector initiative. New lending is more likely (1) for highly profitable ventures oriented towards local sales, (2) for export projects involving known commodities, products and markets, (3) for projects with some debt conversion by the lending bank, and (4) for projects sponsored by important corporate customers.

New partnerships. There may be increased cooperation, innovation and risk-sharing among commercial banks, private insurers and private investors, suppliers or buyers. Highly profitable ventures may be developed through more equal sharing of risks and returns. In the past, banks have borne much of the risk for relatively small returns, while insurers have rarely been involved in investment projects.

New trade patterns. Trade patterns may continue to diversify in the 1990s, with a shift away from the OECD countries toward Asia and possibly Eastern Europe and Latin America. This may encourage short-term secured and unsecured lending by banks from those regions. Impetus may also come from the intermediation of increased aid flows from Japan and other Asian capital-surplus countries, providing their banks with more experience and confidence in Africa. If these aid flows increase, there will be more interest from suppliers to Africa, with pressure on banks for risk lending. South African companies and banks may become more active in the greater southern African region and beyond, as seen in their competition for a lead role in the Lesotho Highlands Water Scheme and their participation in diplomatic initiatives.

Export processing zones are being established in African countries. Typically, the investors have control over export proceeds (or the zones are located in convertible CFA countries, such as Togo and Senegal) and they benefit from tax and tariff incentives. Many zones will be managed by companies with mandates for developing infrastructure and vigorous promotion. Although EPZ projects may be relatively small and labor-intensive, banks may be attracted by the projected flow of funds to provide banking services, revolving trade facilities and loans to larger projects, to groups of projects, or to the management companies.

Whatever may happen in the next few years, Sub-Saharan Africa will not achieve targeted rates of private investment or attract the desired commercial, and even official, financing unless there is a satisfactory enabling environment. This implies not only a policy framework conducive to investment, but a broader approach, including the protection of rights and properties and wider political participation and consensus.

References

Stymme, Joakim. 1989. "Debt, Growth and the Prospects for Debt Reduction: The Case of Sub-Saharan African Countries." IMF Working Paper 89/71. Washington D. C.

World Bank. 1989. *World Debt Tables*. 1989-90 Edition. Washington, D.C.

Comment

Yvonne D. Jones

What is often striking when dealing with Sub-Saharan African countries is the relative lack of communication, and therefore, understanding between governments and banks of each party's constraints. While providing information to each set of actors on the concerns of other negotiating parties is not alone sufficient to bring about a resolution of outstanding problems surrounding commercial bank debt negotiations, in many cases it can make for a more substantive exchange of views.

I also wish to underscore the importance of the analysis of the data on commercial bank debt presented in the paper. It is clear that having a good handle on the data is a prerequisite to analysis in Sub-Saharan Africa on both an aggregate and an individual country level. It has been the experience of the Financial Advisory Services Unit that even where data for an African country is considered accurate, there is a high degree of uncertainty associated with both the estimate of the total volume of commercial bank debt, as well as with the division of that debt between medium- and long-term and short-term debt. Without accurate debt data it is difficult to understand how a country developed a debt problem, as well as how to develop a reasonable strategy for negotiating debt access to appropriate levels of financing on commercial terms. (It may seem like belaboring the point, but we have yet to deal with a country case in Sub-Saharan Africa where the issue has not arisen).

Because one of the objectives of the paper is to offer suggestions for future action for improving commercial bank flows where feasible, it is particularly useful that it specifies where medium- and long-term and short-term commercial bank disbursements have been concentrated in recent years. This information provides a basis for a more realistic assessment at an aggregate level of the future probable interest of commercial banks in providing new lending. If historically only 18 of 44 Sub-Saharan countries borrowed substantial amounts of medium- and long-term debt on commercial terms, we already have a more sense of the limited future scope for this lending. For example, of the seven countries cited as recipients of substantial, long-term commercial bank lending between 1983 and 1988, only two (Kenya, Zimbabwe) are fully servicing their commercial debt.

In contrast to medium- and long-term debt flows, to learn from the paper that short-term debt has been more widely available to Sub-Saharan African countries confirms at an aggregate level, what one sees on a country by country basis. The wider availability of short-term credit also underscores the importance of carefully choosing appropriate mechanisms to reduce or transform the stock of commercial bank debt, mechanisms that would not contribute to a cutting off of the countries from essential commercial flows.

As I address the issues in the paper, my comments will be limited to a comparison of the authors' presentation of the views of commercial banks with the experience of the Financial Advisory Services Unit has had in facilitating contact between Sub-Saharan African debtor countries and commercial creditors.

The section on constraints underscores the complexity of finding solutions for provision of commercial financing, where appropriate to country circumstances. First, on commercial bank constraints. Debtor countries need to be made more aware of the effects of provisioning and capital adequacy requirements on commercial bank negotiating positions. It gives them a broader perspective on why banks offer certain options in restructuring and conversion packages.

As a positive note in a difficult situation, both multilateral institutions and banks have an overlapping view of the constraints associated with foreign commercial financing of projects that generate no foreign exchange, unwieldy government foreign exchange allocation mechanisms, and lending to nonperforming public borrowers. Unfortunately, there has been less consensus on means of enhancing prospects for cofinancing, although clearly more consensus is needed if commercial bank financing is to be available to Sub-Saharan Africa. The degree to which consensus exists between multilateral institutions and commercial banks on necessary changes in country economic structures and policies and institutional structures is important because it is clear that for most countries in the region increased lending where appropriate by commercial banks will depend upon the tripartite agreement on mechanisms by multilateral institutions, banks and governments.

I would like to note at this point a difference between the authors' summation of commercial bank views on credit experience and the handling of the debt crisis, and the experience of our unit in dealing with debt negotiations country by country. On the issue of the perception by commercial banks of the lack of African country political will to service debt, undoubtedly this is a reflection of multiple reschedulings and arrears accumulation on the part of some countries. However, there is a countervailing and nonintuitive situation in the secondary market for African commercial bank debt which contradicts this perception. There are some debtor countries which have continued to service (and in a few cases) amortize their debt, so that the price of their debt in the secondary market is higher than the price of the debt of some Latin American countries. About half a dozen countries fall into this category.

As to donor underestimation of the negative impact on future bank lending of requiring more concessional terms for commercial bank rescheduling, there has been an implicit and explicit feeling that country ability to service its debt is the fundamental criterion which commercial banks should consider in setting rescheduling terms. The history of commercial bank reschedulings in the region suggests that unrealistic terms have often led to an immediate abrogation of signed agreements, which contributes to the perception that African countries are financially irresponsible.

On donor and creditor inability to distinguish differing types of commercial credits, it has been our experience that borrower countries are themselves very sensitive to the potential impact on trade lines of rescheduling medium- and long-term debt and that they are reluctant to consider packages that could result in a negative impact on these trade lines. Use of a menu of options also helps to deal with this problem. The menu approach not only permits banks to select the options that meet their regulatory and tax considerations. It permits a range of treatments for different categories of debt. Costa Rica, where interest arrears were given separate treatment, bears this out. I am also a bit puzzled by the assertion that official creditors and donors can "require" commercial bank debt restructuring on Paris Club terms. While this has often been suggested, I don't believe that any commercial rescheduling has yet been granted these terms. Different treatment for loans to healthy projects is a more difficult issue because debt reduction deals are not usually developed on a loan-by-loan basis.

The authors have emphasized the important role that restructured bank debt can play as a financial resource. It is our experience that debtor countries are open to debt conversion programs that could promote more direct foreign investment. Several countries that have sought assistance from the Bank for debt-restructuring packages already have or are considering debt for equity mechanisms. The problem does not lie in the perceived utility of the instrument. The problem lies in developing an investment environment and appropriate mechanisms for structuring the investments. Using such a tool will require a great deal of tolerance for negotiating the terms of specific deals and one would expect that principally banks with a historical relationship with the region would use this tool.

The main question to ask is, are the objectives in the paper reasonable and feasible? The historical data suggest that even if future commercial flows were to be directed primarily at the private sector, there is limited scope for absorption, at least in the short term. Flows of medium- and long-term commercial finance were highly skewed toward a limited number of countries, of which only a limited subset can today borrow on commercial terms.

The question of the reasonableness of this proposal is tied to the success of the adjustment experience in Sub-Saharan Africa. The success of adjustment programs will determine whether the climate will encourage increased direct foreign investment. Furthermore, given the proposals the paper makes for restrictions on the decision-making powers of African governments in the allocation of export cash flows to service debt and provide for dividend repatriation, which basically addresses the motivations of commercial borrowers, one could reasonably ask what would motivate governments to accept such restrictions (were it deemed appropriate to accede to them in certain instances). It seems to me that governments would ask that these "protected investments" offer improvements in management techniques and technology transfer, so that clear development benefits would accrue to the country's development process.

10

Short-Term Trade Credit

Sudarshan Gooptu
Richard Brun

One word best sums up short-term trade finance for Sub-Saharan Africa: confusing. There can be discrepancies of 100 percent between estimates of short-term indebtedness for the same country. Why? The IMF, the OECD, the World Bank, and the Bank for International Settlements use different definitions and statistical sources for trade finance, which includes short-term bank credit, medium-term trade credit, short-term suppliers credit, short-term financial credit, and interbank lines and so on.

The focus here is on nonguaranteed short-term trade finance—these credits extended by commercial banks to entities in the developing countries with a maturity of one year or less. "Commercial banks" are those involved in traditional banking and only short-term trade credits not guaranteed by the borrower's government or external agencies (such as Ex-Im banks) of creditor governments are included.

Since the beginning of the debt crisis, most developing countries (especially the low-income ones) have relied on official creditors for medium- and long-term financing because commercial banks reduced their exposure and diverted resources to industrial countries. Short-term trade financing from official sources (e.g., export credit agencies) has been insufficient for the needs of developing countries and, anyway, is often tied to exports of the donor country and is too inflexible for the borrower.

The need for short-term trade finance in developing countries is particularly acute. As mainly primary goods exporters (and consumer goods importers), developing countries require short-term trade finance during the short primary production cycle. Crucial for developing countries today, access to short-term trade lines will become more important as international trade flourishes.

Between 1982 and 1986, when banks were reducing medium- and long-term lending to developing countries, short term lending did not decrease proportionately—even when short-term obligations were rescheduled as part of a more comprehensive debt restructuring agreement. It just became costlier. Despite payments difficulties on other debt, most countries serviced short-term debt. When a country went into arrears (eg, Peru), short-term trade credits became even costlier and more difficult to obtain.

Today, reduction of (both bilateral and commercial) debt is being used as a way to help resolve Africa's debt problems. This is seen as a means of easing the debt overhang of the debt-distressed less-developed countries so that economic growth will be resumed and access to international financial markets reopened. But will a country continue to receive short-term trade lines after commercial debt-reduction?

Trade credits can be provided in the form of several investments (not all directly used by commercial banks) and lots of ways to increase the cost for risky clients. Because of the many influences on short-term trade lines—fees, interest rates, penalty structures, currency denominations, exchange rate movements)—the effects of debt reduction on the availibility of short-term trade credits dirrer from one country to another. Each is determined by banks case-by-case. For example, trade lines were still available to Bolivia after its buyback operations —and on improved terms. For Brazil, short-term trade financing was more costly and difficult to obtain after a moratorium on debt service payments to commercial creditors. But, short-term trade lines were restored after the interim financing agreement with commercial banks in late 1987.

Since the 1982 crisis, most low-income African countries have relied more on private short-term trade financing than on medium-term financing. Compare short-term trade financing and total commercial debt in middle-income countries (mainly in Latin America) and in low-income African countries. In 10 African countries, short-term lines represent around 34 percent of the medium and long-term debt, in Latin America only 5.7 percent (table 10.1). Two caveats: the figures partly reflect the limited access of poorer countries to medium- and long-term financing, and these countries rely more than others on short-term financing.

Table 10.1 ***Share of short-term trade lines in total commercial debt, selected countries (as of end-1988)***

Country	*Total commercial debt*	*Millions of U.S.dollars*	*Short-term trade finance 1/ percent*
AFRICA			
Burundi	20	20	100.0
Congo*	310	125	40.3
Guinea	30	15	50.0
Madagascar*	110	24	21.8
Mozambique*	279	23	8.2
Niger*	105	55	52.4
Senega	180	55	68.8
Tanzania*	140	20	14.3
Togo	49	21	42.9
Zaire	441	150	34.0
Subtotal	1,564	508	32.5
LATIN AMERICA			
Argentina	30,400	1,000	3.3
Brazil	67,600	3,300	4.9
Chile	11,000	2,100	19.1
Venezuela	26,600	2,900	10.9
Mexico	63,400	4,200	6.6
Subtotal	199,000	13,500	6.8
Total	200,564	14,008	7.0

Source: World Bank "World Debt Tables", 1989-90 except those indicated by an '*'. For those countries, the data has been obtained more recently by the Government of the countries concerned.

1/ World Bank Staff estimates.

How the debt crisis hit trade finance

Before the debt crisis in the early 1980s, trade financing was one of the most traditional activities of the banking business, and considered the most secure among loans to countries. With a worsening economic situation in a country, bankers could easily cut a line or increase its cost. At the end of the 1970s, however, some developing countries, facing external deficits, dramatically increased short-term indebtedness—interbank lines and trade lines—to finance part of their balance-of-payments gap. When the crisis came, banks with trade or interbank lines to developing countries were trapped. Short-term lines became effectively long-term credit. Between 1982 and 1985 almost all trade lines to the major developing countries were rescheduled or extended, and in some cases were included in the base for the calculation of concerted new money requirements for the countries. Since then, bankers have become more reluctant to open new lines to developing countries, especially in Sub-Saharan Africa.

The curtailment of classical trade financing

The economic factor. The richer a country and the sounder its economic situation, the simpler and cheaper the techniques of trade applied to that country. In Africa the worsening economic situation led to a dramatic decrease of letters of credit (L/Cs) for exporters from OECD countries. For U.S. exporters, "The World Guide for Exporters," a widely circulated professional publication, showed in the first quarter of 1989 that no more L/C was available for Africa (see table 10.2).

In OECD countries, exporters rely on international publications giving the rating of developing countries and the techniques recommended for business with these countries. The Export Credits Clearing House in London regularly surveys commercial conditions in 114 countries (85 developing countries and 29 Eastern and Arab

Table 10.2 ***Main trade financing techniques used for exports outside the United States***

	Open Account	Sight Draft	Time Draft	Unconfirmed L/C	Confirmed L/C
EEC	65	16	18	0	1
Other Europe	51	11	9	6	22
Latin America	3	9	11	1	77
Africa	0	No S/D	No T/D	No ILC	No CILC
Middle East	6	10	15	0	69
Asia	10	15	12	14	49

Source: The World Guide for Exporters, GBC Inc. Publication, First Quarter of 1989.

countries). At the end of 1988, in a survey, 34 IDA-only countries are mentioned; it recommended to exporters to work on the basis of irrevocable letters of credit (ILCs) for nine countries, and confirmed irrevocable letters of credit (CILCs) for 19 countries. Trade is recommended without limitation on techniques in only 6 countries, none in Sub-Saharan Africa. Of the 51 other developing countries mentioned, ILCs are recommended for 14 countries and CILCs for only nine.

A CILC, the worst classification, implies an unfavorable economic situation, and may not, in fact, be available for a country. In theory, a confirmation of credit can be obtained from a bank in the importer's country but in practice few banks in the OECD will accept it, requesting confirmation from another OECD bank. So, some countries (including most in Sub-Saharan Africa) must rely on other techniques to import goods from developed countries.

U.S. banks have important commercial links with Latin America and are generally prepared to confirm L/Cs, but they have very little trade finance with Africa using letters of credit. European banks, mainly French and British, are more flexible in confirming L/Cs in Africa. But some countries cannot obtain any confirmation from any OECD bank; these were the first to suffer a dramatic reduction in imports to minimum levels. In Madagascar, letters of credit were reduced by more than 50 percent in 1983, and documentary collections disappeared. Since 1987, with an improving economy, the country is back on the market. But countries in this situation must also rely on other techniques—cash collateral and countertrade or barter.

The institutional factor

The problem of short-term trade financing in Sub-Saharan Africa differs from country to country.

- If a country belongs to the Franc zone, the situation is manageable. Since the country has access to any foreign currency through the CFA Franc, the availability of trade financing depends only on the cash flow of the domestic bank offering the credit. Moreover, in the Franc zone, the main "domestic" banks are subsidiaries of French multinational banks and which continue to receive some lines of credit from the head office to improve their liquidity. So, they are still able to provide some short-term financing to importers. In this zone, short-term trade lines were cut only in countries where the banking system went almost bankrupt.
- Outside the Franc zone, access to trade financing is more difficult. Those countries, too, rely on credit lines from multinational banks to their subsidiaries, but when there are real problems, more exotic and expensive techniques, like countertrade, must be used.
- The financial situation of most African countries is worsening, and some multinational banks are closing their subsidiaries. U.S. and British banks were less involved in Africa anyway, but now French banks are also trying to withdraw from some small countries. If this continues, short-term financing could be very difficult to obtain, and the flow of imports could become even smaller.

The cost and maturity factor

Besides decreasing volumes of classical short-term trade financing, African countries also saw a dramatic increase in the cost of trade lines associated with L/Cs. Trade lines are charged on the basis of a spread over LIBOR (the London interbank offered rate), similar to medium-term Eurocredits, but they can vary wildly between countries, even in the same country —generally, from half a percentage point to nine points annually. Discussion has revealed that the cost of trade lines is determined by:

- The country's present financial and economic situation
  - Relations with the official international community (adjustment program or not)
  - Economic prospects the country in the next two years
  - Past relations with bankers (moratorium, rescheduling of short-term lines, and the like)
  - A country's size and its political or strategic importance
  - The size of industries and the importance of foreign trade

There are often hidden charges in trade lines to a country. Take one African country, where the cost of trade lines is officially quoted to be LIBOR + 3/8 percent. With maturity stretched to as much as 18 months, bankers agreed to extend new lines only at LIBOR + 5 percent. Probably for political reasons, the country did not want to pay more than the official price. So, it was agreed that banks would maintain trade lines at LIBOR + 3/8 percent but would receive a commission on the value of exported goods. In reality, the banks are receiving LIBOR + 5 percent from the country when adjustments are made to the price paid for its imported goods. This technique, widely used between OECD countries and LDCs, might help explain why a recent World Bank study showed a higher average price paid by African countries on some imports from OECD countries than paid by other developing countries.

Table 10.3 ***Cost of trade financing, selected countries***

Country	*Spread over LIBOR (percentage points)*	*Maturity*
Brazil	3-4	Up to 1 year
Colombia	1-1/2	Up to 180 days
Côte d'Ivoire	3-4	Up to 180 days
Ecuador	1-1/2	Up to 170 days
Madagascar	2	Up to 180 days
Mexico	7/8	Up to 1 year
Mozambique	6	Up to 180 days
Venezuela	2	Up to 1 year

Source: Bank staff estimates.

For a large country in a difficult financial situation, banks will cut some trade lines and charge more, as in Brazil. For small low-income countries, such as those in Africa, they will cut most short-term lines or even halt commercial relations.

The evolution of trade lines in specific countries depends on the evolution of their financial situation. After Brazil declared a year's moratorium on commercial debt service at the end of 1986: trade lines were cut by US$1.5 billion to $2 billion, the spread was increased from an average of 2-3 points to 3-6 points over LIBOR, the maturities of all trade lines not subject to government restrictions were reduced from 180/360 days to 30/60 days, import financing was reduced and most Brazilian importers had to operate on a cash basis during the moratorium.

When Brazil agreed to an interim financing agreement with commercial banks at the end of 1987, short-term lines were restored. Meanwhile, however, Brazil had to maintain a larger trade surplus, deplete international reserves, and probably suffer a negative impact on investment. World Bank estimates show that the cash flow impact for the country would have accumulated to US$3.5 billion over the year, and the financial cost may have averaged US$500 million.

Brazil could manage because its financial system is almost as developed and efficient as most industrial countries. Thus, it found ways to finance important exports, albeit at a higher cost. For most African countries in similar straits, banks would have completely cut trade lines to the country, thereby making them unable to maintain current levels of foreign trade.

Prefinancing exports, barter, countertrade, cash collateral, and other techniques may now account for 20 percent of trade financing in Sub-Saharan Africa, compared with less than 5 percent in the 1970s—and could increase further.

Prefinancing exports

Normally collateralized by commodity exports, this is the last defense before recourse to very expensive techniques, such as countertrade or barter. For example, an exporter of cocoa in a developing country arranges for credit to finance working capital requirements from a foreign financial institution by pledging a quantity of yet-to-be-harvested cocoa to the bank or its assigned beneficiary—say, a cocoa importer in the OECD country. The LDC exporter may also have to negotiate a preferential price for the cocoa. Until recently, the cost of these lines has been relatively low (table 10.4).

African countries are mainly Primary commodity producers, so this technique has grown in importance during the past few years and been widely used for financing imports. But, this is not a panacea. In the case of prefinancing of exports, trading companies are often used to provide the technical aspect of trading operations. In these deals, some risks (product quality of products, delivery, timing) are generally taken on by banks. As the economic situation in a country worsens, the risks can increase, and banks may not provide this financing even with higher spreads and more expensive techniques will be needed. Indeed, some IDA countries in Africa have reached this point.

Table 10.4 ***Cost of pre-financing of exports, selected countries, end-1989***

Country	*Spread over LIBOR (percentage points)*	*Product pledged*
Central African Republic	2.00	Coffee
Côte d'Ivoire	0.40	Cocoa
Kenya	0.75	Coffee
Madagascar	1.25	Cotton
Zimbabwe	0.875	Coffee

* End 1989.

Countertrade and barter

These are generally relied on by poorer countries, whose economic and financial situation is so bad that they have no choice—mostly in Africa but also Asian and Latin American countries. An example of one such deal, with an IDA-only African country in 1987, shows some of the problems of this type of financing.

This country had no access to regular credit lines and did a coffee-oil countertrade deal with two commodity traders and an international bank. It is said to have worked as follows:

• The International bank opened a US$ 50 million oil facility for the country to purchase crude oil. Each time an oil shipment was completed, oil documents were presented to the bank for payment.

• At the same time, the country entered into an agreement with four commodity brokers, under which 50 percent of its coffee was sold at auction and 50 percent to the brokers at a price calculated with a formula based on London and New York prices, adjusted for grade and other market factors.

• Net proceeds were paid into a coffee account with the international bank, which could be drawn on by a public bank of the country—a typical countertrade, where the import (oil) facility is secured from the export of commodities (coffee).

The bank's fee charged seemed reasonable (banker's acceptance rate + 1.375 percentage points) but under this agreement, the country paid 28.2 percent above the spot-market price for its oil imports and received about 10 percent less than the market price for its coffee—for a real fee of about 25 percent of the facility conceded.

For most involved in this business, fees of 15 to 20 percent are normal. This explains why some countries who relied on these techniques between 1983 and 1985 are now trying to finance their trade in a more orthodox way by improving their economic situation and their relations with bankers.

Cash collateral

The technique is simple—an importer who cannot obtain CILCs from a bank sends cash to a banker who authorizes delivery of goods on receipt of the money. Neither the banker nor the exporter has any risk, but the bank still takes a commission that in some Latin American deals has been between 1 and 2 percent of the value of the order. In Africa this technique is used less, but some countries have relied on it in critical times.

Short-term trade lines and their determinants to developing countries

What factors influence the short-term trade lines that commercial banks make available to developing countries? And is a country's access to short-term trade lines hampered by a commercial debt-reduction operation? To answer these questions, a cross-section of 32 countries—17 highly indebted countries and 15 low-income countries in Africa for which data were available in December 1987—were studied. (For a full exposition of the regression analysis summarized here, see Goopta and Brun 1991.)

Since there is no precise estimate of short-term trade finance from commercial banks to developing countries, the analysis began with a proxy estimate of pure short-term trade lines from banks—using World Bank data and assuming that these lines are used to finance noncapital goods—consumer goods and basic necessities—imported from OECD countries. It is not appropriate to look only at the value of imports of the developing country to get an idea of the short-term trade lines available. The complex techniques of trade financing (e.g., countertrade, barter, and prefinancing of exports) often affect the price and volume of exports of the developing country to an OECD country. The objective here is to identify the primary determinants of short-term financing from banks to developing countries.

The proxy estimate was computed by multiplying the trade deficit of a country in end-1987 (U.S. dollars) by the share of its noncapital goods imports. It was assumed (1) that the entire trade deficit in that year would be financed by external borrowing and (2) that capital goods imports would be financed by medium and long-term borrowing while non-capital goods imports (mainly food, fuel, and essential consumer goods) would be financed by short-term trade lines from commercial banks. So, it is implicitly assumed that the component of the trade deficit due to noncapital goods imports is financed by short-term trade lines. Given the quality of the data on short-term trade financing to developing countries and the need to use a proxy measure for the levels of such financing on a given year, any conclusions must be treated with caution.

The ratio of commercial bank debt to total debt outstanding and disbursed indicates the exposure of commercial banks in a country. As this ratio rises, a country's access to short-term trade lines from commercial banks will be drastically reduced. This illustrates the "burden sharing" that banks talked about — they would like to reduce exposure when the share of commercial bank debt to total debt is very large, and they want official creditors to lend more instead.

As expected, a moratorium on commercial bank debt service payments had a negative impact on availability of short-term trade lines. The existence of a World Bank adjustment program had a positive impact. Such a program, therefore, indicates the effort by a country to implement economic reform for growth and development. When the Bank adjustment record of the past five years was incorporated in the analysis, the positive effect on future access to short-term trade lines was much more significant. This shows the importance commercial banks place on Bank adjustment experience of a country over the medium-term.

An IMF Fund adjustment program was important in determining short-term trade lines, but the impact was negative, perhaps because such a program indicates severe short-run balance of payments difficulties. This would color the banks' assessment of repayment capability during the short run — so, short-term trade lines would be less.

Short-term trade lines were directly related to a country's trade deficit but not significantly so. The same was true for a country's international reserves, which banks took into account when determining the short-term trade lines to make available.

The secondary market price of a country's sovereign debt could indicate the creditworthiness of a country and expectations about future repayment —the higher the secondary market price, the higher the probability of repayment (as perceived by the market) and the easier the access to short-term trade lines from commercial banks. In fact, the secondary market price is not particularly important in determining access to short-term lines.

The spreads over LIBOR at which short-term trade lines were extended were negatively related to the amount of short-term trade lines borrowed by a country, but they were not statistically significant. This observation could be explained because the relationship between the cost of trade financing and the amount made available by banks is not one-sided. It may be that once the country requests short-term trade lines, the spread is determined case-by-case. The risk premium may also be charged as an up-front fee, not as a higher spread over LIBOR. On the other hand, if the transaction for which the short-term trade lines is required is essential to the country, it might be coerced to pay a higher rate to the bank providing the lines.

Although most banks would like to pull out of developing country lending in general, and from Sub-Saharan Africa in particular, this did not turn out to be significant in determining the amount of short-term trade lines that commercial banks made available to a country. Evidence shows that (except for Mozambique) short-term trade lines were rescheduled/ refinanced for the highly indebted countries that already had large short-term trade lines outstanding from commercial banks. Trade lines might be included in bank restructurings if the short-term trade lines being extended to a country by commercial banks is large in absolute terms. For countries in Africa, the inclusion of trade lines in reschedulings could lead to a drastic reduction in access to new lines. In the short run, they might be cut off.

Consolidating all commercial bank debt and charging uniform terms might therefore be seen as a positive step by the country to reconcile its figures with its commercial bank creditors and improve future debt management. To gauge the effect of each component of a bank rescheduling agreement on future access to short-term trade lines, case-by-case analysis of countries would be necessary over time. The cross-sectional "snapshot" data nevertheless prove conclusively that the inclusion of trade lines in bank rescheduling agreements is important in determining future access to short-term trade lines from commercial banks.

The reality of trade

The economic and debt crisis of Sub-Saharan Africa

had hurt the region's unfavorable relations with commercial banks. Most medium and long-term credit has been cut, though it has been substituted by public funds, bilateral and multilateral. Access to short-term trade financing, for which there are few public substitutes, has nevertheless declined dramatically. And there has been a marked shift to financing techniques that are much more complex and expensive.

Adjustment is a prerequisite for any improvement in the role and cost of trade financing in Sub-Saharan African. An effective banking system can provide the technical skill necessary to any trade financing. Multilateral organizations can help by providing assistance to improve the technical capacity of the banking system (public or private). It may also be appropriate to design new financial products to attract trade financing. In addiition, some third-party guarantee or enhancement schemes could be hammered out with donors and multilateral institutions to bring fees down.

References

"Attractions of Financing Trade Paper." 1986. *International Financial Law Review* (U.K.) 5, p.8-13.

Bowen, David. 1985. "Trade Finance in Britain—The Consumer's View." Euromoney Trade Finance Report (U.K.). No. 26. June 1985.

Chase Trade Information Corporation.1981. *International Trade Financing: Conventional and Nonconventional Practices*. 2nd ed. New York.

Eisemann, Frederic, Charles Bontoux, and Michael Rowe(eds). 1985. *Le credit documentaire dans le commerce exterieur : commentaire reglementaiton uniforme internationale et formules normalisees*. Paris: Jupiter.

Gmur, Charles J.(ed). *Trade Financing*. 2nd ed. London: Euromoney Publications.

Gooptu, Sudarshan, and Richard Brun. 1991. "The Role and Cost of Short-term Credit." PRE Working Paper no. Washington, D.C.

Guild, Ian. and Rhodri Harris. 1985. *Forfaiting: an Alternative Approach to Export Trade Finance*. Cambridge: Woodhead-Faulkner.

Hall, Michael. 1986. "Export Finance." British Business (U.K.) 21:26-27.

Hammond, Grant Tedrick. 1990. *Countertrade, Offsets and Barter in International Political Economy*. London: Pinter Publishers.

International Chamber of Commerce. 1983. *Uniform Customs and Practice for Documentary Credits*. Rev. ed. New York, N.Y.

Jones, Stephen F. and Ashley Jagoe. 1988. *Third World Countertrade*. U.K.: Produce Studies Ltd.

Kingman-Brundage, Jane, and Susan Schulz. 1986. *The Fundamentals of Trade Finance: the Ins and Outs of Import-Export Financing*. New York: Wiley.

Knight, Martin. and James Ball, and Andrew Ingliks-Taylor(eds). *Export Finance*. London: Euromoney Publications.

Louberge, Henri and Pierre Maurer (eds). *Financement et assurance des credits a l'exportation : aspects theoriques et pratiques en vigueur dans les pays europeens*. Geneve: Librairie Droz.

Lowenfeld, Andreas F. 1981. *International Private Trade*. 2nd ed. New York: M. Bender.

Mills, Dominic. 1986. "USA: Trade Finance Means Taking the Country Risk." *Euromoney Trade Finance Report*, No. 42.

Rowe, Michael. 1989a. *Countertrade*. London: Euromoney Publications.

—. 1989b. "Using Letters of Credit in Trade." *International Financial Law Review* (U.K.)5:290-31.

Schneider, Gerhard W. 1974. *Export-Import Financing: A Practical Guide*. New York: Wiley.

"Trade Financing: The Official Agencies; How the Consensus Survived." 1984. *Euromoney*, January.

Usunier, Jean-Claude. 1985. *Environment international et gestion de l'exportation*. Paris: Presses Universitaires de France.

ANNEX I

List of Variables Used in the Econometric Analysis of Trade Financing

Variable Name	Description	Source
STTLEST1	Short-term trade line estimate 1.	CFS Estimate using World Debt Tables, World Bank Country Briefs & The World Development Report, 1989.
RCBTDOD	Ratio of commercial bank debt to total debt outstanding	BIS Statistics
RDODXGS	Ratio of total debt outstanding and disbursed over exports of goods and services	World Debt Tables, 1989.
BADJCUR	Current adjustment program with the Bank (1987)	CTRMI, World Bank FDB database, 1989.
BADJ5	Adjustment program with the Bank over the last 5 years (1982-87)	CTRMI, World Bank FDB database, 1989.
FADJCUR	Current adjustment program with the Fund (1987)	IMF, Treasurer's Department, 1989.
RTDSXGS	Ratio of total debt service to exports of goods and services.	World Debt Tables, 1989.
RDODGNP	Ratio of total debt outstanding and disbursed to GNP	World Debt Tables, 1989.
TRDEF	Trade deficit	Computed from the World Debt Tables, 1989 as difference of exports and imports
INTRES	International Reserves	World Debt Tables 1989.
SPREAD	Spread over LIBOR charged by commercial bank first	CFS, World Bank.

	to that country.	
SMP87	Secondary market price of sovereign bank debt in Dec. 1987	Salomon Brothers
MORAT87	Declaration of moratorium on debt service payments to commercial banks between 1985 and 1987	"Commercial Banks' Restructuring and New Money Facilities Agreements", CFS. World Bank, July 6, 1989

Comment

Ronald Johannes

Wittgenstien wrote "Whereof we cannot speak, thereof we must be silent." That is basically my feeling on the subject of short-term private trade credit, because of the formidable obstacles to collecting reliable data on what is going on. We are indebted, therefore, to the authors, Brun and Gooptu, for a useful step forward regarding nonguaranteed trade credit, based on not only a careful appraisal of publicly available data, but also numerous interviews—some confidential—with commercial banks worldwide. What is beyond doubt is that the share of private export credits (both short and longer-term, officially guaranteed and unguaranteed) in resource flows to developing countries has fallen sharply over the past decade. Estimated annual net flows exceeding $11 billion at the start of the 1980s turned negative at the end. The picture is similar for Sub-Saharan Africa.

The central issue posed by the restriction of trade credit guaranteed by an export credit agency (ECA) is whether and at what cost a debtor country can develop alternative ways of conducting trade. The implications of the study on this issue are not particularly optimistic. In essence, the conclusion is that, in current circumstances, unguaranteed private export credits offer an expensive stopgap of limited availability, with residual financing provided by complex and efficient transactions. The policy conclusion to be drawn is that the official sector, which in the past has accounted for as much as half of all private flows to Sub-Saharan Africa, should increase its support, with ECAs going back in "on cover" and providing insurance and guarantees, on the basis of risk-adjusted premia, in countries undertaking a credible adjustment effort.

Two key differences between (unguaranteed) short-term trade credit and medium-and long-term commercial debt are:

- Perceived seniority
- Price elasticity

It is generally perceived that a debtor country will accord seniority in servicing to its short-term trade credits over medium-and long-term commercial debt (and even, in a few cases, over multilateral official debt), so as to protect its international trade and maintain its imports. Nevertheless, a problem for severely indebted low-income countries has been to credibly convince editors of that seniority (e.g. Senegal), so as to avoid a precipitous cut in the availability of trade credit lines. At best (in the CFA zone), these countries have been forced to use expensive confirmed irrevocable letters of credit, characterized by high upfront fees on small transactions and disguised fees in the import price. At worst, the issue has been one of not merely seniority but capacity to pay, and countries have had to resort to countertrade, barter, and cash collateral. This has been the story in the 1980s on guarantees provided by export credit agencies for Sub-Saharan Africa.

Whether, in fact, inclusion of trade lines in rescheduling has hurt a country is an open question, as shown by the data assembled by Brun and Gooptu. Generally, Sub-Saharan countries have not been able to reschedule trade lines—important exceptions are Nigeria and Mozambique. But countries that have included trade lines in rescheduling agreements, such as Brazil, Mexico, and the Philippines, do not seem to have suffered as severe a diminution in those lines. What this suggests is that causality runs from the availability of trade lines to their rescheduling, rather than the other way around: in other words, commercial banks risk substantial costs (both lost business and portfolio losses) in cutting off trade lines to big countries, but not to small ones. The relationship also indicates, of course, the benefits of concluding a negotiated agreement, rather than announcing a unilateral moratorium.

By "price elasticity" I mean the elasticity of the supply of trade credits with respect to their interest rate cost. We may infer from restructuring packages for medium-and long-term commercial debt that the supply curve for voluntary new money slopes upwards and eventually backwards. That is, as the interest rate rises, there comes a point at which expected return actually declines, because the high cost overburdens the country. Thus, there exists no equilibrium interest rate at which voluntary new money is forthcoming. For short-term trade finance, the situation appears to be different and interest rate cost seem to play an allocative role. Perhaps the explanation for the difference is the presence of collateral, characteristic of LDC trade finance.

Of course, the true cost of trade credit for developing countries is usually much higher than the nominal spread over LIBOR, as pointed out by Brun and Gooptu. The effective spread may easily range from 5 percent to 10 percent, while for countertrade and barter, the costs may be stratospheric (possibly reflecting fraudulent practice), equal in present value terms to a significant fraction of the principal amount of the deal (such as Nigeria's bartering of oil for military supplies with Brazil). Incidentally, the paper mentions cash collateral and barter as two possibilities. For countries running arrears, these methods face the legal problem of attachment of assets (except government-to-government barter). It would be interesting to know how this problem has worked out in practice.

After a careful examination of World Bank, OECD, and BIS data, Brun and Gooptu conclude that none of the data, as it stands, is satisfactory. Instead, these construct a proxy for short-term trade lines: the trade deficit multiplied by the share of noncapital goods in imports. This seems a sensible way to proceed, but it does emphasize the unreliability of the data. Incidentally, there is a low correlation between this proxy for unguaranteed trade lines and short-term borrowing. For example, short-term borrowing by Nigeria and Côte d'Ivoire far exceeds the proxy, whereas the reverse is true for Mozambique and Madagascar.

Brun and Gooptu find that the most important determinants of the availability of trade credit are the ratio of commercial bank debt to total external debt, the size of the trade deficit, and the level of reserves by contrast, the secondary market price of debt is unimportant. This accords with the notion that the assessment of general creditworthiness on medium- and long-term debt, as expressed by the secondary market price, is not necessarily the same as the country's determination to service trade lines. To take a simple analogy, a man who has run up unserviceable credit card debts will probably continue to pay his electricity bill.

An alternative and not inconsistent interpretation of these results is that the absolute size of a country's economy is a principal determinant of the availability of trade credit. We would expect this relation to hold true, because size expresses the strategic importance of a country to a commercial bank's business and balance sheet. Thus, ratio of commercial to total debt, trade deficit, and reserves may be proxies for size of economy. We must acknowledge, in addition, the importance of strategic and geopolitical interests: for example, Zambia's servicing the debt of its copper company, or trade credits to finance military imports. It is interesting to note that Brun and Gooptu find a positive relation of availability of trade credit to a World Bank adjustment program, and a negative relation to an IMF program. While the positive relation to a Bank program is encouraging, the negative relation to the Fund program is understandable in view of the balance-of-payments disequilibrium that would have induced recourse to the Fund.

The direct role of the Bank in export credits is exercised through the EXCEL (Export Credit Enhanced Leverage) program. which cofinances with ECA's medium-term credits to the private sector through financial intermediaries. Substantial volumes (about $13 billion) of export credits have been cofinanced over the past decade.

The contribution of the Bank is not simply finance, but its expertise on project financing. Additionally, of course, the Bank is providing substantial sums for import financing through structural and sectoral adjustment loans. The benefit is twofold: the immediate injection of liquidity, and the improvement in creditworthiness stemming from the adjustment program.

Finally, through the 1990s, developing country exporters are likely to call upon bank loans as a primary means of finance. The need for rehabilitation of domestic banking systems in a number of countries, (e.g., Angola, Benin, Mozambique) is highlighted by the Bank's study on Sub-Saharan Africa (*Sub-Saharan Africa: From Crisis to Sustainable Growth*). The study notes that the growth rate of exports from Sub-Saharan Africa turned negative in the 1980s and that Africa's share of world markets declined from 2.4 percent in 1970 to 1.3 percent in 1987. Banking systems that have been obliged to finance government subsidies or arrears, for example, are ill-equipped to meet the export potential that must be achieved for a return to growth.

11

Officially Supported Export Credits

Asli Demirguc-Kunt and Refik Erzan

How important were officially supported export credits (OSECs) in Sub-Saharan Africa's external financing in the past two decades, and what are the prospects for the 1990s? OSECs are suppliers' and buyers' credits officially supported by export credit agencies (ECAs) with direct credits, refinancing, interest subsidies, guarantees, or insurance.

The surge in OSECs came when most OECD countries saw them as an economic policy tool, mainly to boost exports, following the new protectionism and mercantilism that swept the industrial countries in the early 1970s. OSECs soon became a big source of external capital for developing countries and Eastern Europe, second only to private bank lending. Soon most OECD countries agreed on guidelines for official export credit practices to avoid "destructive competition," particularly in credits to industrial countries.

Following the debt crisis in 1982, most export credit agencies had financial difficulties due to widespread payment arrears and, later, many Paris Club debt reschedulings. Countries with severe debt servicing problems were increasingly taken off-cover by the agencies. The cutbacks were in response to the agencies' growing portfolio problems, waning budgetary support, and charges that, having given export guarantees too freely, they contributed to the debt crisis. Low rates of investment in debtor countries also drastically reduced demand for capital goods, and net OSEC flows became negative as new commitments fell. But with the recent move toward matching the cover policies with adjustment progress, countries which did not have to reschedule debt (or rescheduled in an orderly fashion) received substantial new commitments. Increased flexibility in agency operations, particularly reliance on market forces for pricing decisions, also contributed to this turnaround. So did better demand for capital goods. It was not before the end of the 1980s that OSECs again yielded net flows for developing countries.

Most OSECs were extended to middle-income developing countries and to the OPEC countries. Like all low-income areas, Africa had a modest share, but officially guaranteed credits covered a more important chunk of capital flows to Africa from private financial sources compared with higher-income developing countries. Although private capital flows to Sub-Saharan Africa are relatively small, this close link suggests the importance of official support in realizing these flows.

In many countries, the export credit agencies are under increasing scrutiny, and their existence is being questioned. Ideally, these agencies should disappear, leaving export credit and insurance to the market—and aid to aid agencies. However, given the shortcomings of international capital markets and the political economy of aid, they do mobilize additional resources for development.

Financial structure of export credit agencies

International trade is financed by export credits, the bulk of which are short-term credits with maturities of around two months and are extended by the exporters—i.e, suppliers' credits. A fraction of exports—mostly investment goods to developing countries and Eastern Europe—are financed by export credits with maturities of several years. These can be suppliers' credits, but banks and other financial institutions play a big role by taking over the exporters' claims or directly extending credits to the buyers abroad or their banks—i.e., buyers' credits.

More than 60 percent of commodity exports of industrial countries are financed by suppliers' credits (over 10 days), of which less than 10 percent have a maturity over six months and less than 5 percent over one year. The rest are advance and cash payments (and credits up to 10 days). Financial credits over one year—that is, buyers' credits and suppliers' credits taken over by banks and other financial institutions—are maybe 5 percent of the total exports. The average payment period is over two years, and roughly 10 percent of exports are financed by credits with a maturity over one year.

Initially, official support was mainly for these medium- and long-term export credits, and OECD guidelines on these did not even address short-term export credits. Lately, there has been a big increase in short-term credits, and subsidies for grain and raw material sales are common. But this chapter is limited to medium- and long-term financing.

Operations

All major exporting countries support export credits to promote exports of their goods and services. The increasing prominence of export credit agencies in industrial countries coincided with balance of payments problems after the 1973 oil shock. For many smaller OECD countries, however, putting their industry on equal footing with other exporters—i.e., "neutralization"—was a real concern. Relatively advanced developing countries set up agencies as a trade policy tool to accelerate exports. Export credit systems vary from country to country. They promote exports and carry out governments' industrial, commercial, or foreign policies. They provide funds directly, to refinance or guarantee other providers—called, in the case of export credit agencies, "official export credit." They have no mandate to ensure that the resources contribute to the development of the importing country.

ECAs subsidize credits in two ways. They advance loans at interest rates below market rates. To restrict competition through these subsidies and to increase transparency, the OECD countries adopted in 1976 a gentlemen's agreement. This so-called "Consensus" is amended periodically and establishes guidelines for OSECs with a repayment term of over two years. Interest rates for different loan currencies and borrowing countries are defined, and down-payment requirements, maximum repayment periods, and the like are established. The minimum interest rates have moved closer to market rates, and for high-income developing countries and industrial countries the gap was eliminated in 1987.

The agencies also provide a subsidy through guarantee and insurance schemes. On direct loans, they self-insure or give cover to institutions that provide funds against the political or commercial risks of nonpayment. This is a subsidy because the premium charged is below the market rate for assuming the same risk. The agencies have traditionally charged a fixed premium and went "off cover" when countries started running into debt-servicing difficulties. Recently, however, there has been a move toward a differentiated premium structure. Generally, premiums depend on the term of the contract and the risk category of the recipient country. With variable prices, agencies can provide cover even for countries with payment difficulties. Some agencies also try to price each contract individually to reflect the risk of nonpayment by the buyer.

Most export credit agencies provide a controversial form of finance called "mixed credits"—commercial tied aid credits with a concessional element, produced either by mixing grants and commercial loans or by direct interest subsidies on commercial loans. According to the Consensus, this element has to be more than 35 percent of a mixed credit, and more than 50 percent for poorer developing countries. However, implicit subsidies through insurance and guarantees are not regulated.

It is likely that the 1976 Consensus which regulated interest subsidies but not the official insurance and guarantee schemes has led to the growth of implicit subsidies in total export credit subsidies. The cost is potentially huge. The US Eximbank recently made a US$4.8 billion provision on 40 percent of its loans and loan guarantees.

Trends during the 1970s and the 1980s, and the profile of OSECs

The importance of OSECs in the external financing of developing countries can be gleaned from the following:

The annual net flow of medium- and long-term OSECs from OECD to developing countries (around $2 billion to $3 billion in the early 1970s) increased to over $13 billion by the end of the decade (table 11.1). In 1977 OSECs accounted for 27 percent of all net external capital flows to developing countries. This has declined to 8 percent in 1984, and in the following year was negligible. From 1986 to 1988, net OSECs were apparently negative. The pattern was similar for Sub-Saharan Africa. From less than US$500 million in the early 1970s, OSECs reached US$2 billion in 1977, and Africa's share of total OSECs to developing countries climbed from less than 10 to over 20 percent. In the peak year, 1977, OSECs accounted for 35 percent of all external funds to Africa. The decline in OSECs was more rapid for

Table 11.1 ***Net flows of officially supported medium- and long-term exports to Sub-Saharan Africa and to all developing countries***

	1970	*1975*	*1980*	*1981*	*1982*	*1983*	*1984*	*1985*	*1986*	*1987*	*1988*
					(millions of US$)						
Direct Official	4	151	-32	189	95	168	-69	177	-79	-79	-29
Guar. Private	230	983	1729	1326	1499	749	-30	-70	-483	-1062	-1603
Total OSECs	234	1134	1697	1515	1594	917	-99	107	-562	-1141	-1632
					(percentages)						
Total OSECs/ Total Inflows	16.6	25.2	17.3	14.7	14.2	11.2	n.a.	n.a.	n.a.	n.a.	n.a.
Guar. Private/ Total Private	51.2	47.3	44.1	30.0	28.0	31.5	n.a.	n.a.	n.a.	n.a.	n.a.
OSEC Credit Composition											
Direct Official	1.8	13.3	n.a.	12.5	5.9	18.3	n.a.	n.a.	n.a.	n.a.	n.a
Guar. Private	98.2	86.7	n.a.	87.5	94.1	81.7	n.a.	n.a.	n.a.	n.a.	n.a.

Note: n.a = not applicable. Direct Official = export credits extended directly by official institutions. Guaranteed Private = officially insured suppliers' credits plus guaranteed bank credits.
Source: ECD, Creditor Reporting System.

Africa, however, and 1983 was the last year yielding a positive net flow. Long before, its share of total OSECs dropped considerably.

Overall, direct official export credits were around 15-30 percent of all OSECs but considerably lower for Africa. The share of private export credits, which are officially insured or guaranteed, in total private capital inflows was generally around 15-30 percent, but for Africa significantly higher at 30-60 percent. These comparisons show the importance of official guarantee and insurance schemes in providing external resources, particularly in attracting private capital to Africa, although the share of private flows in total resource flows to Africa is considerably lower than for most developing regions. For all developing countries, the share of private capital in total resource flows was well above 60 percent in 1975-82, declining to about 30 percent in the late 1980s. For Sub-Saharan Africa, the comparable figure was around 40 percent, and by 1984, private flows became negative.

Outstanding stock

The decline in the importance of OSECs in the 1980s can also be seen in data on the outstanding debt of the developing countries. The share of OSECs in total outstanding debt, and in public and publicly-guaranteed debt of selected Sub-Saharan African countries, which were respectively 17 and 24 percent in 1985, declined sharply to 9 and 12 percent, respectively, in 1988.

New commitments

While net flows continued to be negative, new commitments of OSECs to developing countries turned up in 1988 and 1989, indicating that the post-1982 decline might be over (table 11.2). New commitments to developing countries (US$30.4 billion in 1987) rose by 8 percent in 1988, mainly an increase in long-term credits (with repayment periods over five years) which went up 80 percent to US$11 billion. A 23 percent rise in 1989 was due to medium-term credits; long-term commitments declined.

OSEC commitments to low-income developing countries increased parallel with the general development in 1988 and 1989, with Africa seeing rises of 10 percent (to $3.6 billion) and 23 percent (table 11.3).

The profile of OSECs

Since the mid-1980s a quarter of all medium- and long-term commitments were to industrial countries and high-income developing countries (table 11.2). Low-income countries received another quarter, and middle-income developing countries a half. A third of new commitments to low-income developing countries was to Africa (table 11.3). The share of long-term credits in total OSEC commitments (with an initial term of over one year) bobbed around 20 percent but used to be lower for high-income countries and higher for low-income countries. Recently this trend reversed.

By sector, transport accounted for 32 percent of OSECs in 1989, followed by industry at 30 percent, and telecommunications and energy at 9 percent each (table 11.4) For Africa, transport took 53 percent, and industry only 16 percent.

Distortions from export credit subsidies

Because subsidies maintain or expand employment and economic activity in some sectors and presumably boost exports—but not necessarily value added in international prices—governments are tempted to promote them as instruments yielding a high social return. Moreover, OSECs (mixed credits) can be disguised development aid, which often is politically unpopular. It is tempting to create a constituency for such aid by tying it to exports that benefit certain industries. But how are importing countries affected by export credit subsidies? They benefit the importer because they mobilize additional external resources at low cost. Yet they may cause major distortions, and their overall costs might be high. Based on World Bank staff experience, there are five main problems: excess flows, inappropriate projects, design weaknesses, overpriced goods, and corruption.

In the late 1970s and early 1980s, export credit agencies extended credits even if the recipient country could not use the additional resources. If the credits were not supplied by one country (it was said), they would be supplied by another, and the local exporter would miss a golden opportunity. Some OSECs were used to promote duff projects—those not essential to development or poorly rated due to high risk and low return. Some, considered inappropriate by the World Bank (such as nuclear power stations), were supported by export credit agencies because they satisfied objectives of the agency's government.

Overpriced goods and corruption are harder to prove. Overpricing stems from credits that finance purchases only from the country granting the credits. This discourages buyers from seeking competitive tenders—possibly local producers and suppliers in other developing countries, that lack export credit schemes. Corruption—i.e., the collusion of buyers and sellers in defrauding export credit agencies—is a big problem and would explain why Africa pays about 20 to 30 percent higher prices for its imports.

Using OSECs to finance bad projects, overpricing of goods, and corruption were not only the result of the agencies' indifference to development priorities of the recipient countries. A fundamental cause was the problem of "moral hazard" and "adverse selection," brought about by the mispricing of guarantees.

Moral hazard and adverse selection

There is a moral hazard when the insurer's liability is affected by the insured's actions, about which the insurer has incomplete information. Adverse selection is where the insured knows the risks but the insurer does not. In the case of OSECs, export credit agencies were encouraged to disregard information for pricing purposes, let alone try to improve commercial intelligence.

Exporters had little incentive with these guarantees to minimize the risk of nonpayment. Indeed, they had every reason to seek riskier projects because the guarantees put their expected value—for the exporter—on par with sound projects. The exporter could cash in the (implicitly) subsidized risk premium by charging more to the importer. Relieved from risks, a rational exporter would simply try to find customers willing to pay the higher price.

For developing countries, export credits are scarce resources that need to be allocated efficiently. The incentive structure leads to an inefficient allocation of these resources. "Were ECAs a relatively minor source of finance for developing countries, these considerations would not merit attention. Given the importance of ECAs, however, the potentially distortive effect of their activities warrants major reform efforts" (Krueger 1989). As the subsidy in some export credits comes from the donor country's aid budget (e.g., mixed credits), sharing this subsidy with the exporter is a loss to the recipient country.

Needs and prospects for external finance in the 1990s

For many developing countries, access to external borrowing was sharply curtailed in the 1980s, and real interest rates and therefore the cost of debt-servicing greatly increased. GNP growth dropped sharply, partly because of a decline in investment, which may in turn have been caused by the heavy debt burden. The debt burden reduces the ability of the country to attract new capital, making investment too costly relative to forgone consumption. There is also the "debt overhang" effect: debt servicing needs a large percentage of investment returns to be transferred abroad, so investment is less attractive relative to consumption. To restore investment and growth in the 1990s, these disincentives for investment must be corrected. Nevertheless, debt and debt-service reductions are necessary to eliminate debt overhang.

Table 11.2 ***Flow of new commitments of officially supported medium- and long-term export credits, 1981-1989***

	Category I[a] *(mainly industrial countries)*	*Category II*[a] *(middle-income developing countries)*	*Category III (low-income developing countries)*	*Categories II and III*	*Total*
Medium- and long-term credits with an initial term of over one year,[b] billion SDRs (billions of US$)[d]					
1981	...	...	...	...	70.2 (82.8)
1982	...	...	...	...	77.5 (85.6)
1983	...	...	...	...	63.1 (67.5)
1984	...	...	...	...	56.8 (58.2)
1985	11.8 (12.0)	24.1 (24.6)	10.5 (10.7)	34.6 (35.3)	47.1[c] (47.8)
1986	10.0 (11.7)	19.0 (22.2)	9.7 (11.3)	28.7 (33.6)	39.3[c] (46.1)
1987	12.4 (16.0)	16.2 (20.9)	7.3 (9.4)	23.5 (30.4)	36.4[c] (47.1)
1988	7.3 (9.8)	15.9 (21.3)	9.5 (12.7)	25.4 (34.0)	33.2[c] (44.6)
1989	9.2 (11.8)	20.8 (26.6)	10.4 (13.3)	31.2 (39.9)	41.4[c] (53.1)
Long-term credits with an initial term of over five years,[b] billion SDRs (billions of US$)[d]					
1981	...	...	...	...	18.2 (21.5)
1982	...	...	...	...	18.5 (20.4)
1983	...	...	...	...	13.0 (13.9)
1984	1.8 (1.9)	6.8 (7.0)	2.5 (2.6)	9.3 (9.6)	11.1 (11.4)
1985	1.0 (1.0)	4.8 (4.9)	2.5 (2.6)	7.3 (7.4)	8.3 (8.4)
1986	0.8 (0.9)	4.4 (5.1)	2.7 (3.2)	7.1 (8.3)	8.0 (9.4)
1987	1.8 (2.3)	2.9 (3.7)	1.7 (2.2)	4.6 (5.9)	6.4 (8.3)
1988	1.4 (1.9)	3.5 (4.7)	4.7 (6.3)	8.2 (11.0)	9.6 (12.9)
1989	2.4 (3.1)	3.6 (4.6)	1.9 (2.4)	5.5 (7.0)	7.9 (10.1)
Share of long-term credits in total (percent)					
1981	...	...	...	...	25.9
1982	...	...	...	...	23.9
1983	...	...	...	...	20.6
1984	...	...	...	...	19.5
1985	8.5	19.9	23.8	21.1	17.6
1986	8.0	23.2	27.8	24.7	20.4
1987	14.5	17.9	23.3	19.6	17.6
1988	19.2	22.0	49.5	32.3	28.9
1989	26.1	17.3	18.3	17.6	19.1

a. The country categories correspond to the classification used by the OECD consensus on Export Credits. Since 1982, this Arrangement has classified as Category I all countries with a GDP per capita of over $4,000 per annum according to 1979 data published in the 1981 World Bank Atlas; as Category II all countries not classified in Categories I or III; and as Category III all countries eligible for IDA credits plus any low-income countries or territories whose GNP per capital would not exceed the IDA eligibility level.
b. The value of commitments includes principal and insured interest.
c. Includes unallocated credits, so total exceeds the sum of the categories.
d. SDRs converted to US dollars using yearly average exchange rates from IMF, International Financial Statistics.
Source: OECD, Secretariat of the Export Credit Group; and Johnson, Fisher, and Harris (1990, table 1).

Table 11.3 ***Flow of new commitments of officially supported medium- and long-term export credits, 1981-1989*[a]**

Year	*Millions of SDRs*	*Millions of US$*	*Share in lower income developing countries (percent)*	*Share in all developing countries (percent)*	*Share in all recipients*[b] *(percent)*
1987	2,584	(3,341)	35.3	11.0	7.1
1988	2,652	(3,564)	28.0	10.4	8.0
1989	3,274	(4,196)	31.4	10.5	7.9

a. See notes to table 11.2.
b. The denominators are from columns 3, 4, and 5 of the top part of table 11.2.
Source: OECD, Secretariat of the Export Credit Group.

Table 11.4 ***Flow of new committments of officially supported long-term export credits by major sectors, 1989***
(percentage distribution)

	Total (millions of U.S. dollars)	Transportation	Telecommunications	Energy	Industry	Other
To all countries	10,215	32	9	9	30	20
To Sub-Saharan Africa	513	53	6	11	16	14

Note: Long-term credits are those with an initial term of over five years.
Source: OECD, Secretariat of the Export Credit Group.

Moreover, with debt reductions there must be new money since most debtor countries need to fill financing gaps as minimum investment is made in infrastructure Capital flows to developing countries come mainly from official development assistance, private flows (commercial bank lending and foreign direct investment), and export credits.

Commercial bank lending will be slow to recover in the 1990s, because of the losses suffered since the debt crisis began and the problems for developing countries of debt overhang. By increasing loan loss reserves and lowering portfolio exposure, commercial banks have given a strong signal that voluntary financing will resume only if they see debtor country prospects improving. In the 1990s, credit flows to developing countries will probably shift toward trade and project and private sector financing. Developing countries will have to adopt adjustment programs to attract foreign flows. Foreign direct investment has become an important source of external finance for many developing countries and may increase, helped by the role of the World Bank and regional development banks in adjustment programs, promotion of private sector development, and insurance of investment flows.

OSECs can also help foreign direct investments. In mining, for example, there was a fall in the equity capital-loan ratio in foreign direct investments in the 1970s. Heavy investment requirements and expropriation risks led the investors to dilute the risk on equity capital, and OSECs were an important source in financing machinery and equipment. In the 1990s less risky and relatively cheap capital of OSECs will be exploited by foreign investors and augment the investment volume.

Enhancing the efficiency of OSECs in the 1990s

The efficiency of OSECs as external financing for developing countries can be improved through the export credit agencies, cooperation between them and multilateral development agencies, and the institutional and economic environment in the developing countries.

With fiscal considerations as the main motive, the driving force in reforming the export credit agencies is increasing scrutiny by the authorities and national legislatures. Some discipline imposed by super national bodies of the European Community is also likely.

To induce direct lending to the private sector, borrowing developing countries need to do more than implement adjustment policies and general creditworthiness. Often it is domestic distortions and the related rents that lie behind wasteful investment decisions and corruption—with or without OSECs. Furthermore, some export credit agencies that are eager to expand their nonguaranteed lending to the private sector face many practical problems. Lack of adequate accounting standards and legal complications in potential claims discourage business with the private sector.

Cooperation between multilateral development agencies and export credit agencies can improve the efficiency of the OSECs for recipient and exporting countries. Sound project appraisal is the key to efficient use of export credits. Developed countries cannot be unconcerned about an investment project financed by export credits. If a success, the project will give exporters access to growing markets that do not require subsidies. More directly, good quality projects will decrease the cost of ECAs and save their taxpayers money.

The quality of projects servicing (importance and compatibility with the country's development aims) is the main determinant of a country's debt servicing capacity in the long run. Effective project screening processes by the recipient countries themselves require an efficient administration and technical competence. For those without such a system, cooperation between multilateral development agencies and export credit agencies is invaluable. A direct means of cooperation is cofinancing, through which the multilaterals provide the recipients and the ECAs with assessments of projects and technical judgment. Multilaterals also provide lists of projects eligible for financing to many potential cofinanciers.
All this eases the financing of approved projects and helps borrowers by allowing competitive international bidding for projects. In large projects the multilaterals act as an "umbrella." They receive OSECs from many sources and make purchases from the best supplier for each component. Furthermore, the procurement procedures of multilaterals could be applied to the whole project for price and quality control—something the ECAs oppose.

In 1980-89 the World Bank (including IDA) was involved in about a thousand "packages" with a total value of US$57 billion, to which OSECs contributed 22 percent. Cofinancings in the lowest income countries (with per capita GNP less than US$425) were US$ 21 billion, with OSECs' share 18 percent. For countries in the US$426-835 income bracket, OSECs' share of US$10 billion was 24 percent. OSECs' contribution was the highest in industrial projects, power and energy, and telecommunications.

In the 1990s there will be more emphasis on developing the private sector— and on credit flows to that sector in developing countries. But it is hard for ECAs to assess the viability of private enterprises. The recent EXCEL (Export Credit Enhanced Leverage) program of the World Bank will promote the flow of export credits and Bank loans to development banks and financial intermediaries in the recipient countries. These institutions, which will be responsible for placing the loans, will intermediate between foreign lenders and domestic borrowers. The Bank will provide some financing and help identify the intermediaries and evaluate individual loans. Although the ECAs will not have preferred creditor status, the Bank will seek full repayment of loans.

For Sub-Saharan Africa, in particular, given the acute shortage of technical and administrative skills, the cooperation between multilaterals and ECAs can be crucial in increasing the flow, and efficient use, of OSECs.

References

Claessens, Stijn. 1988. "The Debt Laffer Curve: Some Estimates." Washington, D.C.: World Bank.

Erzan, Refik. 1980. "Officially Supported Export Credits in a Broad Perspective" Study commissioned by AB Svensk Exportkredit, Stockholm.

Fitzgerald, Bruce, and Terry Monson. 1988. "Export Credit and Insurance for Export Promotion" *Finance and Development*.

Fleisig, Heywood, and Catherine Hill. 1984. "The Benefits and Costs of Official Export Credit Programs of Industrialized Countries: An Analysis." World Bank Working Paper 659.

Grassman, Sven. 1973. *Exchange Reserves and the Financial Structure of Foreign Trade*. Westmead/ Lexington: Saxon House/Lexington Books.

Henry, D.P. 1987. "The Financial Cost of Export Credit Guarantee Programs." R-3491-USDP. Santa Monica, Calif.: RAND Corporation,

James, Cristopher. 1989. "Empirical Evidence on Implicit Government Guarantees of Bank Foreign Loan Exposure." *Carnegie-Rochester Conference Series on Public Policy* 30: 129-62.

Johnson, G. G., Matthew Fisher, and Elliott Harris. 1990. "Officially Supported Export Credits:

Developments and Prospects." *IMF World Economic and Financial Surveys*. Washington, D.C.

Kohler, Daniel F. 1984. "Incentives and Insurance in International Financial Markets. " N-2117-USDP. Santa Monica, Calif.: RAND Corporation.

Kohler, Daniel F., and Peter H. Reuter. 1986. "Honor among Nations: Enforcing the Gentlemen's Agreement on Export Credits." Santa Monica, Calif.: RAND Corporation.

Krueger, Anne O. 1989. "Resolving the Debt Crisis and Restoring Developing Countries' Creditworthiness." *Carnegie-Rochester Conference Series on Public Policy* 30: 129-62.

Larkum, C. 1985. "The Role of Export Credits in Economic Development." Washington, D.C.: World Bank.

Radetzki, Marian. 1980. "Changing Structures in the Financing of the Minerals Industry in LDCs." *Development and Change* 11.

Radetzki, M., and S. Zorn. 1979. *Financing Mining Projects in Developing Countries*. A United Nations Study, London: Mining Journal Books Limited.

Ray, John E. 1986. "The OECD Export Credit Consensus." *The World Economy* 9 (3).

---. 1990. "The OECD 'Consensus' on Export Credits." Paris: OECD.

OECD (Organisation for Economic Co-operation and Development). 1989. *Development Co-operation in the 1990s. Efforts and Policies of the Members of the Development Assistance Committee*. Paris.

______. 1990a. "Arrangement on Guidelines for Officially Supported Export credits." Paris.

______. 1990b. *The Export Credit Financing Systems in OECD Member Countries*. 4th edition. Paris.

______. 1990c. *Financing and External Debt of Developing Countries: 1989 Survey*. Paris.

______. 1990d. *Geographical Distribution of Financial Flows to Developing Countries*. Paris.

Sachs, Jeffrey. 1988. "The Debt Overhang of Developing Countries." In de Macedo and Findlay, eds., *Debt, Growth and Stabilization: Essays in Memory of Carlos Diaz Alejandro*. Oxford: Basil Blackwell.

Sachs, Jeffrey, and Harry Huizinga. 1987. "U.S. Commercial Banks and the Developing-Country Debt Crisis." *Brookings Papers on Economic Activity* 2.

Salant, Stephen W. 1984. "Export Subsidies as Instruments of Economic and Foreign Policy." N-2120-USDP. Santa Monica, Calif.: RAND Corporation

World Bank. 1989. *World Debt Tables, 1989-90 Edition*. Washington, D.C.

World Bank, IMF, BIS, and OECD. 1988. *External Debt: Definition, Statistical Coverage and Methodology*. A Report by An International Working Group on External Debt Statistics. Paris: OECD.

Yeats, Alexander. 1989. "Do African Countries Pay More for Imports? Yes." World Bank Working Paper 265. Washington, D.C.

Comment

G. G. Johnson

I must say I have a bit of a sense of deja vu here. We went through a dress rehearsal of this seminar six months ago, and I commented at that time on this paper and I think most of my comments were taken into account. So I must have to say it is an excellent paper at this point. That said, I can still find a couple of things to say.

Most of these I will try to address to general issues in the area of export credits, but there is still one problem I have with the paper, which I think should be brought out, and that is the statistics. We all know the problem of the statistics, and I think the paper does a good job of talking about how inadequate they are. However, one conclusion that the paper draws is I think misleading—that there actually have been net outflows from Africa on account of export credits in recent years. In table 11 it shows the net outflows are shown to be on the order of total export credits running from 500 or 600 million credits in 1986, 1.1 billion in 1987, and 1.6 billion in 1988. To some extent, the breakdown of this can be seen by looking at the 15 or 20 recipients of export credits and just what has happened to them.

The striking thing there is that one sees for Nigeria, by far the largest recipient and much more important than all the rest put together, a sharp decline from a stock of $6.3 billion in 1986 to a stock of $3.6 billion in 1988. Almost certainly this is a mistake in one sense. You all know the very difficult times that Nigeria has been through and Nigeria just has not repaid export credits on anything like that scale. In fact, if anything, the amount of debt owed with respect to export credits has probably gone up because in the Paris Club they have been rescheduling interest as well as principal, so the stock of debt owed to the Paris Club creditors has been rising over time.

I think what we are seeing here is the effect of any accounting practice into which some export credit agencies have fallen. I think we are getting into a more uniform practice now, but in the past at least, of a lot of agencies in reporting export credits: once they had rescheduled it, it was in a sense off their books. It became the responsibility of the government rather than the export credit agencies, and as a result these things just disappeared from export credit statistics. They still show up in the overall debt figures but under the headings of other debts instead of export credits. So while its very true that most countries in Africa have received very little in the way of new credit in recent years—except for countries like Kenya that maintained their creditworthiness and have received a lot—at the same time they haven't actually repaid very much of the old debt. Probably the debt if anything has crept up because of capitalization of interest.

Now turning to the substance of the paper the policies talked about in the paper and so on. Surely the paper is right in the way it emphasizes that export credits are not provided as development aid. They are provided to support industrial country exports, which is not necessarily bad. This can be quite helpful in many cases but it is important to keep in mind that it is different from aid and that the motivations and structures and everything else are different. I just know from my own experience in discussions with export credit agencies, some of which have been held under the auspices of the World Bank, that this distinction between export credits and development assistance is more in the minds of those in the multilateral institutions now. I think that is an important thing to keep in mind, not to think of export credits as something that can be mobilized for development assistance. These can be useful for financial flowsx, and thus can also be useful to provide financing for development projects. But it has to be borne in mind that the motivations of those providing the finance are not the same as those who are trying to develop a country.

What can we think of happening to export credits in the future? Looking ahead, most developing countries particularly those in Africa that have relied so heavily on these types of external finance in the past, probably won't be able to count so much on the use of export credits in the future, at least not in the conventional form that they have taken in the past (basically a loan to a government to finance a project). Probably it is good that they are not going to do too much of that in the future. While most of these countries would be better off to really mobilize more of their domestic savings and not to rely so heavily on external savings, we would still want to see a substantial inflow of capital into these countries.

The question is how can the export credit agencies channel those flows. I think a pretty important thing that is going on these days, at least important in the sense of very active discussions, is on the techniques for project finance. When people talk about having a project financed, they really mean limited resource financing where the security for the project relies mainly in the quality of the project rather than in the guarantee of the government of the country. This does not solve everything from the viewpoint of a successful project that adds more to the debt burden of a country. For example, a very important thing for these limited resource projects to proceed is that the country maintain a suitable economic environment. If the economic policies are not appropriate, it is unlikely that the project will succeed, and in the end there will still be some debt problem left. But perhaps more important from a global point of view,, there will have been a waste of resources if these projects are not effectively used. We certainly know more cases in the past where projects have not been terribly effective.

A second kind of project financing that we can imagine are the ones going on under the auspices of the World Bank, and there are quite a few. The paper talks about the various cofinancing procedures. I think the important thing here is that by the World Bank being involved there is some assurance that the project is part of a coherent investment program for the country. There are some countries in Africa and elsewhere where one can still find some projects that are not really well thought out—the wide open projects that are just going to mean problems for the future. I would say a very important consideration for export credit agencies is that any projects they are going to finance should have the blessing of the World Bank. If they can cofinance, fine, if not, have it as some part of a coherent investment program.

A third thing, and perhaps this is where we had

hoped to see most of the developments in the future, would be lending by export credit agencies to private sectors. The paper does talk about some of the problems in this. There is no DXL program, a way in which the World Bank could help promote export credit lending to private sector entities. Again, though, countries themselves have a very important responsibility here. They have to see that the environment is hospitable for private sector development.

Probably, too, the most important thing from this discussion of the way export credit agencies look at these things is quite a liberal foreign exchange system. One of the big problems that private sectors have is the inability to get hold of the foreign exchange to export. Even if they pay their debts, even if they have a viable project that is doing well in terms of local currency it is not going to do the lender much good if they do not have access to the foreign exchange. The second thing is the legal system, as the author has noted. I mentioned at the seminar last spring that one of the real problems is that in many cases export credit agencies do not have any real way of bringing sanctions to bear on a debtor that has not paid its debts. One case is that somebody from the French agency, COFACE, mentioned a problem with a Southeast Asian country where they were told that before they could pursue the debtor in the courts, they would have to provide full documentation demonstrating how equal the treatment would be if somebody in that country tried to pursue a French debtor. They had to provide a translation into the local language of the whole of the French constitution, and in the end the export credit agency simply said that although the unpaid debt was not a trivial sum, it was not worth the $50,000 or so it was going to cost just to do the documentation necessary to pursue the case. So, improvements in legal systems can be quite important as well.

Those are what I see as considerations governing the overall future of project financing with export credit agencies. But these agencies do other things as well. There was a paper this morning on short-term credits. One of the key issues with short-term credits from export credit agencies' point of view is that generally speaking, short-term credits have been excluded from reschedulings. They have been included sometimes, but by and large export credit agencies through the debt strategy followed in the Paris Club have managed to keep short-term credits out of the rescheduling and that contrasts with the problems the banks have had.

So what does this mean? First of all, the short-term credit is perhaps more important than the medium-term credit to keep the country going. If youcan't get spare parts and raw materials, things obviously are going to grind to a halt. One can perhaps suffer an interruption for a period of time in the flow of medium-term credit. But if short-term credit is cut off, there is almost certainly going to be a crisis.

Two points should be understood. One is the premium of servicing such debt properly. Export credit agencies want to promote their exports, and they would like to stay on. One agency was recently saying, I think in reference to Bulgaria, "Don't they know if they would just pay us the short-term debt, we would be providing them with new credits." Its something which they have very much as part of their debt strategy. Short-term credit gets serviced. But in this area one worry about the future is that export credit agencies are increasingly moving toward privatization, particularly of the short term arm of their operation. In Britain, for example, the ECGD is going to be selling off the short-term arm of their operations. It leaves less security and less confidence that a private enterprise may keep the short-term credits flowing the way the public enterprises do. Something to keep in mind is that developing countries, even more than in the past, need to keep servicing their short-term credits.

Another point is the mixed credits that were mentioned in the paper. In some countries, particularly in Asia, they have really used mixed credits very successfully, They have managed to get export credit agencies to compete with each other to provide favorable terms, and this can be a very useful way of concessional finance—not as concessional as IDA terms perhaps, but still highly concessional.

It is not clear, though, that these mixed credits would be so important in the future. In the OECD consensus they are working toward trying to reduce the competition in this area, trying to reduce exports subsidies of one sort or another. The economic summit this year called for some more action on that.

A final thought: We always have to keep in mind the relationship between export credit cover policy and new flows and what happens to the old debt. I think that a lot of countries clearly have to get rid of their old debt through writeoffs to be able to move ahead with their economy. Other countries have a choice, and I am troubled by the fact that some industrial countries are providing aid in the form of new loans, even if it is concessional aid. They indicate that they may be going to cut off flows of aid to countries that receive concessions. When we talk about concessions and debt relief, there always is a tradeoff between that and new flows.

Part IV

Other Private Resource Flows and Risk Management

Foreign Direct Investment

Roger Riddell
Lawrence Cockcroft

Two major obstacles to higher economic growth in Sub-Saharan Africa in the 1990s are low investment and shortages of foreign exchange. Foreign investment could address both. It brings in foreign exchange, supplements domestic savings, and raises investment. Import-substituting investment can reduce import bills, while investment in export industries will increase foreign exchange earnings. There are other benefits: the creation (or expansion) of local industries to supply inputs to the new plant; the rise in domestic demand; the boosts in incomes and, through taxation, in state revenues; and the transfer of labor (including management) skill, and technology. Foreign investment could also increase efficiency of the domestic economy even before the anticipated investment flows.

Big inflows of new external private investment will materialize only in a country where projects are profitable and it is easy to do business. This means dealing with many problems endemic in Africa over the past 20 years—the overextended state, bureaucratic inefficiencies, and financial and infrastructural constraints. Tackling (if not resolving) these problems is probably a precondition for new foreign investment, but will also enhance the efficiency of the domestic economy.

The record

Up to the mid-1970s foreign investment in Sub-Saharan Africa was much the same as in other developing regions, except that most went into the primary sectors of agriculture and mining. In the 1980s there was a marked change. Foreign investment in Africa now plays a small part in overall investment and total external resource flows.

Africa (including North Africa) accounted for 14 percent of the developing country *stock* of foreign investment in 1985, falling from 27 percent 10 years before—an 8 percent fall in real terms compared with a 76 percent rise for all developing countries (table 12.15. In 1982 the division of foreign investment in all developing countries was primary sector, 19 percent; secondary sector, 44 percent; and tertiary sector, 38 percent. In Asia the ratios were 12 percent, 49 percent, and 39 percent, and for Latin America and the Caribbean 21 percent, 58 percent, and 22 percent. For Africa, however, the figures were 55 percent, 28, percent and 20 percent. Up to at least 1987 there was a fall in net investment flows to all developing countries, even in current prices. But for most subregions it was small, less severe than the fall in net in-flows, so that foreign investment flows formed a rising share of total foreign resource inflow. For Africa, however, there has been a dramatic fall in both the net inflow of foreign investment—and because of a rise in official development assistance, in the share of private investment to foreign resource inflow. According to the OECD, direct private investment in 1980-82 accounted for 9.9 percent of total net resource flows to Africa and just 2.3 percent in 1985-87, compared with a rise from 10.8 percent to 14.4 percent for all developing countries. It fell only marginally (from 5.3 percent to 4.2 percent) for all low-income countries, stayed roughly the same for Asia, and almost doubled for Western countries. (table 12.2) Little appears to have changed since, either relatively or absolutely, for Sub-Saharan Africa.

Aggregate flows include reinvestment of unremitted (often unremittable) profits, which account for more than half of the inflow of private investment.

So, foreign corporate investors have been even less committed than the figures suggest. Zambia, for instance, halted dividend outflows for three to four years, and re-investing profits is the "least bad" answer to idle dividends.

Structural adjustment and foreign direct investment

The long-term objective of structural adjustment programs is to raise the productive capacity of the economy through macroeconomic and institutional intervention that create an environment in which both domestic and foreign private investment can flourish. Yet in the *short term*, or even the *medium*, it is unlikely to prove an incentive for FDI. In its 1989 annual report, the International Finance Corporation (IFC) said; "A number of African countries have embarked on economic and institutional reforms. These reform programs often make the business environment more difficult in the short to medium term by introducing the need to adapt to more competitive circumstances. Furthermore, measures aimed at reducing deficits often result in restrained overall demand and depressed local markets. Many businesses find it difficult to adjust to trade reforms and industrial restructuring measures and to absorb increased input and debt service costs caused by local currency devaluations. In this kind of environment, investors adopt a wait-and-see attitude before making new investments or expanding operations. In the long term, however, the success of such reforms should increase the scope for private sector activity" (IFC 1989). The potentially unattractive character of structure adjustment programs to FDI (in the short term) can be seen from a breakdown of the key components of typical programs.

- The removal of import quotas.
- The reduction tariffs.
- The introduction of positive "real" interest rates.
- A revision of energy prices.
- A revision of agricultural prices.
- Introduction of energy conservation measures.
- A revision of industrial incentive schemes.
- Introduction of policies to increase the efficiency of public enterprises.
- More support for agriculture (marketing, etc.).
- Improving support for industry and its subsectors (such as removal of price controls).

This list excludes devaluations, a common feature of most adjustment lending packages, and severe in the extreme. In Ghana the cedi fell from 3 to the dollar to 30 in 1982-83; the Tanzanian shilling fell by more than a half in 1985-86; Sudan devalued by 40 percent in 1984-85; and in Zambia, the kwcha fell from 2.74 to the dollar in 1985 to 16 in October 1989. A one-off devaluation would encourage foreign investment. In practice, one has often been followed by more, and potential investors wait for further falls before committing funds.

A reduction in protection in import-substituting industries through lower tariffs is likely to mean lower sales in domestic markets and a profit squeeze for uncompetitive manufacturers. Significant devaluation makes imported inputs more expensive, while higher interest rates erode opportunities for cheap local borrowing, which has encouraged foreign investors. Higher prices for energy, transport, and other services have the same adverse effect on current and expected profit flows.

Most holders of FDI in Africa have viewed structure adjustment programs with a wait-and-see attitude—or withdrawn. Bennell's study on British interests in African industry shows substantial disinvestment, and a recent survey of French investors already in Africa revealed little enthusiasm for expansion. Other data suggest at best a slowing of foreign investment inflow, at worst a net outflow. Programs of the 1980s have resulted in much interest in short-term trading deals, which take advantage of freeing the market in foreign exchange. But they have not reversed the trend to disinvest and may have accelerated it. Witness Ghana, where there has been scant new foreign investment interest, despite a vigorous structural adjustment program.

Improvements to the enabling environment. The 1980s, and particularly the last six years, have seen two important changes in Africa. Because of growing foreign exchange shortages, policymakers in Africa began to realize that FDI brings in foreign exchange from the initial investment and from earnings of export-oriented enterprises. Governments began to be less hostile toward foreign companies. Latin America and Asia began to end restrictions on FDI in 1976-77, well before the second oil-price rise or the recession of 1980-82 and the debt crisis (suggesting that the need for foreign exchange was not the main motive for the policy changes). Coming in many cases earlier than in Africa, these must diminish the impact of the African changes, especially as the 1980s have also seen a sharp fall in net private investment flows to Latin America. Through signing

Table 12.1 *Inward stocks of foreign direct investment, 1975 and 1985*

Region				
Africa	16.5	26.8	22.3	14.0
Asia	13.0	21.4	49.6	31.2
Latin America & Caribbean	29.7	48.2	80.5	50.6
Other	2.3	3.7	6.6	4.2
Totals	61.5	100	159.0	100

Source: United Nations data.

Table 12.2 *Direct private investment as share of total net resource flows, 1980 to 1987*

	Direct investment (billions of dollars)	resource inflows (billions of dollars)	1980-82	1985-87
All developing countries	41.2	38.1	382.3	264.4
All low-income countries	5.8	5.8	109.0	137.3
Sub-Saharan Africa	5.0	1.3	50.4	56.2
Western Hemisphere	21.4	14.2	170.6	62.1
Asia	11.0	11.3	84.0	83.7

Source: OECD (1989), Table III.

agreements promoted by the United States Overseas Private Investment Corporation (OPIC), almost all African countries have participated in international investor insurance schemes. Fewer have joined organizations such as the recently formed Multilateral Investment Guarantee Agency (MIGA). OPIC is seen as a *sine qua non* for most US investors to look at all favorably at a country; it forms an important part of the perception potential investors have of African countries. Many African countries—a third of them between 1982 and 1987—have introduced (or changed) investment codes or guidelines for doing business, including speeding up decision making, often through one-stop investment centers. In January 1989 Nigeria changed its laws on foreign investment, reversing the indigenization decrees of 1972 and 1977. Foreigners can now own any enterprise, except banks, insurers, and petroleum exploration and mining companies. In April 1989 Zimbabwe launched new investment guidelines, while in July 1989 Kenya's Investment Promotion Center was overhauled. Even countries with a reputation for hostility to private foreign investors, such as Mozambique and Guinea, have introduced guarantees and opportunities for foreign investors. It is doubtful, however, whether these moves are enough for major inflows of new foreign investment.

Foreign investment in the 1990s

The prospects for Africa generally in the 1990s are probably as poor as they were in the 1980s, maybe poorer. There is little optimism that much higher real per capita income will be achieved, that the debt and foreign exchange crises will be eased, or that infrastructural problems of transport and communication (and the shortage of key skills) will be solved in the short term. There are opportunities in some mineral extraction and mineral and food processing and in some export-oriented manufacturing,

Table 12.3 *Cumulative Investment Flows, by Country of Investor, 1976 to 1986*

Country source	Investment in (millions of dollars)	Percentage (of total)
United States	2,297.0	27.4
United Kingdom	1,919.7	22.9
Japan	1,745.2	20.8
France	1,012.1	12.1
Belgium	645.2	7.7
Germany	369.5	4.4
Italy	296.5	3.5
Netherlands	105.1	1.2
World total	8,390.7	100.0

Source: OECD, derived from Githongo and others. (1988:75).

but in general, Africa is likely to be less attractive to foreign investors than Latin America and Asia. Prospects have also been affected by the single European market. There has been a significant increase in the flow of private investment to EC member states as companies jockey for position before 1992. There has been, and is likely to continue to be, an increase in investment in Europe by those currently trading with the EC. So, in the early 1990s especially, there is unlikely to be a major shift of attention to Africa by foreign investors.

Events in eastern Europe and the Soviet Union since mid-1989 and the new political orders emerging there will lead to the opening of at least the Polish, Hungarian, and Czechoslovakian economies. These changes, and the reunification of Germany, have not only raised the *prospect* for new private foreign investment inflow into these countries, but significant inflows are already occurring in Germany, Hungary, and Czechoslovakia, including investments from countries, such as India, which might be thought to look favorably on Africa. Such investment may intensify in the next few years, eclipsing the efforts of those trying to encourage private companies to invest in Africa. So too could the growing economic importance of east Asia. The US government reckons that East Asia will be the largest economic regional group by early in the 21st century, exceeding North America and the EC in market size. As a result, American and European companies especially have been focusing on trade and investment opportunities there—to the detriment of Africa—and will continue to do so as the 1990s unfold.

The recent World Bank report on Sub-Saharan Africa sends out two powerful messages. First, the rate of return on investment in Africa is low (indeed lower than the current U.S. prime rate, adjusted for inflation), having fallen steeply over almost 30 years (see figure 12.1). Second, that rate of return in the 1980s compares starkly with the high and growing rates on investments in South Asia.

A major impediment to increased foreign private investment in Africa is the low level of domestic saving and investment, best summed up by the vice-president of Equator Holdings, which operates in 20 African countries:

> The Africans keep talking about the need for a Marshall Plan for Africa or about the need for massive foreign private investment, and our feeling is that the rest of the world has pretty much abandoned Africa as an attractive place to invest. Conditions are going to have to change to the extent that indigenous Africans see business opportunities, take advantage of them, and demonstrate success. When they are given the scope in the economy to become productive, retain and reinvest the proceeds of their endeavours, that will attract the attention of the rest of the world. And to the extent that those opportunities are attractive, foreign investment will come in. But

until Africans themselves can generate some kind of positive results in Africa, the rest of the world is certainly not going to pay much attention there.

Figure 12.1 *Rates of Return on Investment Sub-Saharan Africa and South Asia, 1961-87*

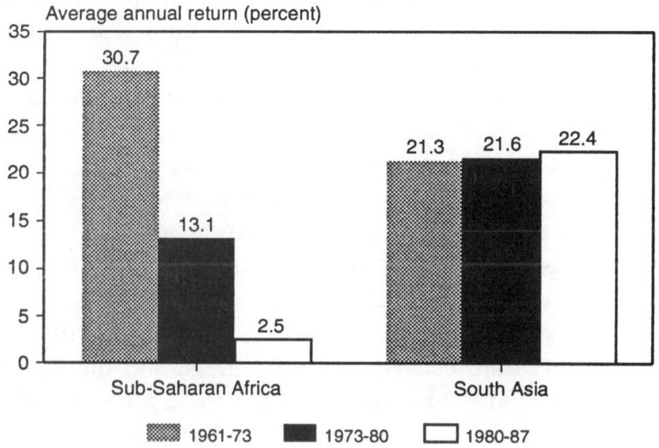

Source: World Bank (1989b:26).

The implications are grave. Aggregate direct foreign investment, if it rises at all in real terms, will not bridge the gap between foreign capital inflows and the shortfall in investment funds needed to raise economic growth rates. FDI as a share of total resource inflow will remain low (less than 5 percent) and play a minimal role in raising investment to GDP ratios in Africa. Even if African economies grow at higher rates in the 1990s, this is unlikely to boost new inflows of foreign investment. Africa has low levels of capital utilization, and higher growth will merely lead, for some considerable time, to higher levels of plant and machine use.

The subregion of Sub-Saharan Africa excludes South Africa because of abhorrence at apartheid and the nondemocratic political system. Yet not only has foreign investment played a big role in the South African economy, but its impact has been almost as important as for the whole of Africa. In 1985 the total stock of foreign private investment in South Africa was about $11 billion, compared with $23 billion for all Africa. And in 1965-74 the inflow of private investment to South Africa averaged $190 million a year.

Since the mid-1970s, however, there has been a net outflow of private capital, which accelerated from the mid-1980s largely because of disinvestment by United States corporations. From 1976 to 1988 there was a net outflow of $2.7 billion. This lack of investor confidence in the future of South Africa, together with trade and foreign financing restrictions, not only affected adversely the growth of its economy but rippled throughout the economies of the neighboring states of southern Africa, depressing their growth rates. What is more, most investors who withdrew from South Africa left the continent completely.

The release of Nelson Mandela, the unbanning of the African National Congress, the willingness of the South African government to talk about ending apartheid, and the discussions about a political system based on universal suffrage raise the possibility of a resolution to the South African conflict. This could have a major impact on the prospects for foreign investment not only in South Africa but the rest of Sub-Saharan Africa. Without being overly optimistic, a political settlement could:

- Provide the catalyst for investors to take an "upbeat" look at the continent.
- Halt private capital outflow and encourage new foreign inflows to South Africa.
- Higher growth rates for the South African economy. These would boost regional economic growth and so improve the climate for private investment in the Southern African Development Coordination Conference (SADCC) countries. If foreigners did increase investments in South Africa, there could be ripple effects in the rest of Africa because a South African economy more integrated with the rest of Africa would allow the exploitation of regional opportunities.

Improving the investment climate

It is widely assumed that Africa's future investment inflows will be related to incentives that influence the expected rate of return, the security of the investment, and ease if disinvestment. The tax regime, the investment code, and overall macroeconomic policies (including access to foreign exchange, domestic borrowing by foreign companies, price setting, and wages and employment regulations) are all central to the overall package. In most of Africa, much is changing to make it more favorable for new foreign investment inflow and the productive use of retained earnings of established foreign companies. These trends will continue at least in the first half of the 1990s. But that still leaves much to be done:

Lack of formal legislative provision for foreign investment. Some governments have still not published investment codes or have a clear-cut policy for foreign investment. In these few cases, foreign companies are reluctant to invest because of the greater likelihood that the rules for foreign investors will change. Concern about the absence of certain legislation is a frequent complaint of foreign investors: if legislation is changed, notice could be given and retro-active legislation avoided.

Lack of legal infrastructure. Some countries urgently need up-to-date company law. So, too, with traditional land tenure legislation, which can impede the exploiting of minerals and agriculture. Strong patent and copyright laws, race in Africa, should be introduced. Their absence is a deterrent to some investment, notably in pharmaceuticals and informatics, as well as to technology transfer.

Price controls lower all returns on investment and routine decisions require government intervention. Some countries also have inconsistent policies on prices. Together with restrictions on access to foreign exchange to purchase imported inputs, this has been one of the biggest obstacles to Japanese investment in Africa.

Labor legislation. Often seen mainly as a hurdle to the employment of expatriates, there are severe restrictions on hiring and firing of workers. These are serious because they are an operational restriction, because companies must deal with unfamiliar legislation, and because they reduce flexibility when demand changes and so increase risks.

Taxation policy appears most important when initial interest in investing is roused (and comparisons with other countries made) and before operating conditions become relevant. Comparisons raise the threshold of what companies expect. Only a few industrial countries give credit for tax not paid under dual taxation agreements (Germans and Belgium among the principal foreign investors), so concessions which may benefit local investors are often less valuable to foreigners, as well as being costly to governments. Concessions more favorable to foreigners are disliked, because of the potential for ill-feeling, either generally or by domestic investors.

Foreign exchange controls, particularly on profit remittances, normally mean that potential investors are unlikely to invest if companies cannot repatriate profits. Yet most of Africa (and many elsewhere in the world) have foreign exchange controls, even in the CFA franc zone. Exchange controls are especially influential if set with reference to the local currency value of the initial investment in a country with severe devaluations, or if they are part of tight restrictions on all outflows. Other problems include requirements that management and know-how fees be denominated in local currency, thus exposing investors to exchange rate fluctuations; pressures to register a corporate presence and so become liable for local corporation and turnover tax; ambiguous corporate tax codes and withholding taxes; high personal tax on expatriates or penalties on remittances.

Exchange rate. Most African countries outside the CFA franc zone devalued significantly in the late 1980s. As a result, the potential returns to investments that generate exports based on domestic resources have improved, including the crucial minerals sector. Where export-oriented projects depend upon imported inputs (such as yarn and, even, woven fabrics), however, increased input costs must be set against the anticipated rise in export values. For foreign investment in import-substituting industries, such as Nigerian textiles, devaluation can devastate an investor's portfolio. The long-run benefits—increased efficiency in the use of assets in the economy—are nebulous. Maintaining the exchange rate between the CFA franc and the French franc at 50:1 has made the CFA franc zone (covering 14 of 45 African countries) a crucial exception to the general pattern of depreciating currencies. With the exchange rate around this level, investors' existing portfolios in import-substituting industries in the CFA franc zone will maintain their value. But new investment in export-oriented industries will be minimal, even with a high domestic resource component.

Addressing these specific problems should improve the investment climate, but anticipated benefits from further "liberalization" are still unlikely to make a major and positive impact. Ironically, one of the (often powerful) attractions of Africa for foreign companies was the lack of competition. As monopoly or oligopolistic powers of potential investors are eroded, these will counterweight the investment-enhancing policies.

Other broader factors nevertheless influence the decisions to invest in Sub-Saharan Africa, which, if addressed, would contribute to a better climate for private foreign investment in the 1990s.

The media

Africa, more than any other developing region, suffers from a bad press. Look at a 1980s survey on U.S. perceptions on African investment:

> Respondents were asked how they obtained their information in making their risk assessments and investment decisions. By far the main source of information on Africa for the business community is the mass media, primarily the press. Since the American press selectively focuses on trouble spots, impres-

sions are more negative than positive. It is not unusual for executives considering investment decisions in Africa to be stopped dead in their tracks by a single unfavorable article. The chief executive officer of one American manufacturing company considering an investment in Zimbabwe reported, for example, that he had decided after reading two recent pieces in the press that the threat of civil conflict and a socialist ideology dissuaded him from further consideration of his project. He made no attempt to corroborate or probe impressions gained in the press, either through contacting US government agencies or sending a company representative to Zimbabwe to verify the judgement. Cited in (1983, pp. 50-51).

This suggests that even if the fundamental conditions for increased foreign investment are met, much time, money, and effort will be needed to counteract this prevalent view of Africa. One way is through past foreign investment ventures, *especially using successful foreign firms as advocates* among potential investors for investing in Sub-Saharan African. Some companies are keen to speak up. Listen to the senior vice-president of the U.S. Corporation, H.J. Heinz:

> Heinz must be prepared to develop an advocacy role for the developing country in which Heinz invests, to intercede on the country's behalf with the US Government and be prepared to put the country's best foot forward in order to attract potential investors among the developed nations. (Letter to one of the authors.)

And to the chairman of the UK's Cluff Resources: Africa is in many respects highly preferable to the more popular exploration areas of the world, such as North America and Australia. Not only is there less competition in Africa but doing business is actually easier than it is portrayed. Far from being bedeviled by bureaucratic obstacles, we find that African politicians and civil servants are more approachable, more practical and more reliable than their counterparts in Canada, the U.S. or Australia, for example. (*African Exchange Digest*, 11 December 1989).

Skill shortages

In many countries, these cover management and accountancy, but even in places like Nigeria, the shallow base of many technical skills leads to inefficiencies and low productivity, which deter foreign investors. They see a large gap between what Asia and Latin America and the average African country can offer in basic education and familiarity with equipment, let alone specific skills. Companies that invest in developed countries (or Latin America or Asia) do not have the wherewithal to deal with severe local skill shortages, and this influences their view of Africa.

There is little doubt that technical training and planned maintenance schemes have been a major factor in the advance, diversification, and competitiveness of manufacturing in Zimbabwe. Likewise, the lack of planned maintenance and shortages of engineers and technical staff in most African countries have held back potential foreign investment, especially in manufacturing. This inhibits opportunities in Africa for launching export-oriented enterprises to penetrate Europe (under Lomé) and the U.S. (under GSP preferences) and also halts the "spread" of foreign investment from sectors to which it is initially attracted.

Attempts to redress the skill shortage through the import of foreign workers are frustrated by restrictions and lengthy bureaucratic delays involved in obtaining work permits--a big problem for foreign investors, for example, in the advanced economies of Kenya, Nigeria, and Zimbabwe. Addressing these issues should be a priority for countries wishing to attract foreign investment.

Inadequacies of the domestic infrastructure

Poor roads, delays in goods shipments on the railways and at ports, faulty telephones, unreliable or unavailable telexes and telefax machines have led to low levels of efficiency in current productive investments and deterred all new investors. But they are likely to disproportionately affect foreign investors, who depend on them more than an "average" company.

So, if the state of (and investment in) infrastructure are poor, foreign investment inflow will be extremely limited. Where structural adjustment conditionality has led to a big contraction of public investment, private investment has already been adversely affected. But well-maintained and efficient infrastructure certainly helps attract potential investors.

Since some infrastructural investment is barred to private (and particularly foreign) investors, improvements and expansion will probably have to come through projects funded by external official assistance or through build-own-transfer techniques seen in some middle-income countries in the Near and Far

East.

Bureaucratic delays and lack of decisions

These often begin in obtaining the initial permission to invest, even when the foreign investment conforms in every way the investment code or guidelines. Delays can stretch into years. Thereafter, managers of foreign (and often domestic) investment projects face many administrative hurdles in running their companies, obtaining import and export licences, permission to hire and fire workers, approval to fix and raise prices.

Some obstruction, as in any country, may be deliberate, particularly when foreign investors try to obtain, say, a concession without formal requirement. But much delay is due to inexperience or red tape. This is particularly damaging to potential foreign investors who, being familiar with procedures in other countries, are more aware of it. They, too, have the choice of where to invest.

One-stop investment centers are helpful in addressing early delays, and more African countries need to introduce them. But the problem of bureaucratic delay is much wider. Unless further steps are taken, this will remain a major deterrent to future investment flows.

Country size and regional markets

Restricted purchasing power associated with the small markets in many African countries is a serious impediment to investment projects aimed exclusively at the domestic market or for export production that requires a strong domestic market base. But the problem goes deeper. The absolute level of profits will be small, and for a firm with limited managerial resources, the costs of gaining information may deter investment in most African countries.

Economic integration may be a key factor in boosting foreign investment. Yet, the reality is that change is distant. The institutional arrangements underlying closer integration--from the UDEAC to the Preferential Trade Area of Eastern and Southern Africa (PTA)--are frail and under financed, and the classic problem of generating benefits to economically weaker states from economic association are unsolved.

In West Africa the picture is particularly bleak. The two Francophone customs unions remain and continue to operate a common exchange rate with all other currencies. Trade with the Anglophone countries of the region is brisk but largely illegal. The Economic Community of West African states (ECOWAS) has attempted to operate a currency clearing system through the West African Clearing House (WACH), but this has been unable to finance the deficits of those countries with a continual trade imbalance (at least officially) with the group. Moreover, members have competitive incentive regimes toward FDI, even though this is against Articles 28-32 of the ECOWAS charter.

In the east and south, the creation of the Southern African Development Coordination Conference (SADCC) and the Preferential Trade Agreement (PTA) of Eastern and Southern Africa is encouraging, and SADCC seems to have stimulated some foreign investment in joint ventures. But problems remain, not least the shortage of trade finance and export credits without which regional trade is likely to grow.

Providing matching finance

Offshore finance. If outside "investors" bring in only token equity finance, this means that (to avoid unacceptable gearing) more must be raised on domestic capital markets. It also means that the aggregate level of investment will be helped if external development finance institutions (DFIs) can increase the equity proportion of project finance. Those DFIs based in the EC--such as the Commonwealth Development Corporation and the Caisse Centrale de Co-opération Economique--have a total stock of investments comprising both loans and equity of about ECU 4.5 billion. Yet the *equity accounts for roughly 4 percent (or ECU 165 million)*. These funds are mainly coinvested with private sector EC companies, and with investors in the host country, frequently parastatal organizations. The DFIs are often associated with projects in which the external private sector investor has a strong interest in the type and structure of the "NFI". (note - define NFI - - - -?

These agencies can play a major role as "facilitator" improving the investment climate for existing and potential private sector investors. Given investors' preference for NFI, high (and so unfavorable) loan-to-equity ratios should be avoided by increasing equity finance from "third parties" such as the FDIs and the IFC. As well as share capital, this should increasingly extend to "near-equity", such as preference shares, and to the underwriting of share and bond issues on African financial markets.

In other ways, too, DFIs should liberalize lending, if they are to continue to expand. Their support for a project is often conditional on a government guarantee of the repayment of principal and interest. Sometimes a supplier of NFI must have a minimum equity stake of 25 percent. And "concessions" granted to one equity holder have to be granted to all. Where a loan is made to a local finance house, the exchange risk is often passed on to the final borrowers, disastrous for the cash flow of many projects in the 1980s. Dealing with devaluation has led to schemes where the final borrower can take a high interest rate with no exchange risk, or a lower rate with the exchange risk. Without such options, the DFIs' ability to participate in financial packages in support of FDI may be limited. In fact, the decline in the projects financed by the IFC in 1988-89 partly reflects these problems.

Local finance. Many potential projects for DFI funding have a problem raising local currency finance to match offshore loan and equity capital. For the European Investment Bank's projects in the African Caribbean and Pacific (ACP) group from 1976-85, more than half the total finance had to be raised outside the host country.

Frequently restrictions are placed on borrowing locally, and foreigners may be prevented from buying into local companies, particularly serious for companies prevented from remitting abroad profits and dividends. Foreign ownership of land, or entry into some sectors, may also be restricted. Where restrictions are uncertain or changeable, such as Zambia, investors will be particularly discouraged.

The relative shortage of domestic capital for lending or investing long term is seldom due to the low time and savings deposits, but more often to the relative profitability of lending short term. In fact, time and savings deposits as a proportion of total deposits in Nigeria grew from 30 to 60 percent from 1960-88. In Zambia in 1988, such deposits accounted for 50 percent of all savings, and in Kenya for 65 percent. This high proportion of long-term saving is not just due to positive real interest rates, engineered as part of structural adjustment in the 1980s. In Kenya quantitative estimates suggest an interest rate elasticity of 0.6. In Nigeria, according to Gothongo (1988), "it is quite possible that saving is relatively interest-inelastic and that other factors — such as distance from and waiting time in banks—may be more powerful influences on saving."

Central banks have responded to the shortage of local capital for investment projects by laying down guidelines on the volume of banks' long-term loans. In Nigeria the target figure in 1988 was 50 percent, but the actual level was only 30 percent. But the crucial shortage is frequently risk (specifically equity) capital. Raising such capital does not depend on a stock exchange. It could be done by launching local investment trusts, whose shares could be bought by local insurance companies, pension funds, and grass roots savings groups, which often find it hard to re-invest deposits. Such trusts might also attract flight capital. Without such initiatives, mobilizing local financial resources to match offshore investment is unlikely.

A more active approach to investment promotion

All these proposals for change are based on two key assumptions. The first is perfect (or near-perfect) knowledge of investment opportunities in Africa, so that once enough restrictions are removed, investment will flow. The second is that there is a known group of "potential investors" for Sub-Saharan Africa to whom this knowledge is available.

These assumptions usually lead to the *passive approach to the promotion of foreign investment.* The passive approach is that it is enough to devise incentives (hopefully longer and better than one's neighbors') and list the areas of the economy or subsectors where foreign investment would be welcome and then to sit back and hope that new investment will flow. Often, host governments cobble together a shopping list of projects in which they would like foreign participation. One reason for this approach in Africa is that many governments are unclear about which areas of the economy they would like developed, by whom and which has priority. It also seems that international institutions (or at least consultants employed by them) have encouraged governments to adopt the passive approach.

An active approach to foreign investment is where governments seek out specifically targeted foreign investors, whom they want to invest in the development of a particular product or at least subsector. This approach is likely to be most effective — and to mean that the host government has decided on its future investment portfolio in detail and on areas where local investors will be involved and on where it needs foreign finance, technology, know-how, machinery, marketing skills, and contacts.

The next step in the active approach is for the host government to:

- Invite companies to examine the proposed project for which foreign participation is sought.

- Propose that they start the conditions under which they might participate.

All would be aware that other (rival) companies were being approached. Then begins the bargaining and negotiation, which hopefully will lead to firm proposals from one company being accepted.

The active and passive approaches should be complementary. General guidelines, the overall macroeconomic environment, and the streamlining of decision making are all necessary to investment strategy. But they are not enough. Nor is a combined active and passive approach. The combined approach nevertheless adds a major (active) bit to the package which is prevalent throughout most of Africa.

The active approach does not assume that potential investors have perfect knowledge of opportunities nor even knowledge that they are potential investors. A direct approach may be the catalyst for a company to begin to think about investing in Africa of greater importance to small countries ignored by the international news media or portrayed in a poor light.

Investment missions from industrial countries with a particular expertise can provide a stimulus to investment, and should be complementary to the passive/active approach. The US OPIC mission to southern Africa in April 1989 led to a joint venture with the Houston-based Interkiln for the manufacture and export of roofing tiles, bricks, and other clay products from Botswana.

Would the wider use of the active approach to foreign investment succeed? The evidence, albeit limited, is encouraging.

- The textile plant privatization in Togo was concluded in February 1987 only after the government had considered 11 competitive bids from investors as far afield as India, Western Europe, and the United States.
- Bridge Oil of Australia became involved in Guinea following an approach to a Swiss banker in 1981 by the Guinean government looking for a joint-venture partner The Swiss banker was a friend of the chairman of Bridge Oil. As a result, Bridge Oil did a feasibility study and "the more it looked at the prospect, the more it felt it should be involved."
- Botswana has declared Selibe Phikwe a special investment zone where a 20-year tax holiday is open to companies willing to invest. The government is sending out special missions to East Asia to sell the idea, targeting textile manufacturers, with the additional carrot of preferential terms of entry to the EC under the Lomé Convention. A mission to Hong Kong, hopes to lure companies considering uprooting from the colony.

Conclusions

Foreign investment will be needed increasingly in Africa in the 1990s to raise the supply of foreign exchange and boost investment levels. Continuing high foreign debt repayments, poor prospects for primary commodity prices in the first half of the 1990s for most of Africa, and low inflows of official development assistance mean that the foreign exchange gap, which widened in the 1980s, will continue to restrain economic growth. Together with other macro-economic influences, this will dampen domestic savings, crucially necessary for boosting the dangerously low levels of domestic investment Both the foreign exchange gap and the savings gap could be partly filled by increased flows of foreign investment

Foreign investment inflow in the 1990s (as in the 1980s) will be in key sectors such as energy and certain minerals, but also some export manufacturing, a new phenomenon and one that will depend much on gaining privileged access to large markets outside Africa. All opportunities should be taken and exploited by a more aggressive and project-specific marketing technique to potential investors. Least attractive for foreign investors in the 1990s will be exclusively import-substituting industries.

There is, however, no realistic prospect for flows of foreign investment to bridge either the foreign exchange or domestic savings gaps. Indeed, despite policies more liberal to foreign investment inflows dismal 1980s. In part, this is based on external factors--prospects in other parts of the world look brighter and less risky and are closer to home. In part, too, the conclusion is based on the *Catch-22* of the 1980s. Potential investors are unlikely to commit pots of money to Sub-Saharan Africa unless and until the prospects for growth improve, but that will not happen until countries succeed in attracting greater amounts of both public and private foreign capital.

References

Baker, P H. 1983. *Obstacles to Private Sector Activities in Africa*. Washington, D.C.: Batelle Memorial Institute.

Bennell, P. 1990. "British Industrial Investment in sub-Saharan Africa: Corporate Responses to Economic Crisis in the 1980s." *Development*

Policy Review, Vol. 8, No. 2.

Cable, V. and B.Persaud, eds. 1987. *Developing with Foreign Investment*. London: Croom Helm and the Commonwealth Secretariat.

Cockcroft, L. 1989. "The Past Record and Future Potential of Foreign Investment." Paper presented to Queen Elizabeth House and Overseas Development Institute, Workshop on Alternative Development Strategies in Africa. Oxford. 1990. *Africa's Way: A Journey from the Past*. London: IB Tauris.

Dunning, J. H., and J. A. Cantwell, 1987. *The Directory of Statistics of International Investment and Production*. London: Macmillan.

Githongo, J. M. and others. 1988. *Investment in the ACP States and Related Financial Flows*. Report by a group of EEC and ACP experts. Brussels, Nairobi and Nice.

International Finance Corporation. 1989 and 1990. Annual Report. Washington, D.C.

Organisation for Economic Co-operation and Development. 1989. *Financing and External Debt of Developing Countries*. Paris.

Page S. B., and R. C. Riddell (1988) "Opportunities for and Impediments to Foreign Direct Investment in Africa." Report prepared for the United Nations Centre for Transnational Corporations. London: Overseas Development Institute. (mimeo)

Riddell R. C., and associates. 1990. *Manufacturing Africa: Performance and Prospects of Seven Countries in Sub-Saharan Africa*. London and New York: James Currey and Heinemann.

United Nations. 1988. "Critical Economic Situation in Africa: U.N. Programme of Action for African Economic Recovery and Development 1986-1990." *Midterm review of the implementation of the United Nations Programme of Action for African Economic Recovery and Development* 1986-1990, Report of the Secretary General Addendum: Investment of transnational corporations in Africa. New York: UN General Assembly, A/43/500/Add2.

U.S. Department of Commerce. 1986. *Direct Investment Update: Trends in International Direct Investment*. Washington, D.C.: International Trade Administration.

World Bank 1989. *Zimbabwe: Private Investment and Government Policy*. Washington, D.C.

Comment

Marcel Yondo

The paper gives an updated situation of FDI during the 1980s and a good overview of the FDI in the 1990s. This useful contribution merits congratulations. My comments on this issue are the following:

Can we have confidence in the FDI figures in the paper? The question is raised because of lack of economic information on the region. These countries experience difficulties in collecting and keeping statistics. The authors have faced these difficulties because the paper deals with problems of different FDI information from one source to another. For example, it says that the World Bank data are different from the OECDs. The OECD data show far more volatility than World Bank's; and only in three out of a possible nine years are the figures at all similar. In 1982 they differ fourfold. In most years since 1980, some sources show a rise in the flow of FDI while others show a fall. Accordingly, we should be very careful in using the paper's data.

As far as the method is concerned, the use of individual examples against trends. The case studies of Nigeria Textile Industry and some particular sectors give details we couldn't have gotten through trends. So, when trends show a fall of FDI during the 1980s, the case studies show increase in some sectors like agriculture, mines, energy, and tourism.

As a matter of fact, FDI in Sub-Saharan Africa decreased by about 12.5 percent in the 1975-85 period while during the same period the FDI in Asia and in Latin America and the Caribbean increased respectively by 10.8 percent and 2.4 percent. Do we accept the paper's reasons for this fall?

The first reason according to the paper is the lower return on investments in Sub-Saharan Africa. The return on investments in this area fell to 2.5 percent in the period 1980-87—from 30.7 percent in 1961-63—while in South Asia it increased to 22.4 percent from 21.3 percent during the same period. The second reason concerns the structural adjustment programs, adopted in Africa during the 1980s to help economic recovery; but according to the paper, some of their conditions have negative effects on FDI in short and medium terms; in the long-term, the paper contends, the program will have positive effects on FDI. The third reason is the small size of African markets and the failure of African economic unions.

Evidently, the lower returns on investments in Sub-Saharan discourage FDI. The effects of structural adjustment programs on FDI need more attention. The programs put in place in the 1980s have generated some interest in the international private sector in short-term trading, which take advantage of the relative freeing of the market in foreign exchange. But it is also sure that these programs have revealed little enthusiasm to make new investments or expanding existing operations. It is worth saying that the paper doesn't say how long the structural adjustment program must last before having positive effects on FDI. Furthermore, we agree that the size of the African markets has negative effects on FDI. But why in the 1970s, when African markets were smaller than in the 1980s, did FDI increase? In the 1970s the size of the theoretical average African Republic was 2.5 million inhabitants; in the 1980s it as about 4.5 million inhabitants, furthermore the per capita income of some countries was lower in the 1970s.

My opinion is that the paper does not develop enough—or not at all—the following main reasons about the fall of FDI in the 1980s.

- Africa has always been an area of minimal interest for foreign investors but it has become more marginal in the 1980s because of the importance of the perceived political and economic environment risks.
- These risks have created and expanded a lack of confidence in African elites, who started transferring large flows of money outside Sub-Saharan Africa.
- The economic crisis of Africa in the 1980s has also discouraged old and new investors. The deep crisis has reduced dramatically the purchasing power of individuals and governments. The African states were suffering from lack of liquidity and could not pay debts to creditors. A lot of companies were sold off. We noticed many disinvestments and a lack of new investments opportunities. Evidently, this is one of many reasons why the United Kingdom and France decreased or halted their FDI in Africa.

How could Sub-Saharan Africa again attract new money? According to the paper, the few new investors in the region prefer management agreements, patent and technology licensing agreements, production sharing contracts, and international subcontracting. This is one of the important issues we should take into account to attract FDI in SSA.

The paper gives too little importance to the big changes happening in the world. The Eastern European countries have rejected communism; they are opening their economies to foreign investments. The Soviet Union is doing the same thing. The German reunification and the new situation of the European Economic Community in 1992 will increase investment opportunities in Europe instead of Africa. Accordingly, Africa must do more to attract new FDI.

The prospects of FDI in the 1990s are not good despite a positive approach to attract investments. In the 1980s African countries have taken the following measures to attract investments: tax holidays for 10 years or more, new investment codes and one-stop investment centers to cancel bureaucratic delays. These measures didn't succeed in attracting more investors. The positive approach won't do better. Nevertheless, if to these measures and a positive approach were added the solution of the political instability and the economic recovery, African countries will improve their image and attract more FDI. Evidently, the political reforms will bring African elites to believe in their own economies and stop transferring money out of the continent.

We are not sure, as the paper says, that the sectors which benefited from direct investments during the 1980s will continue to do the same during the 1990s. The oil sector may continue to benefit because of the Iraqi crisis. Sub-Saharan Africa may attract oil investors. But the agricultural sector, especially some commodity branches will suffer from continued decrease of prices and high costs of production. According to the structural adjustment program, subsidies to the agriculture have been abolished. The costs of fertilizers increase while prices decrease. Furthermore, African governments are encouraging food crops that generally do not attract FDI.

In conclusion, this good paper raises exciting issues whose solutions are necessary to attract FDI. But it must emphasize the political reforms and the economic recovery. Investments are very sensitive to political instability. The economic recovery will create new investment opportunities useful to attract FDI. Debt relief and a great flow and better use of foreign aid will help this economic recovery.

Risk Management in Sub-Saharan Africa

Stijn Claessens and Ying Qian

Sub-Saharan Africa is vulnerable to commodity price, exchange rate, and interest rate uncertainty, but commodity price risk is the most significant, given the large share of primary commodities in total exports and of essential foods in their imports.

Commodity exposures

Exports of most African countries are concentrated in 10 primary commodities—coffee, cocoa, copper, cotton, fish, iron ore, tea, timber, tobacco, and crude oil and petroleum products, which accounted for roughly 75 percent of Sub-Saharan Africa's total exports in 1988. Among 35 African countries in 1984-85, these 10 commodities accounted for more than 80 percent of total exports in eight countries, more than 60 percent in 19 countries, and more than 40 percent in 25. The share of the single largest commodity exceeded 50 percent in 12 countries and exceeded 30 percent in 24 of the 35 (table 13.1).

Table 13.1 ***Commodity export concentration in SSA, 1984-85***

Share of total exports(%)	Numbers of countries: 10 key commodities	Leading commodity
90	3	2
80	8	5
70	15	1
60	19	3
50	2	1
40	5	6
30	28	6

Source: World Bank.

This high degree of commodity dependence continues into the 1990s for most African countries. For some, the concentration of exports in the leading commodity increased in the 1980s, as production of secondary commodities fell due to increased competition from other regions, falling prices, and domestically caused disincentives. A few, such as Kenya, have diversified commodity exports but remain heavily dependent on primary products. Successful efforts to diversify into intermediate and final export products have been few (Mauritius).

Primary commodity prices are the most volatile. During the past decade, the annual volatility of an index of nominal prices for 33 primary commodities prices has been more than 20 percent. The annualized standard deviation of the monthly price changes during the previous 24 months has reached 55 percent and in recent years has not been below 20 percent. Some commodities have seen not only large but rapid price changes. Coffee, for example, fell by a third in the last three months of 1987 and again by 45 percent in April-August, 1989. Because all commodity prices move in much the same way, exporting several commodities is not an effective diversification strategy.

In the 1980s the trend underlying volatile price swings has been down. A price index for 33 primary, non-oil commodities has declined by 33 percent in real terms since 1980, and is now at its lowest level since World War II (figure 13.1). Beverage commodities, especially, have seen a sharp decline in prices. Real crude oil prices fell by 60 percent in 1980-89, reaching their lowest level since 1973 and some international price stabilization schemes have collapsed (tin, coffee, and cocoa).

While export prices for African countries fell, their import bills rose considerably, partly because of worldwide increase in prices, but also due to factors peculiar to Africa (their relatively small markets and limited access to competitive suppliers) which increased import prices relative to the world average. Africa's terms of trade in 1989 were roughly 25 percent below 1980, implying a big income loss. A few countries saw a terms-of-trade gain in the 1980s, but most earned less foreign exchange in real terms from exports in 1989 than in 1980, despite export volume increases (figure 13.2).

It is unlikely that Africa will reduce its reliance on primary commodity exports in the near future. In the longer term, if competitive exchange rates are adopted and the antiexport bias of current protectionist policies is softened, the volatility of export earnings will be reduced.

Figure 13.1 ***Indices of Volatility and Real Price***

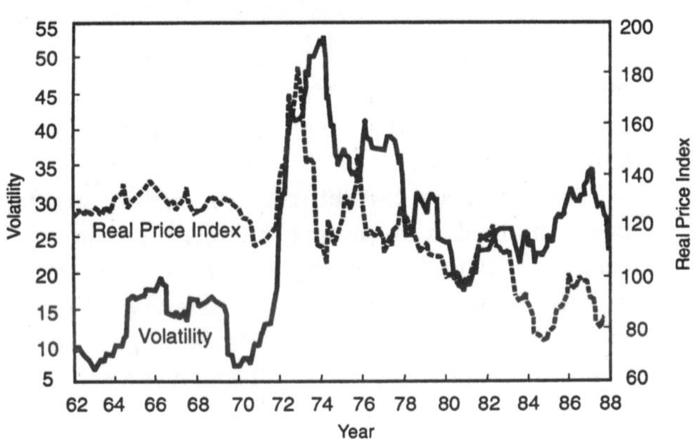

Figure 13.2 ***SSA Exports and Imports Trends***

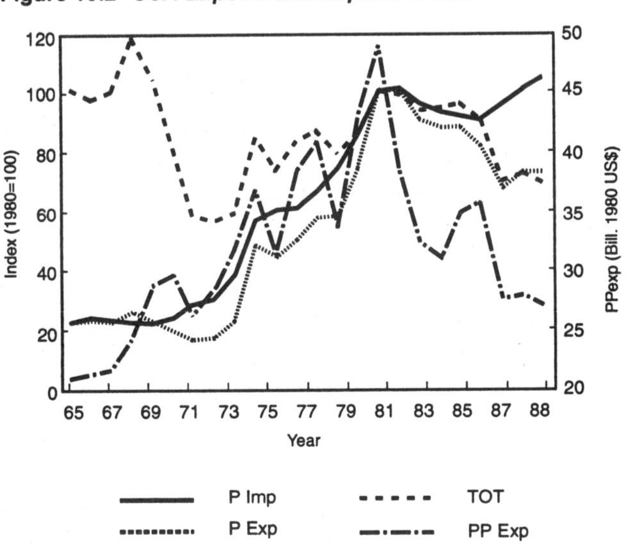

The World Bank reckons that none of the 10 commodities most important among Africa's exports will see a significant increase in real price in the 1990s, and some may decline significantly. Import prices for Africa will probably increase by at least as much as the price index of developed countries' manufactures exports (and likely more), leading to a small improvement (or deterioration) in terms of trade. In any case, primary commodity prices will remain volatile in the 1990s and for many African countries, export revenues will still be uncertain in nominal and real terms.

Currency and interest rate exposures

Many African countries also have external debt that exposes them to other risks: interest rates and cross-currency exchange rates (table 13.2). Of the external debt of Sub-Saharan Africa, 33 percent is variable rate (either debt indexed to a floating rate, or short-term debt rolled over). This is well below the variable-rate share for all developing nations but still exposes African countries to changes in international interest rates, which have been highly volatile over the past decades.

Currency risk arises because the external debt of Africa is denominated in several hard currencies. Roughly 40 percent of medium- and long-term debt is in U.S. dollars, 14 percent in French francs, 8 percent in yen, and 43 percent in other currencies (table 13.3). This implies that Africa's debt service will be affected by movements in cross-currency rates between these hard currencies. For instance, the depreciation of the dollar in 1985-88 increased the dollar debt service of Africa by around 7 percent annually, compared to cross-currency rates that remained at their end-1985 level (table 13.2). Measured in non-U.S. dollar currencies (such as French francs) the debt stock has decreased since 1985 due to the appreciation of these currencies.

Table 13.2 ***Debt outstanding and disbursed (DOD), net flows, and currency valuation effects***

Year	*DOD* (billions)	*Net flows* (billions)	*Current value* (billions)	*Current value* (percent)
1982	70.3	10.2	-2.3	-3.3
1983	79.3	7.9	-3.1	-3.9
1984	82.7	5.3	-3.6	-4.4
1985	96.0	2.7	6.2	6.5
1986	112.7	5.9	6.7	5.9
1987	137.7	6.8	10.8	7.8
1988	139.5	4.2	-6.0	-4.3
1989	148.5	4.1	n.a.	n.a.

Source: World Bank.

Table 13.3 ***Currency composition of Sub-Saharan Africa's debt, 1988***
(percentages)

	U.S. dollar	*French franc*	*Yen*	*Swiss franc*	*Mix*	*Deutsche-mark*	*Other*
Medium-and long-term outstanding and disbursed including IBRD loans	38.3	13.8	4.2	2.5	11.0	7.1	23.1
Medium-and long-term outstanding and disbursed including IBRD loans	40.5	13.8	7.7	4.5	n.a.	8.9	24.6
Disbursements, public and publicly guaranteed including IBRD loans	37.8	15.2	3.8	0.2	10.5	3.8	28.7
Disbursements, public and publicly guaranteed including IBRD loans	39.9	15.2	7.2	2.1	n.a.	5.5	30.1

Note: IBRD loans about one-third dollar and two-third non-dollar.
Source: World Bank.

The volatility of nominal (and real) cross-currency exchange rates has been high in the 1980s, with the annual standard deviation of the nominal and real effective U.S. dollar rate being above 20 percent. The fluctuations in debt stocks and debt service (measured in U.S. dollars or any hard currency) are likely to continue, given that the share of non-U.S. dollar currencies in Africa's debt and in new borrowings remains high (table 13.3) and that cross-currency exchange rates will remain volatile. The composition of funds borrowed in 1988 is similar to that of existing debt stock—U.S. dollar liabilities, 40.5 percent and 39.9 percent respectively, and non-dollar liabilities, 59.5 percent and 60.1 percent—implying that the dollar value of debt will continue to fluctuate as currencies fluctuate.

Debt service changes (because of interest and currency fluctuations) could have affected African economies if they were not offset by changes in net hard currencies export earnings and so the capacity to service debt.

Impact of exposures

Because of Africa's dependence on volatile primary commodities exports and the interest and currency composition of its external debt, income and consumption are highly variable. This lowers welfare. It also complicates government and private sector planning and investment and likely leads to lower (private) investment and output in the long run. It may also lead to Dutch (or Nigerian) disease, whose symptoms are high external prices for major exports, resulting in other exports becoming uncompetitive or unprofitable following appreciation of the real exchange rate and other distortions as a result of the commodity boom.

Does Africa's current external liability structure mean optimal risk-sharing between creditor and debtor countries? Or is there a better structure that benefits both parties? *Ex post*, external shocks on ability to service external debts have been shared between creditor and debtor, through reschedulings, debt write-offs, and internal and external adjustment. This has resulted in much lower growth rates and lost output which could have been avoided through a better *ex ante* structuring of the country's external debt structure.

Concept for measuring risks

Exposures cannot be measured by contractual (accounting) concepts alone. Commodity price risks can be offset by quantity risks. In the case of a net commodity exporter, if the price elasticity of demand is different from zero, quantity changes will offset the effect of price changes on earnings. The net exposure to commodity price risks would then be less than the nominal value exported. In the extreme case—when the price elasticity is -1—revenues would be independent of price movements as quantity movements will perfectly offset price movements, and there would be no need to hedge against price movements. Figure 13.2 shows this relationship: the dollar value of exports for Africa behaves differently from the price index of exports.

In the finance literature, measurement of risk has been in mainstream thinking since the capital asset pricing model (CAPM) was developed in the early 1960s. The CAPM maintains that the risk of holding a single asset (or income stream) needs to be defined with respect to a measure of aggregate risk, such as holding a diversified portfolio of assets. Risks that are diversifiable do not receive any higher expected return (risk premium); non-diversifiable (systematic) risks do. For a country receiving an income stream through (net) exports, this implies two things. Risks arising from commodity price and interest and exchange rate movements need to be defined in an integrated fashion and relative to the country's aggregate economic risks. Also, diversifiable risks in the world capital markets need not be carried by the country, and, if they are, will not receive a higher rate of return.

Both have big implications not only for measuring commodity price risks, where quantity movements can be important, but also for measuring interest and currency price risks. Changes in debt service (resulting from interest and exchange rate movements) only represent a change in the country's burden—i.e., "risk"—in that debt-service capacity does not move commensurately.

Africa's ability to generate foreign exchange, which determines the true burden of exchange rate changes on debt service, depends on the relationship between primary commodity prices and the value of the dollar. In general, commodity prices move inversely with the value of the dollar: when its value increases, value commodity prices tend to decline, and vice-versa. This manifests itself over long cycles, not shorter periods.

In 1974-89 changes in nominal cocoa, coffee, cotton, copper, and sugar prices had a negative relationship with changes in the index of the nominal effective U.S. dollar exchange rate. This could imply that a combination of primary commodity exports and nondollar debts may have benefits, since when debt service payments go up due to dollar depreciation, primary commodity export revenues (in dollars) are likely to go up too. And vice-versa.

Measures, such as exports, are nominal and need to be translated into real terms through, say, the concept of the purchasing power of exports—the nominal value of exports divided by import prices. Similarly, normal debt service payments can be adjusted for price movements.

All this means that a country's exposure to commodity prices, interest rates, and exchanges rates is different from what contractual and nominal measures, such as exports and debt service due, would indicate. Trying to manage these risks on contractual values could only be misleading.

Practical models for risk measurement

Some models to determine real exposures have been applied to Turkey, Indonesia, Mexico, Brazil, Costa Rica, Algeria and Papua New Guinea. The results indicated that there are some offsetting effects between commodity price, quantity, import price, and exchange rate movements. For most, however, these were small, and effective exposures largely coincided with nominal measures.

In determining a country's optimal liability structure, external risks should be measured and managed with respect to net liabilities—ie, external liabilities minus all external assets, such as foreign exchange reserves. Also, management of (net) external liabilities has to bc donc by a tradeoff between the expected effective cost of a financial instrument and the uncertainty of its effective cost (where both cost and uncertainty have to be measured in relation to the economy's ability to pay). This is just another way of saying that the optimal external liability structure has both a speculative and a hedging component. The speculative bit depends partly on the expected costs of the different liabilities. Even though costs of different liabilities will vary, these will not be significant enough to justify speculative positions. For instance, the expected costs of borrowing in different currencies will not differ much, since movements in cross-currency exchange rates can be expected to compensate for nominal interest differentials. Similarly for other liabilities. The result of equal expected borrowing costs is that the speculative portfolio disappears, leaving the hedging portfolio. This is based on risk minimization.

Africa can benefit greatly from improving its liability structure, and there are a number of financial hedging instruments in developed countries' financial markets to manage risk.

Sub-Saharan Africa's optimal liability structure can be approached from the economy as a whole and the government's budget alone. Each can be based on historical data and on a sensitivity analysis of expected future flows (ie, four analyses). But the approach here (see annex 1) is an empirical analysis only on historical data, using the model by Myers and Thompson (1989). This implies that the optimal liability portfolio will be the hedging portfolio, the one that minimizes the impact on Africa from external factors. The inputs are total exports earnings, the commodity prices for which financial hedging instruments exist, population numbers, and import prices. Since commodity risk is the most important, only commodity-price bonds and general obligation dollar loans are included. Population

Table 13.4 ***Optimal portfolios: hedging exports (as a proportion)***

r	*Cocoa*	*Coffee*	*Cotton*	*Copper*	*Oil*	*Total*	*General obligation debt*
3%	14.22	5.66	14.87	36.23	6.20	77.18	22.82
5%	11.63	4.83	18.93	30.84	4.57	70.81	29.19
7%	9.57	3.94	21.65	25.99	3.39	64.54	35.46
9%	8.15	2.70	23.45	21.61	2.52	58.42	41.58

Source: World Bank estimates.

numbers are used to scale data and import prices to calculate terms of trade for each commodity.

The model was run using annual data from 1965 to 1988 for the five commodities—coffee, cocoa, copper, cotton and crude oil—which accounted for more than 70 percent of Africa's total exports in 1980-88. The model calculated the dollar amount to be borrowed in each of five different commodity-linked bonds, assuming different real interest (table 13.4). The optimal portfolios in 1988 should have contained about 70 percent commodity-linked bonds. It also shows that an optimal liability portfolio would include about 30 percent of copper liabilities in its debt portfolio, corresponding to an average 11 percent of copper exports in total exports in 1965-88. The shares for the nonmineral commodities (coffee, cocoa, and cotton) may have to be treated cautiously. Africa exports some products whose prices tend to follow these commodities (tea and, in general, agricultural products). So, including these liabilities shows that instruments whose servicing obligations are linked to these commodities also hedge against other commodities whose prices are correlated.

The optimal portfolios depend on the assumed real interest rate. The proportion of the commodity bonds decreases as real interest increases, and the share of four out of five declines when real interest rises. The main reason for this is that higher real interest implies higher servicing cost, so reducing demand to borrow and lowering the dollar amount of the bonds.

Since the total amount of debt is not changed, the commodity-linked bonds shares decline as real interest goes up. This also implies that the hedging effectiveness of commodity bonds is reversely related to real interest rates. This is clear from table 13.5 showing the absolute amounts to be borrowed per capita in each commodity bond. The total external debt per capita of Africa in 1988 was $291.50.

The optimal risk reduction using commodity-price-linked bonds can be significant (table 13.6): a variance of about 90 percent is achieved.

The effectiveness of the optimal commodity-bond portfolio as a hedge against relative price (terms of

Table 13.5 ***Optimal portfolios: hedging exports (as an absolute dollar amount per capita)***

r	*Cocoa*	*Coffee*	*Cotton*	*Copper*	*Oil*	*Total*
1%	50.16	19.49	26.69	122.24	24.67	243.25
3%	41.45	16.51	43.35	105.60	18.08	224.99
5%	33.91	14.08	55.19	89.91	13.32	206.41
%	27.91	11.48	63.10	75.75	9.88	188.12
9%	23.75	7.86	68.36	62.99	7.34	170.30

Source: World Bank estimates.

Table 13.6 ***Risk reduction benefits (variances)***

r	*Without hedging*	*With hedging*	*Risk reduction*	*Risk reduction as a percentage*
1%	750.18	52.12	698.07	93.1
2%	627.24	57.28	569.95	90.9
5%	548.99	60.36	488.63	89.0
7%	499.51	61.77	437.74	87.6
9%	469.89	62.11	407.78	86.8

Source: World Bank estimates.

trade) changes depending on the commodity-price linked bonds used. The portfolios were reestimated with four, instead of five, bonds. This showed that the cocoa and cotton-price-linked bonds are the most effective. Without them, the risk reduction of the optimal portfolio falls to about 65 percent.

Surprisingly, the total dollar amount to be borrowed in commodity bonds increases when cocoa is dropped, because the dollar amount of the copper bond increases. When cotton is dropped, the amount borrowed in bonds drops. The other three commodities are less effective hedges since the risk reduction of the portfolio remains about the same (90 percent) when any is dropped.

A problem with estimating the optimal liability portfolios is stability. Estimates can change from period to period, which reduces their effectiveness.

Table 13.7 *Optimal portfolios: hedging exports*

r	Cocoa	Coffee	Cotton	Copper	Oil	Total	General obligation debt
1965-1982							
Dollars	9.66	17.95	44.71	11.37	54.69	138.35	55.25
Percentage	5.00	9.26	23.09	5.87	28.26	71.46	28.54
1965-1988							
Dollars	33.91	14.08	55.19	89.91	13.32	206.41	85.09
Percentage	11.63	4.83	18.93	30.84	4.57	70.81	29.19

Source: World Bank estimates.

So the optimal portfolio shares were calculated for a subperiod, 1965 to 1982 (table 13.7). Using a real interest rate of 5 percent, the (real 1980) dollar amounts to be borrowed in coffee and cotton commodity bounds for 1965-82 are similar to those for 1965-88. The big changes—for copper, oil bonds, and cocoa bonds—are largely due to differences in expected future prices. For example, the real oil price expected for the next year is almost twice as high in 1982 as in 1988. Changes in expected prices influence the optimal portfolio, and since those changes were the largest for oil, copper and cocoa, the borrowings in these bonds were most affected.

The percentage to be borrowed in general obligation debt was, at 30 percent, the same for both periods. The relative risk reduction was still high and similar to that for 1965-88 (85 percent), which shows that a portfolio of commodity bonds can mean high risk reduction (although rebalancing from year to year may make it too costly to aim for the highest degree of reduction).

Economy versus government exposures

The economy's exposure to international price changes will differ from the government budget's exposure when movements in export earnings are not one-to-one translated into changes in government revenues. For instance, many African taxes (direct and indirect) do not depend proportionally on commodity prices but are likely progressive. Taxes on export companies' income are likely progressive, while earnings of state enterprises will not depend in a proportional manner on commodity prices. The impact of price fluctuations on government revenues may be mitigated by stabilization schemes, as long as these involve external liabilities or assets.

No attempt has been made to estimate the optimal portfolios for hedging the government budget—given the incompatibility of various definitions of government revenues and expenditures. But the difference in government and economy exposure should be kept in mind when interpreting the results and designing for individual countries.

Future exposure

Future exposures to international prices will differ from the historic and current, as the composition and level of exports or imports change. For the future exposure of an individual country to international price movements, sensitivity analyses can be performed on projections for balance of payments and government finances. Deviations in forecasts for balance-of-payments and government budget from a baseline for alternative commodity or goods prices and interest and exchange rates (compared to base case prices) can then indicate the sensitivity of the economy and budget to different external shocks and, so, the optimal portfolios.

Implications and conclusions

The matching up of the external exposures of Africa with the different type of external liability instruments available indicates that the region could improve its liability structure significantly. Africa could achieve a big reduction in the uncertainty about resources available for imports after debt service, especially by using commodity-price-linked instruments. Sovereign risk factors will impose constraints on their type and the amount of risk sharing feasible between Africa and its creditors.

However, sovereign risks do not rule out all financial risk management instruments, and those can be made available to Africa through, say, collateral and marked-to-market mechanisms. The extensive use of long-dated currency, interest-rate, and commodity-price risk management tools by firms in developed countries suggests that credit risks can be overcome.

Most important, there is scope for the intervention of international official institutions and governments of developed countries to encourage the use of these instruments—providing technical assistance on the use of hedging instruments; direct intermediation of (and providing guarantees for) financial instruments such as commodity-price-linked instruments; facilitating technical solutions to problems associated with marked-to-market (commodity) swaps; providing a regulatory and accounting framework for these instruments in developed countries; and encouraging structural changes in the developing countries which will better allow for the use of such instruments. There is a big opportunity in restructuring the external debt of many developing countries, providing for changes in contractual terms and in ownership of claims, which could include more risk-sharing. But since there is a free-rider problem (introducing more risk-sharing by one creditor generates benefit to all creditors), public intervention may be necessary.

Annex

Estimation of the optimal hedging portfolio starts with a vector auto regressive (VAR) process, which helps to predict the future export revenues and commodity prices. More important, the VAR process generates the conditional covariance matrix, from which the theoretical optimal hedging portfolio can be derived. The stationarity of variables used in the model was investigated before the estimation was made. According to results of a set of standard unit root tests, the unit root hypothesis was rejected for all variables used in the model, including export earnings, and commodity prices for cocoa, coffee, cotton, copper and crude oil. Annex table 13.1 presents statistics from stationarity tests without time trend. As confirmed by the Durbin-Watson (CRDW) test statistics, export earnings, prices of cocoa, coffee, and cotton are stationary at a 95 percent significant level. The stationarity of the coffee price is confirmed by the Augmented Dickey Fuller (ADF) test at a 95 percent significance level. When a time trend is added (as in Annex table 13.2), all variables are validated to be stationary according to the CRDW test at a 95 percent significance level, and prices of cocoa, coffee and cotton are stationary at the same level according to the Dickey-Fuller (DF) or ADF tests.

Before the unrestricted VAR specification was finalized, the SAS stepwise procedures were applied to search for the best fitted model, with the most significant variables and lag structures. Annex table 13.3 defines the variable names used in the model. Annex table 13.4 presents the VAR model in its reduced form.

The seemingly uncorrelated regression technique (SUR) was applied to estimate the VAR system. It was used given that the maximum likelihood estimation method is not available in Africa. The coefficient matrix A(L) defined by the VAR process, and the conditional covariance matrix derived from the VAR residuals, are then used to determine the optimal portfolio.

Annex table 13.5 presents two covariance matrices for variables in the model. The first is the simple unconditional covariance matrix before the VAR process. The second is derived from residuals of those variables after the VAR process, which represents the conditional covariance matrix, because any systematic inter-relationship among variables has been filtered out. What has been left over in the matrix after the VAR process are the truly stochastic errors (according to the data then). The optimal portfolio of commodity-linked bonds is now determined by the conditional covariance matrix of prices and real export earnings multiplied by the inverse of the conditional covariance matrix of commodity prices.

Annex table 13.1 *Stationary/unit root tests for export earnings and commodity prices (without time trend), 1965-88 (annual)*

Series	*CRDW Crit. Val (95% 0.386)*	*DF Crit. Val (95% 3.37)*	*ADF Crit. Val (95% 3.17)*	*Lags (ADF)*	*F(3,20) Crit. Val (95% 8.66)*
Export	0.535*	1.370	1.231	1	0.845
Cocoa	0.731*	2.199	3.057	1	0.072
Coffee	1.138*	2.892	3.227*	1	0.024
Cotton	0.465*	1.453	0.839	1	2.323
Copper	0.199	1.556	2.897	4	1.180
Crude oil	0.233	1.373	1.556	4	0.123

95% significance level.

Annex table 13.2 ***Stationarity/unit root tests for export earnings and commodity prices (with time trend), 1965-88 (annual)***

Series	*CRDW Crit. Val 95% 0.386*	*DF Crit. Val 95% 3.37*	*ADF Crit. Val 95% 3.17*	*Lags (ADF)*	*F(3,20) Crit. Val 95% 8.66*
Export	0.598*	1.757	1.630	1	1.110
Cocoa	0.750*	2.314	3.179*	1	0.080
Coffee	1.203*	2.923	3.287*	1	0.052
Cotton	1.853*	4.351	4.826*	1	0.470
Copper	0.816*	1.735	1.770	1	2.834
Crude Oil	0.484*	0.792	1.077	3	0.100

95% significance level.

Annex table 13.3 ***Index of variable names (in units of constant 1980 dollars)***

XT:	Total exports per capita
CC:	Price of cocoa
CF:	Price of coffee
CP:	Price of copper
OL:	Price of crude oil

Note: The notation L# is used to denote the #th order lag of the variable.

Annex table 13.4 ***Estimation results, 1965-88 (annual)***

XT =	-32.23 + (-3.29)	0.27XTL1 + (2.88)	0.055CFL3 + (3.84)	0.21CNL1 + (5.36)	
	0.25CNL3 - (5.96)	0.01CPL2 (-6.02)			R2 = 0.93 DW = 2.01
CC =	103.36 + (1.84)	1.18CCL1 - (7.51)	0.41CFL2 + (-3.88)	0.72CNL1 - (2.41)	
	0.78CNL2 - (-2.85)	0.06CPL1 + (-5.06)	0.06CPL3 (4.78)		R2 = 0.88 DW = 2.62
CF =	218.32 + (2.54)	0.43CFL1 (2.01)			R2 = 0.17 DW = 1.72
CN =	14.71 + (0.29)	0.20CNL1 + (1.30)	0.70XTL3 + (1.73)	0.03CPL3 (4.94)	R2 = 0.83 DW = 2.90
CP =	1214.10 + (1.41)	0.77CPL1 + (5.03)	3.69CCL1 - (2.72)	6.59CCL3 + (-4.44)	
	5.55CFL3 - (4.41)	6.16CNL1 - (-2.13)	6.04CNL2 - (-1.87)	4.73CNL3 - (-1.62)	
	0.37CPL2 + (-2.18)	0.89CPL3 (5.82)			R2 = 0.97 DW = 2.40
OL =	-4.93 + (-1.14)	0.86OLL1 + (8.37)	0.02CFL3 (2.15)		R2 = 0.80 DW = 2.39

Note: Numbers in parentheses are t-statistics.

Annex table 13.5 *Covariance matrix, 1965-88 (annual)*

				Before VAR			
		XT	*CC*	*CF*	*CN*	*CP*	*OL*
XT	417.4	1172.6	829.3	572.8	3527.5	24.9	
	CC	1172.6	10069.7	8524.0	1823.1	6413.3	-41.1
	CF	829.3	8524.0	12959.8	1910.8	22406.4	-232.3
	CN	572.8	1823.1	1910.8	4176.6	3347635.0	-417.7
	CP	3527.5	6413.3	22406.4	89643.5	-14805.0	102.2
			After VAR				
	XTR	*CCR*	*CFR*	*CNR*	*CPR*	*OLR*	
XTR	33.9	6.7	160.7	8.5	4.2	5.6	
	CCR	6.7	1323.8	1395.7	-2.1	1693.9	-1.1
	CFR	160.7	1395.7	10987.2	-71.3	-2214.1	-96.9
	CNR	8.5	-2.1	-71.3	729.3	1655.3	33.1
	CPR	4.2	1693.9	-2214.1	1655.3	197.6	19.5

Note: Where XXR denotes the residual of variable XX after the VAR process

Notes

All opinions expressed in this paper are those of the author and do not necessarily reflect the views of the World Bank. We are grateful to Brian Pinto, Michael Dooley, Theophilos Priovolos and participants in the April seminar for comments.

References

Balassa, Bela. 1986. "Policy Responses to Exogenous Shocks in Developing Countries." *American Economic Review: Papaers and Proceedings* 76 (2).

Birati, A., J. Deutsche, and M. Ungar. 1986. "Exchange Rate Risk and Efficient Debt Structures." Working Paper No. 8609. Department of Economics and Business Administration, The Economic Research Institute, Bar-Ilan University, Israel.

Claessens, Stijn. 1990. "Integrating Commodity and Exchange Risk: Implications for External Debt Management." In Theophilos Priovolos and Ron Duncan, eds., *Commodity Risk Management and Finance.* New York: Oxford University Press.

Cuddington, John. 1989. "Commodity Booms in Developing Countries." *World Bank Research Observer.* 4 (2).

Dornbusch, Rudiger. 1987. "Exchange Rates and Prices." *American Economic Review* 77.

Engle, R, and C. Granger. 1987. "Co-integration and Error Correction: Representation, Estimation, and Testing." *Econometrica* 55 (2).

Folkerts-Landau, David. 1989. "Marked-to-Market Swaps." In Jacob A. Frenkel, Michael P. Dooley, and Peter Wickham, eds., *Analytical Issues in Debt.* Washington, D.C.: International Monetary Fund.

Gilbert, Christopher. 1989. "The Impact of Exchange Rates and Developing Country Debt on Commodity Prices." *Economic Journal* 99.

Hansen, Lars Peter, and Thomas J. Sargent. 1980. "Formulating and Estimating Dynamic Linear Rational Expectations Models." *Journal of Economic Dynamics and Control* 2.

Kroner, Ken, and Stijn Claessens. 1991. "Optimal Dynamic Hedging Portfolios and the Currency Composition of External Debt." *Journal of International Money and Finance.*

Myers, Robert J., and Stanley R. Thompson. 1989. "Optimal Portfolios of External Debt in Developing Countries: The Potential Role of Commodity-Linked Bonds." *American Journal of Agricultural Economics* (May).

Newbery, David, and Joseph Stiglitz. 1981. *The Theory of Commodity Price Stabilization.* New York: Oxford University Press.

Priovolos, Theophilos, and Ron Duncan 1991. *Commodity Risk Management and Finance.* New York: Oxford University Press.

Yeats, Alexander J. 1990. "Do African Countries Pay More for Imports? Yes. " *World Bank Economic Review* 4 (1).

Comment

Michael Dooley

This paper addresses a very important question and provides some practical advice to governments of Sub-Saharan African countries as to how they might deal with uncertainty. Let me put the main theoretical issue in very general terms as follows:

Many developing countries have comparative advantage in the production of commodities which require a substantial investment in land, capital, and human capital. These investments can take years to come to fruition. At the same time, we know from a long history that the prices of commodities are highly variable. Thus, the developing country has a substantial problem. On the one hand, it has a clear comparative advantage in producing a product that we know for the last two hundred years has had a highly variable price. On the other hand, it has a limited ability to absorb poor outcomes for prices. It seems natural to ask why that particular country is best able to absorb the uncertainty of the income stream. Certainly there is no natural connection between a country that has a comparative advantage as a producer of commodities and that country's comparative advantage in absorbing a variable income stream, and so we would like to think that a market should develop to separate these two activities.

One economic activity is risk taking, an economic activity for which there is a market in many cases. The other economic activity is producing a certain commodity which has this highly variable price. Economists for a very long time have wondered why these two activities are not separated. If we look at what actually goes on in the world, however, it is very hard to find examples where these activities are, in fact, separated. Farmers in the United States take a good deal of the risks of their activities; developing countries that are heavily committed to producing one or a few commodities typically bear the risk themselves. Are these countries ignoring markets that place this risk in the hands of someone else? The answer to that is generally no. Markets that do exist provide protection for short time horizons—a few months or, at most, one crop year. Whereas the investment commitment on the part of the country spans several years, maybe a generation. So the question is why haven't such markets developed in the private sector, and if they haven't, can some sort of governmental intervention correct this presumed inefficiency?

I think the answer is that such markets will not develop, and I have some doubts about the ability of governmental intervention to correct this. These commodity prices have a very special kind of statistical property. In short, when they go up there is no particular reason to think that they will go back down again. Or more important, when they go down, there is no reason to expect them to return to "normal" level. Statisticians call that a non-stationary process in levels. What it means in common sense is that bygones are bygones; if commodity prices have fallen for the last eight years, there is no particular reason to think that they are going to go back up again. Moreover, if we look at other kinds of speculative prices, it doesn't seem as if it is possible to diversify this kind of price risk. In other words, it is very hard to find another price that goes down when these go up or vice versa, so that if I produce copper, for example, I might be able to sell my risk in changes in copper prices to someone else who is smart enough to buy some other commodity which, in a predictable way, goes up when copper goes down. The risk of this variability in commodity prices seems to be one that the system is stuck with. It can't be diversified away, and therefore it cannot be sold in to a financial market cheaply.

If we are going to move this financial risk from the developing country to another party in the system, that second party in the system is going to have to absorb the variability in his income which the developing country is avoiding. That means you have to pay the counterparty to accept this kind of variability in his wealth or his income, however you wish to put it.

But there is another implication in this kind of price series which is more serious, and Stijn Claessens mentioned this when he talked about credit or counter party risks. Because these prices do not tend to return to some normal level, one of the two parties in any hedging agreement is going to wish he had not made the agreement almost immediately after the contract is signed. One of the two parties not only is going to wish he had not made the agreement—that is not so unusual—but because of the nature of these price series, he will expect that he is going to be sorry forever. In other words, there is no sense he can wait and say I am sorry today, but two years from now this price is likely to come back, and I'll wait it out. If he knows the statistics, he will say to himself, not only am I sorry that I made this contract today, but I will always be sorry I entered into this contract. This generates a serious problem, because unless I have some way to enforce that contract against my counterparty, he will simply default on it. He will default on it because he has no reason to perform unless I can coerce him to perform or unless he has some collateral that I can collect from him in case he does not perform.

That is why I think that we find that these sorts of contracts are generally for short periods. You cannot lose much, and therefore a small amount of collateral or a small enforcement cost will be sufficient to make the counterparty perform. Over a long time period, however, we know that the variances in these prices is roughly a linear function with time, so if I were to enter into a contract that was five years long, I would face the uncertainty that one of the two people involved would have lost too great a deal of money over the life of the contract. I do not know which one, but I do know that both of them would have very little incentive to actually satisfy the contract. Therefore, the private contract is not credible, and that is one of the reasons it does not exist. It is interesting to note, for example, that most of these kinds of contracts require margin calls. You only maintain such a contract as long as you know the counterparty is going to perform.

From the point of view of developing countries, it may be true that the only way to assure income, given that the country produces a commodity which has this kind of price behavior, is to self-insure and to self-insure in a very old fashioned way—by accumulating assets. Notice that in good years setting aside safe financial assets is not simply to smooth consumption. Instead, if the country experiences a number of consecutive bad draws, as we have for the last 15 years, it is necessary to smooth the transition to producing something else.

To overcome counterparty risk, market participants might trust an international organization. The World Bank, for example, could guarantee a commodity agreement for a developing country and a counterparty in the private market might take the other side. I am uneasy about such an initiative because it means that unless the World Bank has superior resources or superior ability to force the loser in the contract to pay, the World Bank is simply taking the credit exposure. In accounting for such an agreement, the organization should reorganize the substantial credit liability created by the agreement.

Capital Flight in Sub-Saharan African Countries

P. H. Kevin Chang and Robert E. Cumby

Overview

This paper examines the extent to which Sub-Saharan African countries have experienced capital flight during the 1970s and 1980s. After discussing alternative definitions and the measurement of capital flight, we present evidence for a sample of 36 countries using two definitions of "capital flight." The first considers capital flight to be the increase in net foreign assets held by the private sector, which we estimate to be about $ 40 billion for the region overall from 1976 to 1987. The second defines capital flight as the private sector's stock of foreign assets whose income is not reported to local authorities; this stock is estimated to have increased by $ 32 billion for the region over this same period. Comparisons with Latin American countries suggest that, for their size, certain African countries have exhibited capital flight on par with countries such as Argentina or Mexico. We also examine trade data to detect possible capital flight through misinvoicing, and look for patterns in the timing of capital flight through a comparison of private capital flows to the behavior of the real exchange rate and the black market premium for dollars.

Introduction

Previously, analysis of external finance of Sub-Saharan African countries has focused on financing needs and the role of official development assistance in filling those needs. Rather than focusing on inflows of official capital in the Sub-Saharan African countries, this paper examines outflow of capital, especially private outflows, from those countries.

In section 2 we examine alternative definitions of capital flight. The essential problem that one faces in defining capital flight is to distinguish "capital flight" from "normal" capital movements. Two approaches are taken in the literature. The first is to identify specific episodes (or countries) that are characterized by abnormally adverse conditions for domestic investment and to consider all acquisition of external claims by the private sector as flight capital. The second approach distinguishes capital flight from other capital movements by considering capital flight to consist of the acquisition of external claims that are not reported to the domestic authorities.

In section 3 we consider measurement issues and section 4 we present estimates of capital flight from 36 Sub-Saharan African countries. We find that between 1976 and 1987, the private sector in these economies increased their claims abroad by approximately $40 billion. Nearly half of this total is accounted for by residents of Nigeria, with the Sudan accounting for approximately another $7 billion. We estimate that residents of Sub-Saharan African countries increased their holdings of unreported foreign assets by approximately $32 billion between 1976 and 1987. Again Nigeria and the Sudan account for more than half of this total. As is the case with the large Latin American debtors, there are often two-way capital flows, with the private sector increasing its external assets at the same time that the public sector is increasing its external liabilities.[1]

In section 5, we examine the extent to which the estimates of capital flight reported in section 4 are affected by misinvoicing of international trade. We find little evidence of systematic capital flight carried out through misinvoicing of trade flows. Section 6 explores possible trends in the timing of private capital outflows, real exchange rate behavior, and changes in the premia in the black market for dollars. Section 7 concludes.

Defining capital flight

A central problem in explicitly defining capital flight is to distinguish capital flight from other, "normal" capital flows. Residents of an open economy will commonly engage in international transactions, some of which result in domestic residents' increasing their claims on nonresidents. How can "normal" capital flows be distinguished from flight capital? The definitions of capital flight proposed in the literature attempt to distinguish capital flight from "normal" capital flows on more objective grounds.

One possibility, suggested by Kindleberger (1937, 1987) and Walter (1987), is simply to define capital flight as all capital that "flees," regardless of the motivation, which in any case is impossible to measure. Recognizing the subjectivity inherent in identifying countries or episodes in which residents were "fleeing high risks at home" rather than simply "diversifying by investing abroad," we choose to adopt the relatively agnostic approach of defining capital flight as all private sector acquisitions of net claims on foreigners.

Dooley (1986, 1987) is skeptical of the broad definitions of capital flight and the measures they imply, pointing out that many large Latin American debtors received large net inflows of foreign savings during the very years in which capital flight has been estimated to be large.[2] He therefore argues that abnormal risks in the domestic economy cannot alone explain the private outflows. Instead, there must exist an *asymmetry* between residents' and nonresidents' perception of the risks or the returns from investing in the domestic economy.

Why would domestic residents choose to lend to nonresidents who in turn lend to residents of the domestic economy? Possibly because financial markets are more highly developed abroad than at home, resulting in lower transaction costs of intermediation. Or, there may be an asymmetry in tax treatment, as emphasized by Dooley. If taxes (outright or implicit such as interest rate ceilings) on financial positions in the domestic economy can be avoided by lending abroad, domestic residents will have an incentive to do so. Nonresidents may not face these same taxes and would then find recycling the funds an attractive alternative.

Like different tax treatments, different guarantees offered to domestic and foreign residents may induce two-way capital flows.[3] Governments frequently borrow abroad in foreign currency but will not (or cannot credibly) borrow from domestic residents in foreign currency. In effect, the governments provide foreign exchange guarantees to foreign lenders but not to domestic residents, who in turn lend abroad in foreign currency, while foreign residents recycle the funds and lend to the domestic government in foreign currency.

What are the welfare costs of these asymmetries and the resultant shifting abroad of capital? Cuddington (1986) points to several possible reasons this may occur, such as: 1) social returns on domestic projects may exceed private returns, and capital flight reduces domestic investment; 2) capital flight raises a country's gross borrowing requirements, resulting in an increase in the marginal cost of foreign borrowing; 3) capital flight reduces the domestic tax base, requiring the domestic government to raise other taxes that may involve greater distortions or adverse effects on the distribution of income. As Cuddington suggests, in each case one needs to ask whether capital flight is the source of the problem and whether policies to restrict capital flight will solve the problem.

Noting that large private outflows are often accompanied by contemporaneous large capital inflows, Dooley (1986, 1987) finds it difficult to believe that domestic real investment was sharply curtailed during those periods, and focuses on the third problem raised by capital flight: the adverse effect on the home government's fiscal position if residents avoid taxes by investing abroad and fail to report the income from foreign claims. The government may then be led to levy taxes elsewhere that lead to greater distortions or adversely affect income distribution.

Based on these considerations, Dooley (1986, 1988) and Khan and Ul Haque (1986) choose to define capital flight as the stock of foreign claims that generates income that is not reported to the domestic authorities. This definition differs from the broader definition above in three ways. First, it does not require periods of abnormal risk to be identified. Second, it excludes private external investment that generates *reported* income. Third, it measures capital flight as the stock rather than a flow of flight capital.

Which definition seems more appropriate? If the problem with capital flight is that the social rate of return on capital invested domestically exceeds the private rate of return on such investments (or if the shadow value of foreign exchange exceeds the market price), then any movement of funds abroad---reported or not---that otherwise would have been invested at home should be considered in a measure of capital flight. If the relevant problem is instead the erosion of the domestic tax base and the consequent need to levy other distortionary taxes, then unreported capital outflows seem the natural definition. As the above discussion suggests, however, there exists more than one viable definition of the term, and the appropriate choice will depend on the policy questions most pertinent to the country and time period under consideration.

Measuring capital flight

The broad definition of capital flight as the increase in the private sector's net foreign assets has been employed by the World Bank (1985), Erbe (1985), and Morgan Guaranty (1986). All three of these studies choose to estimate capital flight as a residual based on the balance-of-payments accounting identity rather than directly. As shown in table 14.1, computing this "sources of funds" minus "uses of funds" residual first involves adding together two "sources" of funds: inflows of official capital, computed as the increase in external debt reported by the World Bank, and net foreign direct investment flows.[4] These funds can be used to finance a current-account deficit, to increase official reserves, or to increase the private sector's foreign assets. To obtain capital flight estimates, one subtracts the current-account deficit and the increase in official reserves from the inflow of funds.

Measuring the change in external debt, one of the "sources of funds," requires several choices. Using the change in public and publicly guaranteed external debt will produce an estimate of the private sector's *net* acquisition of foreign assets, whereas including private non-guaranteed debt will provide an estimate of the increase in *gross* private sector foreign assets. Since private external indebtedness does represent an actual liability of the private sector that is expected to be serviced and ultimately repaid, we believe that the simultaneous acquisition of a foreign asset and foreign liability should *not* be considered "capital flight." Thus, we choose *net* acquisition of foreign assets by the private sector as the relevant measure.[5]

Should short-term debt be included as well as long-term debt? Calculating net private sector acquisition of foreign assets would require knowing public and publicly guaranteed short-term debt, but unfortunately, separate estimates of private non-guaranteed and public/publicly guaranteed long-term debt are available only for long-term debt. Although short-term debt does also include private trade credits, anecdotal evidence suggests that for a number of Sub-Saharan African countries, a large fraction of short-term debt represents obligations of the public sector (including public sector enterprises). We therefore include short-term debt in computing our estimates of net private capital outflows.

Finally, one must choose whether to measure the change in public and publicly guaranteed debt by examining the change in the stock or the flows of new debt (disbursements less principal repaid). The change in the stock will include exchange rate-induced changes in the dollar value of non-dollar debt but this difficulty can be circumvented by subtracting the exchange rate valuation effect computed by the World Bank (available beginning in 1981) from the change in the stock.

The change in the stock adjusted for exchange rate valuation effects will still differ from the new flows by three items: "discovery" of old debt, private non-guaranteed debt rescheduled into publicly guaranteed debt, and interest rescheduled. Previously existing debt "discovered" during a rescheduling is added to the stock but is often not reflected in the new flows. Thus, the change in the stock of debt is probably the preferable measure but may present a misleading picture of year-to-year changes in debt and therefore in the timing of the private sector's acquisition of external claims. Nonetheless, cumulative totals are more accurately reported, and are unaffected by certain debts' being reported when "discovered" rather than when first incurred.[6]

When private sector external debt is converted to public sector obligations in a rescheduling agreement, the private sector substitutes a liability to the government for a foreign liability. Although no new flow of funds has occurred, the private sector will increase its *net* foreign assets, suggesting that the change in the stock of debt will be the superior measure.

The question of whether to include rescheduled interest is somewhat more difficult. If balance-of-payments data measure interest payments *due* rather than interest payments made, the current-account deficit will be overstated and thus the residual estimates of private capital flows understated. Including interest rescheduled will correct this understatement and will therefore yield better estimates of private sector acquisition of foreign claims.[7] Therefore, we believe that changes in the stock, which do include rescheduled interest, rather than recorded flows, which do not, seem preferable.[8] In sum, for the various reasons listed above, we choose to use the change in the stock of debt, adjusted for exchange rate valuation changes, to obtain the residual estimates discussed in the following sections.[9]

Dooley (1986, 1988), defining capital flight as the stock of foreign claims whose income is not reported, measures the stock of external claims by summing identified capital flows in the balance of payments accounts and making two adjustments to capture unreported capital flows. The first is to add the errors and omissions. The second adjustment is based on a comparison of the World Bank data on the stock of external debt and external borrowing reported in the balance-of-payments accounts, which is often lower. This suggests that in the balance-of-payments accounts, part of the increase in external debt goes unrecorded[10]. This is a liability whose counterpart on the asset side Dooley (1986, 1988) assumes to be private sector acquisition of foreign assets. He therefore adds in the difference between each year's change in external debt as reported by the World Bank and as recorded by the balance-of-payments accounts. He then compares his estimated stock of external assets against the stock implicit in reported investment income (assuming a return equal to the U.S. Treasury-bill rate), calling the difference "capital flight." The accuracy of these figures may also be reduced by discrepancies between balance-of-payments accounts and fiscal authorities' figures for investment income.

Estimates of capital flight in Sub-Saharan African countries

In this section we present estimates of capital flight from a sample of 36 Sub-Saharan African countries using both approaches to defining capital flight.

Characteristics of private capital outflows in Sub-Saharan African countries

Estimates of broadly defined capital flight for 36 Sub-Saharan African countries are found in table 14.2, where we report residual estimates of net private capital outflows from 1976 to 1987, cumulating over 3-year subperiods.[11] Analysis of balance-of-payments aggregates and net private capital outflows for 29 of the 36 countries taken together indicates that the degree of capital movement has varied considerably both across countries and over time, with many countries exhibiting both positive and negative flows. Nonetheless, certain discernible trends emerge:

(1) Cumulative net private capital outflows since 1976 of just over $ 40 billion can be attributed almost entirely to nine countries that experienced outflows in excess of $ 1 billion, with outflows from Nigeria ($ 17.5 b) constituting nearly half the region's total, and Sudan ($ 7.5 b) nearly another 20%. The other seven countries with outflows of at least $ 1 billion were: Gabon ($2.5 b), Zambia ($2.3 b), Zaire ($2.1 b), Congo ($1.3 b), Liberia ($1.8 b), Ghana ($1.5 b), and Uganda ($1.4 b)

(2) Two-way capital flows are common. Large increases in private sector claims often occur at the same time as large increases in public sector liabilities.

(3) While most countries experienced net private capital inflows at some point, no country had cumulative inflows in excess of $ 1 billion. Five out of 36 countries show cumulative net inflows, the largest occurring in Cameroon, whose residents are estimated to have reduced their foreign assets by $ 490 million in the 1976-1987 period, with net inflows recorded every year since 1980.

(4) A sharp increase in net capital outflows from the region occurred in the 1985-1987 period, which accounts for 40% of the cumulative outflows since 1976. In Nigeria, for example, over half the outward movement of capital occurred in the past few years, with flows of $2 billion, $4 billion, and $5 billion respectively in 1985, 1986, and 1987. In fact, before 1985, Sudan had exhibited the largest cumulative outflows of all Sub-Saharan African nations.

(5) The estimates of private capital outflows are determined almost entirely by the difference between current account deficits and increases in official external indebtedness. The estimated increase in private capital outflows during 1985-1987 corresponds to a substantial improvement in current account balances accompanied by a sizable increase in external debt.

(6) Although individual countries' outflows, except perhaps Nigeria's, are smaller than those in Latin America, total outflows for the region are comparable to flows from a country such as Argentina, Brazil, or Venezuela.

(7) Relative to external debt or GDP, several Sub-Saharan African countries have experienced capital outflows of similar or greater magnitude than the more visible Latin American debtor countries.

Estimates of capital outflows using alternative measures of external debt

Table 14.3 summarizes the effect of using different debt measures on the residual estimates of private capital outflows. If short-term debt is excluded, the estimate of 1976-87 private outflows falls from $41.6 billion to $27.6 billion, for the Sub-Saharan African countries as a whole. While Nigeria and the Sudan still account for more than half of the total, the estimated outflows from these countries are reduced by \$1.8 billion and \$2.5 billion, respectively. Among other countries, excluding short-term debt most affects the estimates for Zambia, where the estimated outflows fall from \$2.3 billion to slightly less than one billion dollars.

If we wish to estimate *gross* private acquisition of external claims, the measure of external debt should include private long-term debt along with public and publicly guaranteed long-term debt and short-term debt. The effects of doing so are also summarized in table 14.3. Between 1976 and 1987, gross acquisition of external claims for the Sub-Saharan African countries as a whole exceeds net acquisition by approximately \$5.3 billion. The largest impact is found in the estimates for the Cote d'Ivoire, where the increase in gross claims exceeds the increase in net claims by \$3.6 billion.

Capital outflows in Sub-Saharan Africa vs. Latin America

How do these figures compare with those of other regions, particularly Latin America? In magnitude, only Nigeria's \$ 17.5 billion outflows are comparable to outflows from countries such as Argentina, Brazil, Mexico, or Venezuela with estimated cumulative outflows from 1976 to 1987 of \$ 29.0 billion, \$ 17.9 billion, \$ 49.5 billion, and \$ 33.6 billion respectively. Capital outflows from the Sub-Saharan African countries combined, however, are in fact approximately equal to those of a large Latin American nation, though the former appear to have received considerably less notice.

Since the economies of the major Latin American debtors are considerably larger than those of the Sub-Saharan African countries, it is useful to scale the estimates of private capital outflows. In table 14.2 we present estimates of capital outflows relative to the stock of external debt, the change in external debt and GDP. Table 14.4 presents similarly scaled estimates of capital outflows for four Latin American countries, calculated in the same manner as the African estimates.

These scaled comparisons indicate that many African nations have actually experienced more significant capital outflows than some of their more visible Latin counterparts. For example, over the 1976-1987 period, cumulative private capital outflows as a function of end-1987 debt levels were: 55% in Mexico and Argentina, 17% in Brazil, 116% in Venezuela—or 47% for these four countries overall. Though the levels are smaller, the ratio of cumulative outflows to outstanding debt is actually higher than 55% (i.e. higher than countries like Mexico or Argentina) for six of the thirty-five Sub-Saharan African countries: Liberia (125%), Gabon (106%), Uganda (85%), Sudan (73%), Chad (73%), and Nigeria (68%). These relatively high ratios of capital outflows to debt suggest that, though these nations are currently experiencing difficulties in servicing their debt, private residents' claims on foreigners could offset a significant fraction of debt owed or guaranteed by the public sector.

Measured against GDP, cumulative capital outflows in Argentina, Brazil, Mexico, and Venezuela of \$ 130 billion represent about 25% of the average level of dollar GDP in these countries from 1976 to 1987. Sudan (87%), Zambia (78%), Gabon (75%), Gambia (66%), and Zaire (45%)—with combined cumulative outflows of \$ 14.5 billion—hold more private claims on foreigners, relative to output produced, than do Argentina, Brazil, Mexico, and Venezuela as a group.

Thus, the magnitude of combined cumulative outflows, both in both absolute terms and relative to debt or GDP, indicates that private capital outflows in Sub-Saharan Africa are an issue of non-negligible importance.

Characteristics of unreported private external claims

Estimates of changes in the stock of unreported foreign assets for our sample of 36 Sub-Saharan African countries are found in table 14.5, where we report estimates for 1976 to 1987. While Dooley provides a method for computing the stock of unreported claims given some base-year estimate, we have chosen to report changes in the stock for two reasons. First, doing so facilitates the comparison of these estimates to the residual estimates of private capital outflow reported above. Second, we have little confidence in estimates of base year values. By reporting changes in the stock, we remove any errors induced by base year estimates.[12] Like the residual estimates of private capital outflows, these estimates indicated considerable variation across countries and over time. Nonetheless, several conclusions emerge quite clearly from the estimates.

(1) Residents of the Sub-Saharan African countries have increased their unreported external assets by approximately \$32 billion between 1976 and 1987. This figure is surprisingly similar to the residual estimate of total net private capital

outflows despite the very different notions of "capital flight" behind the estimates.

(2) As with the residual-based estimates, more than one-half of the total is accounted for by two countries, Nigeria ($11.7 billion) and the Sudan ($7.2 billion).

(3) Relatively few countries account for most of the remaining $13 billion. In particular, residents of the Cote d'Ivoire ($3 billion), Gabon ($2.3 billion), the Congo ($1.4 billion), Liberia ($1.4 billion), Kenya ($1.2 billion), Tanzania ($.9 billion), Zaire ($.7 billion), and Zambia ($.6 billion) are all estimated to have substantially increased their holdings of unreported foreign assets. There is considerable overlap between these countries and those with large residual estimates of private capital outflows.

(4) A large increase in private unreported foreign assets occurred between 1985 and 1987, with this period accounting for nearly 40% of the 1976 - 1987 total. The residual estimates of private capital outflows exhibit similar behavior. This period contributed an especially large proportion of the 1976 - 1987 increase for Nigeria, the Cote d'Ivoire, and the Congo.

Capital flight and trade misinvoicing

The systematic misinvoicing of trade data represents an additional potential source of capital flight. Specifically, the overinvoicing of imports and the underinvoicing of exports can result in a country's residents accumulating claims on foreigners that would not be captured by any of the standard measures of capital flight based on balance-of-payments data. With trade misinvoicing, capital outflows are hidden in current account data, which will show a greater deficit than the true current account, and will not be reflected in any capital account items. Therefore, we need to seek an alternative means of identifying capital flight through the misinvoicing of trade.

One may detect such systematic misinvoicing by comparing a country's reported trade data with corresponding figures of its trading partners. Since import data are reported on a cif basis, we deflate import data by the country's cif/fob ratio. To test for overinvoicing of exports for the Sub-Saharan African countries, we compare a country's reported exports to all industrial countries with industrial countries' reported imports from that country. Similarly, to test for underinvoicing of imports, we compare the country's reported imports from industrial countries with industrial countries' reported exports to the country. If the industrial countries' data are accurately reported, then the African country's reported trade flow divided by the industrial countries' figure will give an indication of the degree of misinvoicing. If private accumulation of claims on foreigners are indeed being disguised through misrepresentation in the current account, then this ratio should be greater than one for the country's exports, smaller than one for the country's imports. As table 14.6 indicates, there do indeed exist significant discrepancies between the trade flows reported by these Sub-Saharan African countries and those reported by their industrial trading partners. Differences on the order of sixty per cent for example, are commonplace. For seven (Ethiopia, Gambia, Ghana, Madagascar, Niger, Tanzania, and Zambia) of the thirty-one countries considered, the pattern of misinvoicing is consistent with capital flight through disguised current account transactions: imports are overreported, exports are underreported. This finding, however, does not indicate that capital flight of that nature is occurring in these countries. If countries' misinvoicing of data were randomly distributed around one, for example, we would on average expect about a quarter of the sample to show inflated imports and deflated exports.

The high occurrence of apparent simultaneous underinvoicing of both imports and exports, however, is striking. Sixteen of the thirty-one countries report lower figures for both imports and exports and their trading partners attribute to them. Conversely, only three countries overreport both imports and exports. This distribution suggests that some systematic underinvoicing of all trade transactions may be occurring, presumably to avoid tariffs, quotas, export taxes, or other trade restrictions.

The high variation over time for a given country, evident in the minimum and maximum figures presented in table 14.6, also suggests either that patterns in capital flight through misinvoicing are extremely volatile, or that the quality of the data is inadequate to permit its detection if it does exist. The apparent systematic underreporting of trade figures in both directions to avoid trade barriers in this case seems to overwhelm any discernible capital flight through misinvoicing.

Policy implications

The analysis in this paper has focused on defining and measuring capital flight, rather than on identifying its causes or its effects on the economies involved. As we discuss in section II, capital flight is a problem only if it involves an externality. Without a general equilibrium model that incorporates the relevant externalities and other possible distortions in the domestic economy, it is difficult to make any firm statements about the welfare effects of capital flight or the economic effects of policies attempting to deal with it.

While our approach does not permit us to endorse any particular policy, there are nonetheless some important policy implications that emerge from the analysis in this paper. These implications derive from two features of the data: the high levels of estimated capital outflows, and the sizable inflows of foreign savings that coincide with large private outflows.

The most important implication of the paper is indicated by the large magnitude of private outflows: that investors can and do invest abroad as well as at home. This paper has generated new evidence of both the magnitude and mobility of capital held by domestic residents in Sub-Saharan countries, implying that domestic investment must be made attractive if resident investors are to choose domestic rather than foreign investment. If domestic investment conditions were somehow made more favorable, however, our results suggest that potentially large sums could flow back to these countries.

We have also observed that countries experiencing large private capital outflows often receive large flows of funds from abroad at the same time. There are several possible explanations of this phenomenon, each with different policy implications. One possibility is that financial intermediation may be less costly abroad, so that domestic residents simultaneously lend abroad and borrow from abroad, with little economic consequence other than the value added in the provision of financial services.

Empirically, however, offshore intermediation explains little of the observed flows, since in most countries, private liabilities to foreigners are negligible. Instead, the two-way flow of funds takes the form of the private sector lending abroad while the public sector borrows from abroad. Why might this occur? Dooley (1987, 1988) suggests that an asymmetry of perceived risk or return must be behind such a two-way flow of funds. Two types of asymmetry are discussed in section II: differences in the tax treatment of funds lent abroad and funds lent domestically, and differences in the currency of denomination of public sector borrowing from domestic and foreign residents. In the case of concessional financing from foreign governments or supranational institutions, foreigners and private domestic residents may perceive different total returns in lending to the public sector. The evidence seems to suggest that such asymmetries are important factors underlying observed capital flows and are thus issues that must be addressed in any set of policies aimed at controlling capital flight.

Concluding remarks

In this paper we have examined the extent to which Sub-Saharan African countries have experienced capital flight during the 1970s and 1980s. After discussing alternative ways of defining and measuring capital flight, we present evidence from thirty-six countries based on two definitions of "capital flight," the first estimating the increase in the net foreign assets of the private sector, the second estimating measures the private sector's stock of foreign assets that generate income not reported to the domestic authorities. Despite the large difference in the definition of capital flight behind these two measures, the estimates are strikingly similar. Residents of the thirty-six countries are estimated to have increased their net foreign assets by approximately $40 billion between 1976 and 1987. Unreported foreign assets are estimated to have increased by about $32 billion over this same period. Nigeria and the Sudan account for more than half of the total in both sets of estimates.

References

Cuddington, John T., 1986, "Capital flight: Estimates, issues, and explanations," *Studies in International Finance*, no. 58, Princeton, NJ, Princeton University Department of Economics.

Dooley, Michael P., William Helkie, Ralph Tryon, and John Underwood, 1985, "An analysis of external debt positions of eight developing countries through 1990," working paper.

Dooley, Michael P., 1986, "Country-specific risk premiums, capital flight and net investment income payments in selected developing countries, "International Monetary Fund Departmental Memorandum" 86/17.

Dooley, Michael P., 1987, "Comment," in Donald R. Lessard and John Williamson, eds, *Capital Flight and Third World Debt*, Washington, DC, Institute for International Economics, 79-81.

Dooley, Michael P., 1988, "Capital flight: A response to differences in financial risks, *International Monetary Fund Staff Papers*, 35, September, 422-436.

Eaton, Jonathan, 1987, "Public debt guarantees and private capital flight," *World Bank Economic Review*, 1, May, 377-395.

Erbe, Suzanne, 1985, "The flight of capital from developing countries," Intereconomics, November/December, 268-275.

Gajdeczka, Przemyslaw, 1989, "Financial Flows in Developing Countries," *Quarterly Review*, World Bank, March.

Gajdeczka, Przemyslaw, 1990, "The Measurement of Capital Flight and Developing Country Foreign Assets," mimeo, presented at the Kiel Institute Workshop on Net External Asset Positions.

Gajdeczka, Przemyslaw and Daniel Oks, 1989, "Domestic Deficits, Debt Overhang, and Capital Outflows in Developing Countries," in *Finance and the International Economy*, R.O'Brien and I.Iversen, eds., (Oxford University Press), 103-120.

Khan, Mohsin S., and Nadeem Ul Haque, 1987, "Capital flight from developing countries," *Finance and Development*, March,.

Kindleberger, Charles P., 1937, *International Short-Term Capital Movements*, New York, NY, Augustus Kelley.

Kindleberger, Charles P., 1987, "A historical perspective," in Donald R. Lessard and John Williamson, eds, *Capital Flight and Third World Debt*, Washington, DC, Institute for International Economics, 7-26.

Lessard, Donald R. and John Williamson, 1987, "Introduction" and "The problem and policy responses," in Donald R. Lessard and John Williamson, eds, *Capital Flight and Third World Debt*, Washington, DC, Institute for International Economics, 1-5 and 201-254.

Morgan Guaranty Trust Company, 1986, "LDC capital flight," *World Financial Markets*, March.

Rodriguez F., Miguel A., 1987, "Consequences of capital flight for Latin American debtor countries," in Donald R. Lessard and John Williamson, eds, *Capital Flight and Third World Debt*, Washington, DC, Institute for International Economics, 129-154.

Walter, Ingo, 1987, "The mechanism of capital flight, in Donald R. Lessard and John Williamson, eds, *Capital Flight and Third World Debt*, Washington, DC, Institute for International Economics, 103-128.

World Bank, 1985, *World Development Report*, Washington, DC, World Bank.

Table 14.1 ***Capital outflow estimation***

Balance of payments accounts		
Current account		(A)
Capital account		
Net FDI		(B)
Private capital		
Long-term	(C)	
Short-term		
Nonbanks		(D)
Banking system		(E)
Official capital		(F)
Errors and omissions		(G)
Change in reserves		(H)

Capital flight:
Residual estimate = A + B + F + H
= -(C + D + E + G)
(By balance of payments identity)

Balance of payments accounts supplemented by World Bank debt data		
Current account		(A)
Capital account		
Net FDI		(B)
Private capital		
Long-term	(C)	
Short-term		
Nonbanks		(D)
Banking system		(E)
Change in public and publicly guaranteed debt		(F)
Errors and omissions		
Counterpart item: official capital—change in debt		(I)
Change in reserves		(H)

Capital flight:
Residual estimate = A + B + F + H
= -(C + D + E + G - I)
(By balance of payments identity)

Table 14.2 ***Residual estimates of private capital outflows relative to debt and GDP***

	1970-75	1976-78	1979-81	1982-84	1985-87	
1976-87						
Benin						
Outflow	-39.9	-49.5	104.1	-176.9	NA	NA
Debt	89.4	237.5	543.7	892.2	1103.1	1103.1
Outflow/Debt	-0.45	-0.21	0.19	-0.20	NA	NA
Outflow/ΔDebt	-0.82	-0.33	0.34	-0.51	NA	NA
Outflow/GDP	-0.11	-0.08	0.09	-0.15	NA	NA
Botswana						
Outflow	NA	-110.5	-28.8	-147.3	264.5	-22.2
Debt	147.3	123.6	184.5	303.6	412.7	412.7
Outflow/Debt	NA	-0.89	-0.16	-0.49	0.64	-0.05
Outflow/ΔDebt	NA	4.66	-0.47	-1.24	2.42	-0.08
Outflow/GDP	NA	-0.29	-0.03	-0.16	0.21	-0.03
Burkina Faso						
Outflow	-32.4	79.6	-63.3	-56.9	NA	NA
Debt	63.4	262.7	379.5	544.9	799.0	799.0
Outflow/Debt	-0.51	0.30	-0.17	-0.10	NA	NA
Outflow/ΔDebt	-0.76	0.40	-0.54	-0.34	NA	NA
Outflow/GDP	-0.07	0.10	-0.05	-0.06	NA	NA
Burundi						
Outflow	NA	NA	NA	NA	150.7	NA
Debt	19.4	74.7	186.6	386.0	736.6	736.6
Outflow/Debt	NA	NA	NA	NA	0.20	NA
Outflow/ΔDebt	NA	NA	NA	NA	0.43	NA
Outflow/GDP	NA	NA	NA	NA	0.13	NA
Cameroon						
Outflow	63.0	704.2	348.2	-367.3	-1175.6	-490.6
Debt	386.6	1392	2532.2	2828.4	3327.3	3327.3
Outflow/Debt	0.16	0.51	0.14	-0.13	-0.35	-0.15
Outflow/ΔDebt	0.25	0.70	0.31	-1.24	-2.36	-0.17
Outflow/GDP0.04	0.21	0.06	-0.05	-0.10	-0.07	
Central African Republic						
Outflow	-1.7	22.6	46.9	11.6	60.7	141.7
Debt	77.0	135.1	248.4	331.0	582.9	582.9
Outflow/Debt	-0.02	0.17	0.19	0.03	0.10	0.24
Outflow/ΔDebt	-0.03	0.39	0.41	0.14	0.24	0.28
Outflow/GDP	-0.01	0.05	0.06	0.02	0.07	0.20
Chad						
Outflow	45.8	126.7	50.1	7.8	51.2	235.8
Debt	90.8	210.8	220.2	199.2	323.3	323.3
Outflow/Debt	0.50	0.60	0.23	0.04	0.16	0.73
Outflow/ΔDebt	0.82	1.06	5.33	-0.37	0.41	1.01
Outflow/GDP	NA	NA	NA	NA	NA	NA
Congo						
Outflow	NA	-7.3	80.9	460.3	1359.9	1893.9
Debt	403.5	965.4	1825.3	2560.7	4819.2	4819.2
Outflow/Debt	NA	-0.01	0.04	0.18	0.28	0.39
Outflow/ΔDebt	NA	-0.01	0.09	0.63	0.60	0.43
Outflow/GDP	NA	-0.01	0.05	0.21	NA	NA

Côte D'Ivoire						
Outflow	149.8	1170.1	-647.2	-689.4	748.8	582.3
Debt	955.9	3551.7	6438.5	7346.7	9267.0	9267.0
Outflow/Deb	0.16	0.33	-0.10	-0.09	0.08	0.06
Outflow/ΔDebt	0.21	0.45	-0.22	-0.76	0.39	0.07
Outflow/GDP	2.16	2.42	-0.27	-0.66	NA	NA
Equatorial Guinea						
Outflow	NA	NA	NA	NA	NA	NA
Debt	25.2	39.2	93.8	128.8	183.1	183.1
Outflow/Debt	NA	NA	NA	NA	NA	NA
Outflow/ΔDebt	NA	NA	NA	NA	NA	NA
Ethiopia						
Outflow	77.9	143.4	30.3	117.8	NA	NA
Debt	343.6	563	1153.6	1576.2	2604.4	2604.4
Outflow/Debt	0.23	0.25	0.03	0.07	NA	NA
Outflow/ΔDebt	0.45	0.65	0.05	0.28	NA	NA
Outflow/GDP	0.03	0.04	0.01	0.03	NA	NA
Gabon						
Outflow	1121.0	1151.2	748.8	606.6	21.5	2528.2
Debt	771.6	1511.9	1303.7	1277.3	2390.5	2390.5
Outflow/Debt	1.45	0.76	0.57	0.47	0.01	1.06
Outflow/ΔDebt	1.65	1.56	-3.60	-22.98	0.02	1.56
Outflow/GDP	NA	0.42	0.20	0.17	0.01	0.75
Gambia						
Outflow	-5.8	-10.7	14.0	68.9	45.7	117.9
Debt	13.4	49.8	183	268	322.9	322.9
Outflow/Debt	-0.43	-0.21	0.08	0.26	0.14	0.37
Outflow/ΔDeb	-0.70	-0.29	0.10	0.81	0.83	0.38
Outflow/GDP	-0.08	-0.07	0.06	0.37	0.30	0.66
Ghana						
Outflow	260.9	215.0	244.3	591.8	480.1	1531.2
Debt	720.2	1259.7	1518.8	2082.4	2954.2	2954.2
Outflow/Debt	0.36	0.17	0.16	0.28	0.16	0.52
Outflow/ΔDebt	1.44	0.40	0.94	1.05	0.55	0.69
Outflow/GDP0.09	0.02	0.01	0.03	0.09	0.12	
Guinea						
Outflow	NA	NA	NA	NA	NA	
Debt	790.4	1042.5	1455.7	1535	2208.5	2208.5
Outflow/Debt	NA	NA	NA	NA	NA	NA
Outflow/ΔDebt	NA	NA	NA	NA	NA	NA
Guinea-Bissau						
Outflow	NA	NA	NA	63.8	29.6	NA
Debt	7.0	52.2	150.9	281.9	413.6	413.6
Outflow/Debt	NA	NA	NA	0.23	0.07	NA
Outflow/ΔDebt	NA	NA	NA	0.49	0.23	NA
Kenya						
Outflow	-315.2	405.3	-232.6	191.6	213.1	577.4
Debt	716.0	1888.3	3200.5	3857.2	4704.5	4704.5
Outflow/Debt	-0.44	0.21	-0.07	0.05	0.05	0.12
Outflow/ΔDebt	-0.79	0.35	-0.18	0.29	0.25	0.14
Outflow/GDP-0.14	-0.14	0.09	-0.04	0.03	0.03	0.10
Liberia						

Outflow	NA	404.6	678.7	452.6	273.0	1808.9
Debt	178.6	443.0	829.0	1133.0	1450.8	1450.8
Outflow/Debt	NA	0.91	0.82	0.40	0.19	1.25
Outflow/ΔDebt	NA	1.53	1.76	1.49	0.86	1.42
Outflow/GDP	NA	0.57	0.71	0.42	NA	NA
Madagascar						
Outflow	95.9	68.6	45.0	192.9	-180.0	126.5
Debt	184.0	361.0	1707.7	2603.9	3073.6	3073.6
Outflow/Debt	0.52	0.19	0.03	0.07	-0.06	0.04
Outflow/ΔDebt	1.01	0.39	0.03	0.22	-0.38	0.04
Outflow/GDP	0.07	0.04	0.02	0.07	NA	NA
Malawi						
Outflow	-51.8	70.4	-267.4	-115.1	24.5	-287.6
Debt	259.9	586.1	859.4	1034.1	1321.6	1321.6
Outflow/Debt	-0.20	0.12	-0.31	-0.11	0.02	-0.22
Outflow/ΔDebt	-0.38	0.22	-0.98	-0.66	0.09	-0.27
Outflow/GDP	-0.11	0.09	-0.23	-0.10	0.02	-0.26
Mali						
Outflow	5.9	68.8	-11.0	329.7	-109.0	278.5
Debt	356.1	568.3	901.2	1518.4	1864.0	1864.0
Outflow/Debt	0.02	0.12	-0.01	0.22	-0.06	0.15
Outflow/ΔDebt	0.05	0.32	-0.03	0.53	-0.32	0.18
Mauritania						
Outflow	NA	218.4	-1.5	-41.5	12.5	188.0
Debt	188.9	683.1	1007.2	1480.6	1905.9	1905.9
Outflow/Debt	NA	0.32	-0.00	-0.03	0.01	0.10
Outflow/ΔDebt	NA	0.44	-0.00	-0.09	0.03	0.11
Outflow/GDP	NA	0.40	-0.00	-0.05	NA	NA
Niger						
Outflow	109.8	37.1	-182.2	35.4	5.4	-104.3
Debt	111.3	447.2	770.5	1033.8	1311.7	1311.7
Outflow/Debt	0.99	0.08	-0.24	0.03	0.00	-0.08
Outflow/ΔDebt	1.38	0.11	-0.56	0.13	0.02	-0.09
Outflow/GDP	0.20	0.03	-0.08	0.02	NA	NA
Nigeria						
Outflow	819.4	2898.5	3932.1	-836.9	11541.9	17535.7
Debt	1052.4	4754.7	10846.7	18518.8	25947.4	25947.4
Outflow/Debt	0.78	0.61	0.36	-0.05	0.44	0.68
Outflow/ΔDebt	1.37	0.78	0.65	-0.11	1.55	0.70
Outflow/GDP	0.04	0.06	0.05	-0.01	0.20	0.25
Rwanda						
Outflow	26.1	42.8	-30.5	29.0	-16.0	25.3
Debt	24.1	126.8	202.6	314.4	537.6	537.6
Outflow/Debt	1.08	0.34	-0.15	0.09	-0.03	0.05
Outflow/ΔDebt	1.36	0.42	-0.40	0.26	-0.07	0.05
Outflow/GDP	0.06	0.06	-0.03	0.02	-0.01	0.02
Senegal						
Outflow	47.5	250.6	-128.2	76.4	NA	NA

Debt	325.2	852.2	1642.4	2458.0	3367.6	3367.6
Outflow/Debt	0.15	0.29	-0.08	0.03	NA	NA
Outflow/ΔDebt	0.21	0.48	-0.16	0.09	NA	NA
Outflow/GDP	0.04	0.12	-0.05	0.03	NA	NA
Sierra Leone						
Outflow	-49.3	-10.5	-185.6	-90.5	124.2	-162.4
Debt	156.9	299.7	509.1	575.5	745.4	745.4
Outflow/Debt	-0.31	-0.04	-0.36	-0.16	0.17	-0.22
Outflow/ΔDebt	-0.51	-0.07	-0.89	-1.36	0.73	-0.28
Outflow/GDP	-0.10	-0.02	-0.15	-0.08	0.17	-0.17
Somalia						
Outflow	-5.5	49.0	274.4	82.7	127.2	533.3
Debt	228.8	515.2	1079.5	1577.8	1986.9	1986.9
Outflow/Debt	-0.02	0.10	0.25	0.05	0.06	0.27
Outflow/ΔDebt	-0.04	0.17	0.49	0.17	0.31	0.30
Sudan						
Outflow	392.1	1427.5	2354.9	2594.1	1142.5	7519.0
Debt	1363.8	3088.1	6202.4	9000.5	10268.3	10268.3
Outflow/Debt	0.29	0.46	0.38	0.29	0.11	0.73
Outflow/ΔDebt	0.38	0.83	0.76	0.93	0.90	0.84
Outflow/GDP	0.12	0.18	0.23	0.34	0.13	0.87
Tanzania						
Outflow	-30.6	477.1	68.5	375.8	-25.8	895.6
Debt	890.6	1934.2	2800.0	4056.1	4599.9	4599.9
Outflow/Debt	-0.03	0.25	0.02	0.09	-0.01	0.19
Outflow/ΔDebt	-0.05	0.46	0.08	0.30	-0.05	0.24
Outflow/GDP	-0.02	0.14	0.01	0.06	-0.01	0.18
Togo						
Outflow	45.4	409.0	30.7	-137.6	-78.3	223.8
Debt	119.5	734.1	1073.2	1136.7	1247.3	1247.3
Outflow/Debt	0.38	0.56	0.03	-0.12	-0.06	0.18
Outflow/ΔDebt	0.57	0.67	0.09	-2.17	-0.71	0.20
Outflow/GDP	0.11	0.59	0.03	-0.18	NA	NA
Uganda						
Outflow	105.9	153.2	605.1	400.1	200.1	1358.4
Debt	240.3	426.0	827.9	1127.2	1598.1	1598.1
Outflow/Debt	0.44	0.36	0.73	0.35	0.13	0.85
Outflow/ΔDebt	1.04	0.82	1.51	1.34	0.42	1.00
Outflow/GDP	0.05	0.03	0.05	0.15	NA	NA
Zaire						
Outflow	83.3	953.5	503.2	16.7	578.1	2051.6
Debt	1804.1	4309.8	5299.2	6202.7	8148.2	8148.2
Outflow/Debt	0.05	0.22	0.09	0.00	0.07	0.25
Outflow/ΔDebt	0.06	0.38	0.51	0.02	0.30	0.32
Outflow/GDP	0.03	0.19	0.08	0.00	0.19	0.45
Zambia						
Outflow	160.2	933.5	718.4	-165.1	843.2	2329.9
Debt	1232.6	2435.2	3743.7	4346.3	5988.6	5988.6

Outflow/Debt	0.13	0.38	0.19	-0.04	0.14	0.39
Outflow/ΔDebt	0.26	0.78	0.55	-0.27	0.51	0.49
Outflow/GDP	0.07	0.35	0.19	-0.05	0.38	0.78
Zimbabwe						
Outflow	NA	NA	-165.8	240.8	-178.2	NA
Debt	186.9	446.1	1293.1	563.6	2695.9	2695.9
Outflow/Debt	NA	NA	-0.13	0.09	-0.07	NA
Outflow	NA	NA	-0.20	0.19	-1.35	NA
Outflow/GDP	NA	NA	-0.03	0.04	NA	NA

Table 14.3 ***The effect of debt measures on estimates of private capital outflows***

	1970-1975	1976-1978	1979-1981	1982-1984	1985-1987	1976-1987
Benin						
Residual Estimate	-39.9	-49.5	104.1	-176.9	NA.	NA.
Excl. Short Term	-39.9	-105.5	75.5	-178.8	NA.	NA.
Incl. Private	-39.9	-49.5	104.1	-176.9	NA.	NA.
Botswana						
Residual Estimate	NA.	-110.5	-28.8	-147.3	264.5	-22.2
Excl. Short Term	NA.	-113.5	-33.8	-144.3	264.2	-27.5
Incl. Private	NA.	-110.5	-28.8	-147.3	264.5	-22.2
Burkina Faso						
Residual Estimate	-32.4	79.6	-63.3	-56.9	NA.	NA.
Excl. Short Term	-32.4	1.6	-20.3	-47.9	NA.	NA.
Incl. Private	-32.4	79.6	-63.3	-56.9	NA.	NA.
Burundi						
Residual Estimate	NA.	NA.	NA.	NA.	150.7	NA.
Excl. Short Term	NA.	NA.	NA.	NA.	150.3	NA.
Incl. Private	NA.	NA.	NA.	NA.	150.7	NA.
Cameroon						
Residual Estimate	63.0	704.2	348.2	-367.3	-1175.6	-490.6
Excl. Short Term	62.3	540.8	267.0	-504.1	-1556.1	-1252.5
Incl. Private	96.6	756.8	512.0	-8.1	-1358.0	-97.4
Central African Rep.						
Residual Estimate	-1.7	22.6	46.9	11.6	60.7	141.7
Excl. Short Term	-1.7	13.6	36.4	17.3	35.9	103.1
Incl. Private	-1.7	22.6	46.9	11.6	60.7	141.7
Chad						
Residual Estimate	45.8	126.7	50.1	7.8	51.2	235.8
Excl. Short Term	45.8	112.7	53.4	15.8	24.5	206.4
Incl. Private	45.8	126.7	50.1	7.8	51.2	235.8
Congo						
Residual Estimate	NA.	-7.3	80.9	460.3	1359.9	1893.9
Excl. Short Term	NA.	-126.6	90.4	374.5	910.6	1249.0
Incl. Private	NA.	-7.3	80.9	460.3	1359.9	1893.9
Cote D'Ivoire						
Residual Estimate	149.8	1170.1	-647.2	-689.4	748.8	582.3
Excl. Short Term	149.8	441.1	-1083.2	-163.6	-440.0	-1245.7
Incl. Private	214.8	1358.1	-298.2	697.6	2459.8	4217.3
Equatorial Guinea						
Residual Estimate	NA.	NA.	NA.	NA.	NA.	NA.
Excl. Short Term	NA.	NA.	NA.	NA.	NA.	NA.
Incl. Private	NA.	NA.	NA.	NA.	NA.	NA.
Ethiopia						
Residual Estimate	77.9	143.4	30.3	117.8	NA.	NA.
Excl. Short Term	77.9	91.4	23.4	109.4	NA.	NA.
Incl. Private	77.9	143.4	30.3	117.8	NA.	NA.

	1970-1975	1976-1978	1979-1981	1982-1984	1985-1987	1976-1987
Gabon						
Residual Estimate	1121.0	1151.2	748.8	606.6	21.5	2528.2
Excl. Short Term	1121.0	937.2	815.7	502.7	-129.7	2126.0
Incl. Private	1121.0	1151.2	748.8	606.6	21.5	2528.2
Gambia						
Residual Estimate	-5.8	-10.7	14.0	68.9	45.7	117.9
Excl. Short Term	-5.8	-20.7	5.5	42.0	69.5	96.3
Incl. Private	-5.8	-10.7	14.0	68.9	45.7	117.9
Ghana						
Residual Estimate	260.9	215.0	244.3	591.8	480.1	1531.2
Excl. Short Term	254.1	-137.4	317.6	639.4	651.7	1471.3
Incl. Private	270.9	215.0	244.3	613.8	480.1	1553.2
Guinea						
Residual Estimate	NA.	NA.	NA.	NA.	NA.	NA.
Excl. Short Term	NA.	NA.	NA.	NA.	NA.	NA.
Incl. Private	NA.	NA.	NA.	NA.	NA.	NA.
Guinea-Bissau						
Residual Estimate	NA.	NA.	NA.	63.8	29.6	NA.
Excl. Short Term	NA.	NA.	NA.	18.4	47.8	NA.
Incl. Private	NA.	NA.	NA.	63.8	29.6	NA.
Kenya						
Residual Estimate	-315.2	405.3	-232.6	191.6	213.1	577.4
Excl. Short Term	-315.2	2.3	-299.5	288.1	22.6	13.5
Incl. Private	77.1	446.3	-300.4	254.4	412.2	812.5
Liberia						
Residual Estimate	NA.	404.6	678.7	452.6	273.0	1808.9
Excl. Short Term	NA.	315.3	687.3	463.8	120.1	1586.5
Incl. Private	NA.	404.6	678.7	452.6	273.0	1808.9
Madagascar						
Residual Estimate	95.9	68.6	45.0	192.9	-180.0	126.5
Excl. Short Term	95.9	23.6	-0.4	133.7	-125.0	31.9
Incl. Private	95.9	68.6	45.0	192.9	-180.0	126.5
Malawi						
Residual Estimate	-51.8	70.4	-267.4	-115.1	24.5	-287.6
Excl. Short Term	-51.8	-4.6	-242.4	-107.1	15.8	-338.3
Incl. Private	-51.8	70.4	-267.4	-115.1	27.7	-284.4
Mali						
Residual Estimate	5.9	68.8	-11.0	329.7	-109.0	278.5
Excl. Short Term	5.2	50.7	-64.8	332.0	-103.9	214.0
Incl. Private	5.9	68.8	-11.0	329.7	-109.0	278.5
Mauritania						
Residual Estimate	NA.	218.4	-1.5	-41.5	12.5	188.0
Excl. Short Term	NA.	165.1	-46.3	-70.3	-42.9	5.7
Incl. Private	NA.	218.4	-1.5	-41.5	12.5	188.0

	1970-1975	1976-1978	1979-1981	1982-1984	1985-1987	1976-1987
Mozambique						
Residual Estimate	NA.	NA.	NA.	-1087.2	NA.	NA.
Excl. Short Term	NA.	NA.	NA.	-1167.2	NA.	NA.
Incl. Private	NA.	NA.	NA.	-1087.2	NA.	NA.
Niger						
Residual Estimate	109.8	37.1	-182.2	35.4	5.4	-104.3
Excl. Short Term	109.8	-212.9	-46.0	86.5	-37.3	-209.7
Incl. Private	109.8	196.0	-37.7	-106.0	99.4	151.7
Nigeria						
Residual Estimate	819.4	2898.5	3932.1	-836.9	11541.9	17535.7
Excl. Short Term	819.4	452.5	1950.9	-2154.0	15534.6	15784.1
Incl. Private	910.4	3143.5	4943.1	-783.9	10478.9	17781.7
Rwanda						
Residual Estimate	26.1	42.8	-30.5	29.0	-16.0	25.3
Excl. Short Term	26.1	25.8	-33.5	12.0	-22.9	-18.6
Incl. Private	26.1	42.8	-30.5	29.0	-16.0	25.3
Senegal						
Residual Estimate	47.5	250.6	-128.2	76.4	NA.	NA.
Excl. Short Term	47.5	109.6	-224.2	39.9	NA.	NA.
Incl. Private	64.7	244.3	-126.3	73.3	NA.	NA.
Sierra Leone						
Residual Estimate	-49.3	-10.5	-185.6	-90.5	124.2	-162.4
Excl. Short Term	-51.0	-32.8	-230.9	-67.7	62.7	-268.7
Incl. Private	-49.3	-10.5	-185.6	-90.5	124.2	-162.4
Somalia						
Residual Estimate	-5.5	49.0	274.4	82.7	127.2	533.3
Excl. Short Term	-5.5	27.0	256.6	30.4	103.3	417.3
Incl. Private	-5.5	49.0	274.4	82.7	127.2	533.3
Sudan						
Residual Estimate	392.1	1427.5	2354.9	2594.1	1142.5	7519.0
Excl. Short Term	400.7	873.1	2000.5	2030.5	84.7	4988.8
Incl. Private	392.1	1427.5	2598.9	2594.1	1272.5	7893.0
Tanzania						
Residual Estimate	-30.6	477.1	68.5	375.8	-25.8	895.6
Excl. Short Term	-30.6	224.1	13.6	20.2	77.6	335.5
Incl. Private	23.4	485.5	72.1	378.5	-85.6	850.5
Togo						
Residual Estimate	45.4	409.0	30.7	-137.6	-78.3	223.8
Excl. Short Term	45.4	319.0	9.9	-89.8	-81.0	158.1
Incl. Private	45.4	409.0	30.7	-137.6	-78.3	223.8
Uganda						
Residual Estimate	105.9	153.2	605.1	400.1	200.1	1358.4
Excl. Short Term	105.9	132.2	587.8	396.0	7.3	1123.2
Incl. Private	105.9	153.2	605.1	400.1	200.1	1358.4

	1970-1975	1976-1978	1979-1981	1982-1984	1985-1987	1976-1987
Zaire						
Residual Estimate	83.3	953.5	503.2	16.7	578.1	2051.6
Excl. Short Term	83.3	617.5	507.2	104.7	146.7	1376.2
Incl. Private	83.3	953.5	503.2	16.7	578.1	2051.6
Zambia						
Residual Estimate	160.2	933.5	718.4	-165.1	843.2	2329.9
Excl. Short Term	159.9	284.0	757.4	13.0	-87.7	966.6
Incl. Private	280.2	963.5	618.4	-191.7	819.8	2209.9
Zimbabwe						
Residual Estimate	NA.	NA.	-165.8	240.8	-178.2	NA.
Excl. Short Term	NA.	NA.	-535.8	294.8	-141.7	NA.
Incl. Private	NA.	NA.	-152.6	305.2	-205.4	NA.

Table 14.4 ***Latin American capital outflows relative to GDP and debt***

	1976-1978	1979-1981	1982-1984	1985-1987	TOTAL
Argentina					
Outflow	4902	7152	11101	5845	29000
Outflow/GDP	0.11	0.05	0.17	0.08	0.35
Debt	10174	23491	37418	52717	52717
Outflow/debt	0.48	0.30	0.30	0.11	0.55
Outflow/Δdebt	0.85	0.54	0.80	0.38	0.60
Brazil					
Outflow	1856	1192	6560	8291	17899
Outflow/GDP	0.01	0.005	0.03	0.03	0.07
Debt	37596	60852	80841	105455	105455
Outflow/debt	0.05	0.02	0.08	0.08	0.17
Outflow/Δdebt	0.08	0.05	0.33	0.34	0.20
Mexico					
Outflow	12471	9598	14892	12553	49515
Outflow/GDP	0.14	0.05	0.09	0.08	0.33
Debt	30459	68015	76166	89981	89981
Outflow/debt	0.41	0.14	0.20	0.14	0.55
Outflow/Δdebt	0.65	0.26	1.83	0.91	0.63
Venezuela					
Outflow	1887	15546	11445	4741	33619
Outflow/GDP	0.05	0.27	0.18	0.08	0.62
Debt	14709	28493	28086	29039	29039
Outflow/debt	0.13	0.55	0.41	0.16	1.16
Outflow/Δdebt	0.14	1.13	-28.12	4.97	1.21

Table 14.5 ***Change in estimated stock of unreported foreign assets***

(US$ million)

Country	76-78	79-81	82-84	85-87	76-87*
Benin	-51.6	114.3	-178.8	28.1	-88.0
Botswana	-14.5	-84.5	-79.7	-148.9	-327.6
Burkina Faso	65.7	-24.6	6.8	NA.	NA.
Burundi	NA.	NA.	NA.	NA.	NA.
Cameroon	697.9	728.2	-231.9	-1137.9	56.3
C.A.Republic	-5.0	65.2	22.7	40.9	123.8
Chad	133.5	41.8	39.7	-2.4	212.6
Congo	-27.2	113.9	387.9	896.1	1370.6
Cote d'Ivoire	1568.0	-773.0	357.3	1822.5	2974.7
Eq. Guinea	NA.	NA.	NA.	NA.	NA.
Ethiopia	75.2	71.5	-99.9	489.2	535.9
Gabon	1103.7	856.8	426.6	-136.8	2250.3
Gambia	-9.2	17.4	37.7	66.4	112.3
Ghana	116.0	-386.2	-306.1	418.9	-157.4
Guinea	NA.	NA.	NA.	NA.	NA.
Guinea-Bissau	NA.	NA.	NA.	53.1	NA.
Kenya	894.2	-254.4	151.1	367.0	1157.9
Liberia	386.8	523.9	308.7	184.4	1403.8
Madagascar	87.8	-80.4	101.1	-110.2	-1.7
Malawi	95.1	-392.9	-158.8	-5.5	-462.0
Mali	56.8	-35.6	293.7	-140.9	174.0
Mauritania	259.7	-51.3	-47.7	24.8	185.5
Mozambique	NA.	NA.	216.9	NA.	NA.
Niger	259.4	-63.8	-155.0	102.8	143.4
Nigeria	4392.8	-1025.5	788.5	7525.1	11681.0
Rwanda	51.6	-63.7	75.4	-82.5	-19.3
Senegal	186.7	-198.0	-25.4	-287.3	-323.9
SierraLeone	24.8	-256.7	-130.4	154.0	-208.3
Somalia	104.6	179.4	54.5	73.6	412.1
Sudan	1318.5	2044.1	2582.1	1284.8	7229.4
Tanzania	360.3	130.0	532.7	-70.9	952.1
Togo	406.6	81.9	-102.8	-302.2	83.4
Uganda	145.1	449.3	266.3	351.1	1211.8
Zaire	568.5	295.5	-227.0	86.4	723.4
Zambia	NA.	4.0	-235.5	864.1	568.6
Zimbabwe	NA.	-372.6	53.6	79.7	86.0
Total**	13186.1	1678.3	4500.6	12434.4	32060.7

* Changes for Zambia and Zimbabwe are 1977 - 1987.
** Totals exclude NA's.

Table 14.6 ***Misinvoicing of trade data***

	MEAN	MIN	MAX
Benin			
Overinvoicing of exports	0.78	0.41	0.94
Overinvoicing of imports	0.85	0.41	1.14
Burundi			
Overinvoicing of exports	1.10	0.87	1.64
Overinvoicing of imports	0.79	0.41	1.28
Cameroon			
Overinvoicing of exports	0.96	0.75	1.11
Overinvoicing of imports	0.80	0.44	1.00
Central African Republic			
Overinvoicing of exports	0.88	0.56	1.44
Overinvoicing of imports	0.93	0.59	1.28
Chad			
Overinvoicing of exports	1.03	0.73	1.39
Overinvoicing of imports	1.00	0.13	1.73
Congo			
Overinvoicing of exports	0.67	0.41	0.87
Overinvoicing of imports	0.72	0.39	1.22
Cote d'Ivoire			
Overinvoicing of exports	0.93	0.84	0.99
Overinvoicing of imports	0.95	0.82	1.13
Ethiopia			
Overinvoicing of exports	0.80	0.60	0.94
Overinvoicing of imports	1.01	0.92	1.14
Gabon			
Overinvoicing of exports	0.87	0.67	1.01
Overinvoicing of imports	0.93	0.60	1.29
Gambia			
Overinvoicing of exports	0.94	0.76	1.32
Overinvoicing of imports	1.11	0.83	2.20
Ghana			
Overinvoicing of exports	0.99	0.73	1.78
Overinvoicing of imports	1.02	0.76	1.71
Guinea-Bissau			
Overinvoicing of exports	1.00	0.54	1.75
Overinvoicing of imports	0.40	0.02	1.25
Kenya			
Overinvoicing of exports	0.91	0.84	1.00
Overinvoicing of imports	0.88	0.77	0.95
Liberia			
Overinvoicing of exports	0.27	0.13	0.35
Overinvoicing of imports	0.61	0.47	0.91
Madagascar			

Overinvoicing of exports	0.89	0.73	1.08
Overinvoicing of imports	1.04	0.85	1.17
Malawi			
Overinvoicing of exports	1.14	0.77	1.54
Overinvoicing of imports	1.11	0.80	1.78
Mali			
Overinvoicing of exports	0.83	0.57	1.11
Overinvoicing of imports	0.99	0.62	1.47
Mauritania			
Overinvoicing of exports	0.91	0.65	1.07
Overinvoicing of imports	0.83	0.77	0.91
Niger			
Overinvoicing of exports	0.75	0.38	0.95
Overinvoicing of imports	1.16	0.65	1.83
Nigeria			
Overinvoicing of exports	1.10	1.03	1.19
Overinvoicing of imports	0.98	0.88	1.11
Rwanda			
Overinvoicing of exports	1.10	0.84	1.51
Overinvoicing of imports	1.31	0.10	3.33
Senegal			
Overinvoicing of exports	0.82	0.72	0.92
Overinvoicing of imports	0.96	0.84	1.08
Sierra Leone			
Overinvoicing of exports	0.99	0.87	1.06
Overinvoicing of imports	0.76	0.59	0.86
Somalia			
Overinvoicing of exports	0.63	0.31	0.93
Overinvoicing of imports	0.66	0.39	1.39
Sudan			
Overinvoicing of exports	0.82	0.52	1.04
Overinvoicing of imports	0.90	0.63	1.10
Tanzania			
Overinvoicing of exports	0.95	0.81	1.13
Overinvoicing of imports	1.05	0.77	1.22
Togo			
Overinvoicing of exports	0.78	0.45	1.00
Overinvoicing of imports	0.87	0.72	1.07
Uganda			
Overinvoicing of exports	1.06	0.44	1.43
Overinvoicing of imports	1.01	0.37	1.27
Zaire			
Overinvoicing of exports	0.72	0.52	1.04
Overinvoicing of imports	0.62	0.40	0.84
Zambia			

Overinvoicing of exports	0.80	0.64	0.92
Overinvoicing of imports	1.12	0.64	1.32
Zimbabwe			
Overinvoicing of exports	1.09	0.94	1.41
Overinvoicing of imports	0.99	0.72	1.18

Statistical annex

Sources for calculation of private capital outflows.

A. Current account surplus. Source: International Monetary Fund, *Balance of Payments Yearbook.* Data are in millions of SDRs and are converted to millions of U.S. dollars using the period average SDR/$ exchange rate.

B. Net foreign direct investment. Source: International Monetary Fund, *Balance of Payments Yearbook.* Data are in millions of SDRs and are converted to millions of U.S. dollars using the period average SDR/$ exchange rate.

C. Long term private capital (portfolio investment in bonds and corporate equities). Source: International Monetary Fund, *Balance of Payments Yearbook,* items identified as "Other bonds, assets" and "corporate equities". Data are in millions of SDRs and are converted to millions of U.S. dollars using the period average SDR/$ exchange rate.

D. Non-bank short-term capital. Source: International Monetary Fund, *Balance of Payments Yearbook,* items identified as "Other short-term capital of other sectors". Data are in millions of SDRs and are converted to millions of U.S. dollars using the period average SDR/$ exchange rate.

E. Short-term capital of the banking system. Source, International Monetary Fund, *International Financial Statistics,* line 7ad. Data are in millions of U.S. dollars.

F. Change in debt. Source, World Bank, *World Debt Tables.* Data are the sum of the change in public and publicly guaranteed debt, the change in short-term debt and the estimated valuation effect due to exchange rate changes, all in millions of U.S. dollars.

G. Errors and Omissions. Source: International Monetary Fund, *Balance of Payments Yearbook.* Data are in millions of SDRs and are converted to millions of U.S. dollars using the period average SDR/$ exchange rate.

H. Change in central bank reserves. Source: International Monetary Fund, *Balance of Payments Yearbook.* Data are in millions of SDRs and are converted to millions of U.S. dollars using the period average SDR/$ exchange rate.

Sources for calculation of unreported stock of foreign assets

A. Cumulative Recorded non-FDI Balance of Payments Claims. Source: International Monetary Fund, *Balance of Payments Yearbook,* lines 62-64, 69-71, 77-79, 84, 85, 89, 93, 94, and 98-109. Data are in millions of SDRs and are converted to millions of U.S. dollars using the period average SDR/$ exchange rate. The balance of payments errors and omissions obtained from International Monetary Fund, *International Financial Statistics* is added to the sum of these flows. The sum of the flows is accumulated beginning in 1965. No base year adjustment is made to the accumulated flows.

B. Adjustment for Unrecorded Claims = Stock of Debt - Cumulative Recorded Balance of Payments Liabilities. Sources: 1. Stock of Debt, World Bank, *World Debt Tables.* Data are the sum of public and publicly guaranteed long-term debt, short-term debt and the cumulative estimated valuation effect due to exchange rate changes, all in millions of U.S. dollars. 2. Cumulative recorded balance of payments liabilities, International Monetary Fund, *Balance of Payments Yearbook,* lines 53-61, 65-68, 72-76, 80-83, 86-88, 90-92, 95-97, and 110-111. Data are in millions of SDRs and are converted to millions of U.S. dollars using the period average SDR/$ exchange rate. The sum of the flows is accumulated beginning in 1965. No base year adjustment is made to the accumulated flows.

C. Capitalized Reported non-FDI Income = Reported Balance of Payments non-FDI Income divided by the U.S. Treasury Bill Rate. Sources: 1. Reported balance of payments non-FDI income, International Monetary Fund, *Balance of Payments Yearbook,* lines 15, 17, and 19. Data are in millions of SDRs and are converted to millions of U.S. dollars using the period average SDR/$ exchange rate. 2. U.S. Treasury Bill Rate, International Monetary Fund, *International Financial Statistics,* line 60c.

Comment

Przemyslaw Gajdeczka

It is fair to start my comments on statistical issues by giving credit to the authors for their effort to estimate capital flight out of Sub-Saharan Africa. However, it also seems fair to highlight some of the weaknesses of the employed methods and data sources used to estimate capital flight. These weaknesses are especially iomportant to Africa and are not discussed in this paper.

The biggest challenge is posed by the poor quality of statistical data and methodological inconsistencies between different sources. That is particularly important for capital flight estimates which exploit divergences between data derived from different sources. For example, by applying the "residual" method the authors implicitly assumed that some entries in balance of payments statistics (eg, current account, direct investment, or change in reserves) are more reliable than others. These selected series were then compared with borrowing data from the World Bank's Debtor Reporting System, which, in turn, were assumed to be of better quality than similar debtor data reported through the balance of payments reporting system. This procedure implies the ability to correctly select data that are highly reliable and mutually consistent. However, if the balance of payments reported "uses" of funds (current account and change in reserves) are underestimated, the estimate of capital flight will tend to be exaggerated, other things being equal.

Unfortunately, there are valid reasons to question the quality of trade data. As stated in the recent World Bank report on Sub-Saharan Africa: "In many countries there are no reliable statistics." In addition, there are tremendous difficulties in interpreting the data that already exist. Considerable discrepancies between African and partner-country trade data seriously undermine the reliability and utility of African trade statistics.

Some of the weaknesses discussed above—and evident in the paper by Chang and Cumby—could be reduced by adding trade misinvoicing estimates to other capital flight estimates. This would substantially eliminate double-counting, and in other cases supplement information on the uses of resources, including capital flight. Also, it could be beneficial to limit the number of sources used to derive data for various capital flight estimates eg. by matching all nonlending data (current account balance, foreign direct investment and change in reserves) from balance of payments statistics with debt data from the World Bank's Debtor Reporting System. However, even then considerable problems are likely to remain.

Notwithstanding the statistical difficulties, the value of capital flight estimates for Sub-Saharan Africa lies in their contribution to (hopefully) better understanding of the use of resources and the importance of capital flight in this respect. The authors showed that the relative importance of capital flight from Sub-Saharan Africa, measured by relating the stock of accumulated foreign assets to GDP and the stock of external debt, matched or in some cases surpassed outcomes in the most publicized cases in Latin America.

However some important differences between the two regions were not mentioned in the paper. First, there is a major difference in the timing of major capital flight episodes in the two regions. Second, a major difference is in the pattern of financing of private capital outflows, even though in both regions these outflows were accompanied by the inflow of foreign resources. In Latin America large resource inflows—mostly in the fvorm of public and publicly guaranteed borrowing—were accompanied by significant private capital outflows. In Sub-Saharan Africa a substantial share of total resource inflows consisted of grants and concessional lending, which to a significant degree were under the control of donor governments.

The difference in timing and financing pattern of capital flight were accompanied by the differences in the mechanisms through which capital was fleeing, both in terms of techniques and dependence on the availability of foreign exchange reserves. In many Latin American countries the acquisition of foreign assets was conducted through official channels and was facilitated by the overvaluation of exchange rates and open capital account policies. The governments stood ready to replenish foreign exchange reserves by borrowing abroad. In some cases, the acquisition of foreign assets was financed not only through large foreign borrowing but also was accompanied by considerable trade surpluses. In Africa, the intermediation of foreign capital seems to have played a much more modest role while trade misinvoicing appears to be a major vehicle for capital flight. In aggregate, Sub-Saharan countries excluding Nigeria have had trade deficits since 1970.

The discussion of policy implications of capital flight from Sub-Saharan Africa was very limited in the paper. The discussion of factors contributing to capital flight included in the paper could be usefully extended. The analysis of exchange rate overvaluation effect on capital flight could be extended by examining whether relative exchange rate stability provided by CFA franc arrangements had lowered incentives for capital outflows. More discussion of alternative factors behind capital flight could be provided by differentiating between policy distortions and other sources of risk. Policy distortions can be viewed as more amenable to corrections and by their nature can be short-lived. It seems very likely that policy distortions in other high capital flight countries, extensively discussed in the literature, have also been a factor in Sub-Saharan Africa. The most important policy distortions include exchange rate overvaluation which has been discussed in the paper, and also unsustainable fiscal deficits and financial repression. Recently, a rapid increase in domestic and external debts impaired governments' creditworthiness, thus providing additional stimulus for capital inflows. In Sub-Saharan Africa there are also certain adverse structural conditions that can be conducive to capital flight. These factors create conditions of high risk and low opportunity, providing incentives for capital flight.

The paper barely touches upon the issue of policy recommendations to remove incentives for capital flight—maybe because they are quite conventional, and unfortunately can address only some of the problems at hand. The least can be done regarding the risk inherent in commodity prices. This risk creates tremendous incentives to diversify, including the acquisition of assets abroad. Capital controls can be effective in preventing capital flight in the short run, but they are never able to create incentives for investment. Similarly, foreign currency deposits can attract savings and can be helpful when the policies are good. Such schemes tend to collapse, however, when policies are under the strain and require extra support.

The most important and effective piece of advice is to improve policies. As demonstrated by recent developments in Mexico, sound macroeconomic policies supported by structural reforms, if sustained, can not only stem but also reverse private capital outflows. Furthermore, investment disincentives created by excessive external debt can be removed by an appropriately tailored mixture of debt relief and concessional aid.

Endnotes

1. For sub-Saharan Africa overall, public and publicly guaranteed debt amount to about 95% of all debt outstanding and disbursed.

2. The same is often true of the African countries we examine below as can be seen from Table 3, where we report net private capital outflows as a fraction of the change in external debt.

3. This is emphasized in Eaton (1987) and Lessard and Williamson (1987).

4. This choice presumably reflects a judgement that the World Bank debt data are of higher quality than the official capital flows reported in the balance-of-payments accounts.

5. In choosing to examine *net* private sector acquisition of foreign assets, we differ from much of the previous literature. Dooley et. al. (1985), the World Bank (1985), and Morgan Guaranty (1986) all use private, non-guaranteed debt in addition to public and publicly guaranteed debt in computing residual estimates of provide sector acquisition of foreign assets. Erbe (1985) uses OECD data on medium and long-term gross external indebtedness with estimates of short-term debt for some countries. Cumby and Levich (1987) use public and publicly guaranteed long-term debt and all short-term debt as is done here. Morgan Guaranty (1986) excludes the increase in short-term foreign assets of the banking system from the increase in total private sector claims. Acquisition of foreign assets by nonbank agents, however, continues to be considered capital flight. Since they offer no explanation for treating the banking system differently from other firms and individuals, we do not pursue their distinction here.

6. For further discussion of the difficulties in estimating stocks from flows and vice versa, see Gajdeczka (1990).

7. If, however, only interest paid is measured in the balance-of-payments accounts, using the adjusted change in the stock of debt (which includes rescheduled interest) will result in overstating the extent to which the private sector has increased their claims abroad.

8. In any event, rescheduled interest probably amounts to no more than $2 billion for the sub-Saharan African countries as a whole over the period examined. The same reasoning would suggest that interest arrears ought to be added to the stock of debt if interest due but unpaid is included in the current account data.

9. Previous studies have used the change in the stock of external debt without adjusting for the effects of exchange rate changes on the dollar value of non-dollar debt. Exceptions are Gajdedzka (1989) and Gajdedzka and Oks (1989) who use net flows rather than changes in the stock.

10. Of course, as discussed earlier, exchange rate revaluation effects, debt reclassification, and "discoveries" of existing debt will also cause these estimates to diverge.

11. These figures are obtained from the tables in the Appendix.

12. Base-year problems can be quite serious. If we assume a base year value of 0 in 1965 and cumulate all measured flows from that point, the estimated stock of unreported foreign claims becomes negative and large in absolute value for a number of countries in certain years.